LABOUR IN GLASGOW

Socialism, suffrage, sectarianism

SCOTTISH HISTORICAL REVIEW

MONOGRAPHS SERIES

No. 11

CURRENT AND FORTHCOMING VOLUMES

LABOUR IN GLASGOW, 1896–1936

Socialism, Suffrage, Sectarianism

J. J. SMYTH

TUCKWELL PRESS

First published in Great Britain in 2000 by
Tuckwell Press
The Mill House
Phantassie
East Linton
East Lothian EH40 3DG
Scotland

Copyright © J. J. Smyth, 2000

ISBN 1 86232 137 X

British Library Cataloguing in Publication Data

A catalogue record for this book is available
on request from the British Library

The right of J. J. Smyth to be identified as the author of this work has been asserted
by him in accordance with the Copyright, Design and Patent Act 1988

Typeset by Hewer Text Limited, Edinburgh
Printed and bound by The Cromwell Press, Trowbridge, Wiltshire

For my mother. Frances Livingstone Smyth,
And in memory of my father Edward Smyth

Contents

Acknowledgements

This book has had a long gestation and I have accumulated many debts along the way. I thank colleagues, past and present, at the Departments of Economic and Social History at Edinburgh and Glasgow, and the Department of History at Stirling University. I would like to mention Bob Morris, Roger Davidson, Frank Bechhofer and George Peden for all their help, Ewen Cameron for undertaking the onerous task of editing my typescript and, in particular, Alan McKinlay for all his critical encouragement and friendship. My deepest thank you, as ever, is to Fay.

List of Abbreviations

ASE	Amalgamated Society of Engineers
BSP	British Socialist Party
CP	Communist Party
CSCC	Central Strike Co-ordinating Committee
CWC	Clyde Workers' Committee
CSS	Catholic Socialist Society
DLP	Divisional Labour Party
DORA	Defence of the Realm Act
GWHA	Glasgow Women's Housing Association
GWSSWS	Glasgow and West of Scotland Society for Women's Suffrage
HGB	Home Government Branch
ILP	Independent Labour Party
INL	Irish National League of Great Britain
LEA	Local Education Authorities
LPHC	Labour Party Housing Committee
LRC	Labour Representation Committee
MEA	Municipal Employees' Association
MCU	Middle Class Union
NAC	National Administrative Council
NUWSS	National Union of Women's Suffrage Societies
PLP	Parliamentary Labour Party
SCWG	Scottish Co-operative Women's Guild
SLP	Scottish Labour Party
SocLP	Socialist Labour Party
SLRL	Scottish Land Restoration League
SDF	Social Democratic Federation
SPL	Scottish Protestant League
SSP	Scottish Socialist Party
STUC	Scottish Trade Union Congress
SUTCLP	Scottish United Trades Councils Labour Party
SWRC	Scottish Workers' Representation Committee
UIL	United Irish League
WEC	Workers' Election Committee
WFL	Women's Freedom League
WIL	Women's International League
WLL	Women's Labour League
WPC	Women's Peace Crusade
WSPU	Women's Social and Political Union

Labour and its Electorate

The continuing debate over the rise of the Labour Party and the concomitant demise of the Liberals shows little sign of abating. Each generation
returns to the issue with new questions and fresh insights provoked by
contemporary political developments. With the success of a militant right-
wing Conservatism in the 1980s, Labour's so-called 'forward march' appeared as a problematic, contingent phenomenon.[1] Yet the whole notion of
an uninterrupted progression hardly reflects the reality of an electoral
journey that has been more of a circuitous route than it has been a straight
line. It is only from the vantage point of 1945 that Labour's progress appears
certain or pre-ordained.[2] Prior to this, of course, there had been the great
debacle of 1931 and, after the high point of Attlee's Government, successive
electoral defeats in the 1950s encouraged fears of permanent opposition.[3]
As the current political situation changes – the success of 'New Labour' in
England at the last general election, the creation of a Scottish Parliament
elected under proportional representation – so new questions are posed
about past events. For instance, was the Progressive Alliance between
Liberals and Labour bound to dissolve? Can it be put together again?[4]

While there are a number of recent studies at both local and national
levels which offer analyses and explanations of Labour's rise there is, as yet,
no widely accepted consensus. Was Labour already threatening the Liberals
before 1914, or was Labour's breakthrough after and due to the War? And, if
so, was this the result of a radicalisation of, and increasing unity within, the
working class, or was it due to a more moderate perception by trade
unionists that war-time collectivism showed the State and state intervention

---

[1] Eric Hobsbawm's siren warning, 'The Forward March of Labour Halted?',
originally given as the 1978 Marx Memorial lecture predated the rise of 'Thatch-
erism', but was given greater credence by the result of the 1979 general election.
E.J. Hobsbawm, *The Forward March of Labour Halted?* (London, 1981).

[2] Cole's history of the Labour Party written during the early years of the 1945–51
Labour Government is no panegyric but it does end on a genuinely heroic note.
G.D.H. Cole, *A History of the Labour Party From 1914* (London, 1948).

[3] M. Abrams & R. Rose, *Must Labour Lose?* (London, 1960).

[4] Tony Blair's enthusiasm for a single party of the left and his regret at the split of
the progressive forces is well known and gives added interest to Duncan Tanner's
discussion of the Progressive Alliance in his, *Political Change and the Labour Party
1900–1918* (Cambridge, 1990). It is an historical irony that while the progressive
alliance never operated in Scotland prior to the First World War, there is now a
Labour and Liberal Democrat Administration installed in Edinburgh.

in a more beneficial light? Did the massive rise in the electorate as a result of the 1918 Representation of the People Act explain Labour's increased electoral support?[5] On all of these questions there is no broad agreement and one recent overview offers the almost apologetic conclusion that, 'the rise of the Labour party was still an event of considerable historical importance.'[6]

The emphasis in this study is upon Labour as a political entity and upon the changing electoral fortunes of Labour – at the parliamentary and especially the municipal level – in Glasgow over a forty year period. The start and end dates represent Labour's first, tentative efforts at achieving representation in the mid 1890s, and its eventual capture of the Municipal Corporation in the 1930s. However, this was by no means a constant and steady progression but, rather, was halting and partial. Over this forty year period it went from apparent strength to almost complete annihilation and for many years appeared stuck at a level of local representation which, though significant, was well short of a majority. It is well known that Glasgow went 'red' in 1922 when Labour won ten of the City's fifteen parliamentary seats. What is not so generally recognised was that the City Corporation remained resolutely 'blue' until 1933 when Labour only won a majority under very peculiar circumstances; the dramatic intervention of a militant Protestant party and the split within Labour's own ranks as the newly-disaffiliated Independent Labour Party (ILP) – the heart and soul of Labour in Glasgow – decided to stand its own candidates. Such were the conditions of Labour's ultimate triumph. However, if securing a Labour majority in the Corporation's palatial headquarters in George Square had been an elusive goal for Labour, once achieved it has proven to be more or less permanent.[7]

A study of Glasgow needs no justification. It was one of the major urban centres of the United Kingdom – the proudly proclaimed second city of the Empire – and the largest centre of population in Scotland by some way. In 1911 the population of the City of Glasgow, some 784,496 individuals, represented 16.5% of the total population of Scotland. The continuing physical expansion of the City saw the population rise to over one million after World War One and by 1931 Glasgow accounted for over one fifth of

[5] Amongst the many contributions to the debate the following is a short selection of some of the more influential: P.F. Clarke, 'The electoral position of the Liberal and Labour Parties, 1910–1914' *English Historical Review*, xc (1975); H. C. G. Matthew, R. McKibbin & J.A. Kay, 'The Franchise Factor in the Rise of the Labour Party', *English Historical Review*, xci (1976); A. Reid, 'The division of Labour and Politics in Britain, 1880–1920' in, W.J. Mommsen & H. Husung (eds.), *The Development of Trade Unionism in Great Britain and Germany, 1880–1914* (London, 1985); Tanner, *Political Change,* J. Turner, *British Politics and the Great War: Coalition and Conflict 1915–1918* (London, 1992)
[6] M. Savage & A. Miles, *The Remaking of the British Working Class 1840–1940* (London, 1994), p. 73.
[7] W. Miller, 'Politics in the Scottish City 1832–1982', in G. Gordon (ed.), *Perspectives of the Scottish City* (Aberdeen, 1985), pp. 201–4.

the Scottish population.[8] The post-war expansion of the City's constituencies to fifteen represented a similar proportion of Scotland's total parliamentary seats.

Moreover, Glasgow was the 'capital' of industrial Scotland, where business and labour organisations tended to have their headquarters. Glasgow may have been the home of the skilled worker but, as a major urban centre, it had a complex social structure with all classes – from the very poorest to the super rich – living within its boundaries. As such it was the sort of place crucial to Labour's long term prospects and an accurate barometer of its ambition and success. Gains made in single class constituencies like the mining seats and small towns may have provided the bedrock of Labour's representation before 1914 but succeeding in a city with its mixed occupational and social structure was more problematic and much more significant.[9]

Furthermore, Glasgow has been the subject of the most intense debate within modern Scottish political historiography, the continuing 'Red Clydeside' controversy. The major monograph remains Iain McLean's, *The Legend of Red Clydeside*, which argues that Glasgow's radical war-time militancy was less of a reality and more the mythical construct of participants like Willie Gallacher who, as Communists, sought to bolster their own revolutionary reputations by exaggerating the significance of the industrial unrest of 1914–19.[10] In addition, McLean asserts that the rise of Labour, as evidenced by its vote in Glasgow, occurred after the war and for reasons not directly related to the war – namely the politicisation of housing and rents under specific circumstances in 1922 and the shift in allegiance of Irish-Catholic voters from Liberal to Labour once the issue of Ireland appeared to have been resolved by the Treaty of 1921.

McLean's thesis has proven remarkably influential and resilient. Christopher Harvie's history of Scotland in the twentieth century, *No Gods and Precious Few Heroes*, with its curt dismissal of Clydeside's radical reputation, is clearly indebted to McLean.[11] English historians of Labour, where they do pay attention to events in Scotland, also tend to rely on the same source.[12] Political scientists and sociologists of modern Scotland also focus upon *The Legend*, even where they are in partial disagreement with it.[13] Yet McLean's

---

[8] Census of Scotland, *Report* 1911, 1931.

[9] See Tanner, *Political Change,* p. 129.

[10] I.S. McLean, *The Legend of Red Clydeside* (Edinburgh, 1983); Willie Gallacher, *Revolt on the Clyde* (London, 1936).

[11] Although McLean's book was published after Harvie's, the original Ph.D. thesis was produced in 1971. C. Harvie, *No Gods and Precious Few Heroes* (London, 1981, 2nd. edition Edinburgh, 1992). Published in the debacle of the first devolution referendum of 1979, this may explain the choice of lacerating title.

[12] M. Savage, *The Dynamics of Working Class Politics: The Labour Movement in Preston 1880–1914* (Cambridge, 1987), p. 194.

[13] A. Brown, D. McCrone, L. Paterson, *Politics and Society in Scotland* (Basingstoke, 1996), pp. 131–4.

revisionism has come in for sustained criticism by other historians who insist
that the war-time unrest was both more prolonged and more significant
than McLean allows and was also directly responsible for the post-war shift in
political loyalties towards Labour.[14]

It is within that perspective that this study is located. However, the focus
does not lie narrowly upon the war years of Red Clydeside and it is intended
that, by taking a significantly longer time-span, the nature and complexity of
Labour's progress can be illustrated in sharper relief. At the same time and
contrary to the arguments of McLean and McKibbin, the war can still be
seen as a watershed in Labour's political and electoral development.[15] By
1914 it will be shown that, although Labour had secured itself a place in
Glasgow's political landscape, it remained very much a minor player with
little prospect of becoming a majority party in either parliamentary or
municipal affairs.[16] Only after the War did Labour's ambitions genuinely
rise above this minority status.

Labour's position before and after the war is also linked to the question
of the suffrage. Against the now widely held view that there was no class
bias in the suffrage, the study of the pre-war Glasgow electorate undertaken here indicates that the franchise system did clearly discriminate
against the working class, as was intended.[17] However, while supporting
Matthew, McKibbin and Kay's argument that it was the working class who
suffered under the franchise restrictions, we do not accept that the
passing of the 1918 Reform Act can be disentangled from the War
itself.[18] It may be that by 1914 a further reform of the franchise was
likely but it was only as a consequence of the War that it became
inevitable. Furthermore, while agreeing that the extension of the franchise was crucial to Labour's post-war expansion, it is important not to
interpret this in a mechanistic fashion, that the 'new' voters were simply
waiting to fall into Labour's lap, or that these electors on their own were

[14] J. Melling, *Rent Strikes: People's Struggle for Housing in West Scotland 1890–1916*
(Edinburgh 1983); J. Melling, 'Whatever happened to Red Clydeside? Industrial
Conflict and the Politics of Skill in the First World War', and J. Foster, 'Strike
Action and Working Class Politics on Clydeside 1914–1919', both articles in
International Review of Social History, xxxv (1990); also J. Melling, 'Work, culture
and politics on 'Red Clydeside': the ILP during the First World War', in A.
McKinlay & R.J. Morris (eds.), *The ILP on Clydeside 1893–1932: from foundation to
disintegration* (Manchester, 1991) pp. 83–122. J.J. Smyth, 'Labour and Socialism in
Glasgow 1880–1914: the electoral challenge prior to democracy' (unpublished
Ph.D. thesis, University of Edinburgh, 1987).

[15] R. McKibbin, *The Evolution of the Labour Party 1910–1924* (London, 1974).

[16] This is in broad agreement with Hutchison's conclusion about Labour's parliamentary position in Scotland on the eve of War. I.G.C. Hutchison, *A Political
History of Scotland 1832–1924: Parties, Elections and Issues* (Edinburgh 1986), p. 265.

[17] See Tanner, *Political Change*; M. Pugh, *Electoral Reform in War and Peace 1908–1918*
(London, 1978).

[18] 'the events of the war were only subordinate factors', Matthew *et al*, 'The
Franchise Factor', p. 736.

able to completely transform the balance of political forces.[19]

While the basis of Labour's appeal to voters after 1918 has been examined and debated, it is equally necessary and illuminating to examine Labour's attitude towards the pre-war electorate. By looking at both parliamentary and local elections prior to 1914 it can be shown that Labour was ambivalent, indeed often hostile, to women and the poorer working class, the very groups most affected by the 1918 reform.[20] While Labour was formally in favour of votes for all adult men and women, this did not translate into an active commitment. It is generally recognised that Labour shared a great deal of its 'commonsense' view of the world with Liberalism, and in many respects this shared value system was progressive and democratic.[21] However, it was only partially democratic. It was based upon a view of the franchise as a qualification for citizenship rather than as a natural right. Both Liberals and Labour sought to appeal to the 'respectable' working man, and both were concerned with the lack of respectability among the poorer working class. Matthew *et al* calculate there were some 4,500,000 disenfranchised working class men before 1914 and argue that had they had the vote they would most likely have voted Labour.[22] However, this can only be an assumption given Labour's own lack of concern about the disenfranchised. Beyond the formal commitment to adult suffrage lay deep misgivings about the possible consequences of a fully democratic franchise, perhaps best summed up in Keir Hardie's remark, 'It is the slum vote which the Socialist candidate fears most.'[23]

Afraid of the supposed conservative or reactionary tendencies of the very poor and women, Labour could not grasp the prickly matter of the suffrage and make a complete democratic reform central to its outlook and practice. It was the political and social transformation of the War which effectively solved the problem for Labour by basically getting rid of it. Full employment under the war economy saw the notion of a residuum disappear, at least temporarily. The narrowing of the wage differential between skilled and unskilled and the rapid growth of the general unions shifted the balance within the labour movement away from the skilled man. The politicisation of

---

[19] An astute contribution to the debate over the franchise is made by Dunbabin who takes a long term regional view of party fortunes, 'Each expansion of the franchise between 1832 and 1918/28 inducted the new voters into a going concern. . . . In no case is it contended that the new voters immediately took over the system . . .' J.P.D. Dunbabin, 'British Elections in the nineteenth and twentieth centuries, a regional approach', *English Historical Review*, xcv (1980), p. 265.

[20] Two thirds of the 'new' voters in 1918 were women. Turner, *British Politics*, p. 412. The discrimination against poorer working class men will be discussed below.

[21] J. Smith, 'Labour Tradition in Glasgow and Liverpool', *History Workshop*, xviii (1984).

[22] Matthew et al, 'The Franchise Factor', pp. 739–40

[23] J. Keir Hardie, *From Serfdom to Socialism* (London, 1907), quoted in K. O. Morgan, *Keir Hardie: Radical and Socialist* (London, 1975), p. 208.

the housing question – particularly in Glasgow – gave Labour a direct point of contact with working class women. A truly homogeneous working class may not have been made during the War, but it soon became clear that women and the poor were prepared to vote Labour after all.

Labour's Electoral Journey, 1896 – 1936

While the detail of Labour's electoral progress will be found in the following chapters, a summary is provided here. The concentration is on local, municipal elections since the annual contests in the city wards permit a more accurate reflection of electoral fortunes and trends than the irregular nature of general elections. Moreover, it was at the local level where Labour first made most effort and where its hopes of success were greatest.

The term Labour is used throughout as a form of shorthand. The story of 'Labour's' electoral performance cannot be limited to the Labour Party alone. Apart from anything else, labour candidates predated the formation of the Labour Party. The Mid Lanark by-election of 1888 is usually taken as the obvious starting point, due to Keir Hardie's challenge to the Liberal Party and to the formation of the Scottish Labour Party (SLP) which that campaign brought about. The SLP was a broad and loose coalition of trade unionists (especially miners), socialists, assorted radicals and land reformers, Irish nationalists and various disaffected Liberals. Despite defections and the lack of any electoral success, the SLP did maintain a political presence and gradually became a self-pronounced socialist party. The SLP associated itself with the all-British movement for labour representation which gave birth to the Independent Labour Party (ILP) in 1893 and to all intents and purposes the SLP was, and soon became formally, the ILP in Scotland.[24]

However, it was not until the early to mid-1890s that Labour candidates began to register actual successes, and these were in local elections, not parliamentary contests. By then the SLP/ILP had established a number of branches throughout the City and the Trades Council had become increasingly politicised. It had supported Hardie in 1888, declared itself in favour of state-regulated reforms such as the eight hour day and was a keen supporter of municipal control of services and the extension of municipal conditions. Socialists were becoming dominant on the council and the employers' backlash of the 1890s only encouraged a political perspective.[25]

It was the ILP which was most closely identified with the struggle for Labour representation. This was its raison d'être. Committed to acting in and creating coalitions and alliances, but prepared to act on its own when

---

[24] J.J. Smyth, 'The ILP in Glasgow 1888–1906: the struggle for identity', in McKinlay & Morris, *ILP on Clydeside.*

[25] W.H. Fraser, 'The Working Class', in W.H. Fraser & I. Mavor (eds.), *Glasgow, Volume Two: 1830–1912* (Manchester, 1996), pp. 334, 337–8.

necessary, it was the ILP which provided the thread of continuity in Labour's electoral campaigns from the 1890s through to its eventual disaffiliation from the Labour Party in the early 1930s. In both organisational and political terms, therefore, the role of the ILP was crucial.

While, at times, the ILP would present a more definitely socialist face to the electorate, mostly it was involved in building alliances with other forces around a common programme. In Glasgow in the 1890s these other forces were the Trades Council, the Co-operators and the Irish Nationalists. Together with the ILP these formed the 'forces of the democracy'. The term 'democratic' was used as commonly as that of 'workers' and indicates both the weakness of the ILP and trade union elements and how much wider and inclusive the perception of a labour party had to be. The Irish were an important part in this coalition and, in the figure of John Ferguson, could be said to have played a leading role in the cause of labour representation. Released from the constraints of Home Rule that dominated Parliamentary elections, Ferguson and other nationalists were free to play a more progressive role at the municipal level. Elected to the east end ward of Calton in 1893 Ferguson became the effective leader of the labour or democratic forces on the Town Council, so much so that the first successful ILP candidates declared themselves as his 'disciples'.[26]

Labour representation in Glasgow received a great fillip at the municipal poll of 1896 when all the seats, not just the usual third, fell vacant. This provided the opportunity for the forces of the democracy to establish a more coherent organisational basis under the banner of the Workers' Election Committee (WEC). The success of this Committee saw the emergence of a more coherent and relatively numerous bloc of Labour councillors on Glasgow Town Council. This grouping, known as the Stalwarts, came to be regarded as an exemplar of Labour organisational and electoral success. However, there always had been tensions within this coalition and one by one (starting with the Co-operators) the constituent bodies withdrew until, by the mid 1900s, the ILP was left on its own and labour municipal representation had been effectively nullified.

Over a ten year period, therefore, Glasgow had gone from being a model of local Labour success, offering a possible strategy to be adopted nationally, to being regarded very much as a problem area.[27] In the five or six years up to the outbreak of war, Labour's organisational basis and electoral performance began to improve. The Trades Council became re-involved in promoting Labour candidates and, eventually, a Glasgow Labour Party was formed in 1913.[28] This marked a distinct break with the older structure of the Stalwarts and the WEC and represented a distinct shift from the

[26] *Glasgow Herald,* 6 Nov. 1895.
[27] *Labour Leader,* 10 Nov. 1905.
[28] Hutchison, *Political History,* p. 254; W.H. Fraser, "The Labour Party in Scotland", in K.D. Brown (ed.), *The First Labour Party 1906–1914* (London, 1985), p. 57.

combined forces of the democracy to a more identifiably modern Labour movement. At the same time, however, the electoral success of this re-vamped Labour movement was no greater than that enjoyed by the Stalwarts in their heyday.

In the 1900s, however, the ILP faced a much more difficult task in promoting municipal control. Added to the cost of local services was the cost of statutory obligations in health and education imposed by central government. As the rates rose continuously, so a ratepayers' reaction set in and Labour candidates suffered in the backlash. Labour's organisational weakness was compounded by a drift in terms of policy. The ILP may have done for the single tax panacea but they had yet to replace it with anything similarly powerful.[29] There was a recognition that Labour needed a 'big issue' to regain the initiative.[30] This was achieved in the immediate pre-war years with housing, more precisely the workman's cottages scheme popu-larised by John Wheatley.

The importance of the housing question to Labour's electoral success cannot be gainsaid. This can be seen most clearly after 1918 but is also evident in the more limited context of Labour's pre-war challenge. Whea-tley's scheme, had it been implemented, might have done little to solve Glasgow's housing crisis but, at a propaganda level, it benefited from being straightforward, self-contained (the finance was to come from the tramway surplus), and offered a qualitatively better form of public housing than tenement flats. At the same time the popularity of the housing policy encouraged Labour's organisational growth as a series of housing bodies, though formally non-political, were established to broaden the campaign for Wheatley's cottages.[31]

The position of Labour in Glasgow in 1914 was better than it had been for some time, perhaps better than it had ever been. The Glasgow Labour Party was a more coherent body than the WEC had been (though there was a still a problem of maintaining party discipline over elected members). Labour now had a sizeable number of Councillors though these remained a minority and there was no possibility of Labour forming an administration. Yet, there were a series of elements by 1914, the bloc of Councillors, the organisation of the Labour Party and associated bodies, the political leader-ship provided by the ILP, the politicisation of the housing question, which

[29] The single tax panacea refers to the solution to industrial depression and increasing want offered by the American social reformer Henry George, as outlined in his famous book *Progress and Poverty*. George made a fundamental distinction between land and other forms of property and argued that all forms of taxation should be replaced by a single tax on land values. H. George, *Progress and Poverty* (London, 1906 edition), p. vii. See Chapter One, p. 8 for the significance of the single tax within Labour's early municipal programme. For a socialist critique of this 'panacea' see article in the very first edition of *Forward* (13 Octobr 1906) 'Popular Fallacies – Henry Georgism exposed'.

[30] *Forward*, 13 Nov. 1909.

[31] J. Melling, *Rent Strikes*, pp. 31–4.

together meant that Labour was well placed to respond to the unique circumstances of war-time and to exploit the new opportunities which opened up after 1918.

Electoral politics came to an end in 1914 but it was, ironically enough, during war-time that Labour made its greatest advance. As Liberalism self-destructed, industrial and community issues became the political issues of the moment and class politics dominated. This analysis is not contradicted by Labour's poor showing at the general election of 1918 when it took only one seat in Glasgow, no better than its position in 1906 and 1910. But, from a long term perspective what is most significant about 1918 is the shift in Labour's expectations. While local activists may have been disappointed by their showing, they now had genuine ambitions to be a major political force rather than the marginal grouping they had been for so long. Moreover, Labour's political breakthrough did not occur in 1922 but actually prior to that in the immediate post-war local elections. As in 1896, extensions of the City boundaries saw a belated local general election held in 1920 when all seats in every ward had to be contested. Labour had secured some significant victories in 1919 but the following year it almost doubled its representation and made a Labour Council a possibility where before it had been merely a pipe dream.

Yet it was to be another thirteen years before this was achieved and the gap between Labour's parliamentary and municipal performance is a notable one. In 1922 Labour secured a clear majority in the City's parliamentary representation that it surrendered only in the near universal collapse of 1931. This predominance, however, stubbornly refused to replicate itself in the municipal arena as Labour appeared stuck at a level of representation which, though significant, remained some way short of a majority. What explained this was a local franchise which was significantly less democratic than the parliamentary suffrage; and the uniting of Conservatives and Liberals into an anti-Socialist alliance in municipal affairs which operated as the Moderate Party. For the most part the Moderates were very disciplined in avoiding any split votes and were successful in winning a key number of working class wards which secured their majority. When Labour did achieve an administration in 1933 it was in what appeared to be the most unpropitious of circumstances. The Party was still feeling the deadening effects of MacDonald's treachery and the overwhelming triumph of the National Government. To make matters worse the ILP's disaffiliation in 1932 was followed by the decision to put forward its own candidates, thereby opening up the prospect of a badly divided Labour vote. What tipped the balance, however, was the intervention of the Scottish Protestant League (SPL) which took sufficient seats and, more importantly, votes from the Moderates to allow Labour in. Thereafter, while the SPL quickly departed, Labour maintained its majority.

The Electorate in Glasgow Before 1914

Although there have been five Reform Acts on the way to a full democratic franchise, traditional political historiography tended to recognise only the first three: 1832 which gave the middle class the vote; 1867 which gave the urban working class the vote; and 1884 which enfranchised the rural working class. The two Acts of 1918 and 1928 which gave women the parliamentary vote for some reason tended not to be identified as the Fourth and Fifth Reform Acts. Neal Blewett's seminal article on the pre-1918 franchise was responsible for questioning the assumption that the electoral system then was in no way different to present day practice. In particular his estimate that only 60% of adult males had the vote seriously questioned the democratic credentials of the pre-1918 system.[32]

For Matthew *et al* there is a clear inference to be drawn from this, which is that those disenfranchised were overwhelmingly working class and that the Representation of the People Act of 1918 provided the Labour Party with a new source of electoral support.[33] Other historians are not convinced, either that the 1918 Reform can explain the rise of Labour or that those disenfranchised before then were predominantly working class. Martin Pugh accepts the findings of Blewett and agrees that the assumption, prevalent until the early 1960s, that, 'manhood suffrage had virtually been achieved by 1900 [was] a gross exaggeration'.[34] Nevertheless, he does not agree with Matthew *et al* that a class bias operated. Pugh points out that men could move on and off the electoral register and concludes from this that, 'the dividing line between the enfranchised and unenfranchised was therefore much less significant than the gross numbers would suggest.' In Pugh's estimation the system was, despite any flaws, 'broadly representative'; the electorate was comprised in the main of working class voters who were only slightly less represented than the middle class.[35] Duncan Tanner makes essentially the same argument. The Conservatives may have enjoyed a slight benefit from the workings of the Edwardian electoral system but there was no major bias against any social group; the discrimination in the system was against women and younger adult men who were not householders in their own right.[36]

However, if the working class dominated the Edwardian electorate this

---

[32] N. Blewett, 'The Franchise in the United Kingdom 1885–1918', *Past and Present*, xxxii (1965), pp 27–56

[33] 'We cannot say how many votes the introduction of universal franchise was worth to Labour but we can say that it was a critical element in the emergence of the party as a major political force.' Matthew et al, 'The Franchise Factor', p. 740

[34] Pugh, *Electoral Reform*, p. 3.

[35] Pugh, *Electoral Reform*, pp. 3–4.

[36] Tanner, *Political Change* pp 99–129. See also the same author's article, 'The Parliamentary Electoral System, the 'Fourth' Reform Act and the Rise of Labour in England and Wales', *Bulletin of the Institute of Historical Research*, lvi (1983), pp. 205–19.

did not translate into working class political predominance. Pelling has
estimated that prior to 1914 only eighty-nine constituencies, which returned
ninety-five MPs, were 'predominantly working class in character'.[37] A higher
figure has been given elsewhere which estimates 25% of UK seats prior to
1914 as 'dominated by working class and mining groups'.[38] In Scotland a
recent exhaustive study of the electoral system by Dyer has found that the
industrial areas were still under-represented in numbers of seats even after
the redistribution of 1885.[39] More significantly, however, this study also
argues that the system was biased against the working class: the year-long
residential qualification particularly affected the population of dynamic
urban and industrial areas; the lodger franchise allowed the qualification of
the sons of wealthy householders but not working class single men who were
unlikely to be able to afford a room with a £10 annual rental or, given the
desperate overcrowding of the industrial areas, expect to have a room for
their exclusive use; and the disqualification for non-payment of rates,
exemption from rates or receipt of poor relief also accounted for a
considerable number of men not appearing on the electoral register.[40]

These last exclusions are referred to as the 'poverty clauses' which draws
our attention to the simple fact that it was the poorer members of society
who were least likely to have a vote. This is not to say that all unskilled or
labouring men did not have a vote – they could still qualify – but that the
rules and regulations of the electoral system were stacked against them. In
order to substantiate this viewpoint, however, it is necessary to look at the
pre-war electorate in Glasgow in some detail.

It is widely recognised that, prior to 1918, enfranchisement rates of adult
males varied widely between different types of constituency. Broadly
speaking County divisions had higher levels of enfranchisement than
Burghs: in England & Wales in 1911 the proportions were 69.9% and
58.8%, and in Scotland enfranchisement was lower with rates of 62.5% and
57.3% respectively.[41] Dyer points out that in Scotland the real difference
lay between rural and urban areas generally with much lower levels of
enfranchisement in the urban industrial areas. Giving estimates for *circa*
1900 Dyer shows that on average 56% of adult males qualified for the vote
in Burgh constituencies: but whereas the Border Burghs enjoyed 70%
enfranchisement the figures for Glasgow and Dundee were 51% and 50%
respectively. Individual constituencies were even lower: on Clydeside four

[37] H.M. Pelling, *Social Geography of British Elections, 1885–1910* (London, 1967), pp.
419–20.
[38] After the War this proportion increased to one third. Tanner, *Political Change*, p.
392 referring to the work of D.H. Close, 'The realignment of the British
electorate in 1931', *History*, lxvii (1982), pp. 393–404.
[39] M. Dyer, *Capable Citizens and Improvident Democrats: The Scottish Electoral System
1884–1929* (Aberdeen, 1996), pp. 29–31.
[40] Dyer, *Capable Citizens*, pp. 22–25.
[41] Matthew et al, 'The Franchise Factor' p. 727.

of Glasgow's seven divisions had rates below 50%, as did three of Lanark-shire's constituencies: Greenock had the lowest level of enfranchisement at only 41%.[42]

The most interesting differences for our purposes, however, lie within Glasgow itself. Table 1 below gives the rates of enfranchisement in 1911 for the seven parliamentary divisions of the City.

Table 1: Enfranchisement rates, Glasgow Parliamentary Divisions, 1911.

Divisions	Proportion of Adult males *Enfranchised*
No. 1 Bridgeton	43.7
No. 2 Camlachie	48.7
No. 3 St.Rollox	57.5
No. 4 Central	75.6
No. 5 College	52.0
No. 6 Tradeston	50.0
No. 7 Blackfriars & Hutchesontown	48.3
Total for all Glasgow	53.9

At the extremes lie Bridgeton, in the East End, and Central, which comprised the business heart of the City, and whose exceptionally high figure can be explained by the large number of plural votes which could be exercised there. Even without Central the variation in rates is interesting; but if we then delve deeper into the levels of enfranchisement operating in the smaller municipal wards the contrasts are much more dramatic.

The explanation for the differences in enfranchisement revealed in Table 2 lie in the economic and social make up of the different areas of the City. The two wards which stand out as having the highest rates by far – Exchange and Blythswood – constituted the commercial heart of Glasgow. They were also the two smallest wards and were the preserve of the City's business community. Though Blythswood (Glasgow's early West End) still housed a bourgeois element, the electorate there and in Exchange bore little relation to the actual resident population. The astronomical levels of enfranchise-ment can only be explained by plural votes. Put simply, there were more electors in these two wards than there were men of all ages: in Blythswood in 1911 the ratio was almost two to one.[43]

Nowhere else was the plural vote so evident, though the other wards which together with Exchange and Blythswood made up the Central Division – Anderston, Sandyford and Broomielaw – would have had a

---

[42] Dyer, *Capable Citizens*, pp. 21–2.
[43] See *Glasgow Herald*, 4 Nov. 1896 for a revealing description of the 'commercial electorate' going to the polls in these wards.

significant plural element since they all at least bordered the business area. This was particularly so with Broomielaw which was very much in the City centre and which, though it had a relatively high enfranchisement level of over 67%, was definitely one of the 'poorer class districts' of Glasgow.[44] It is hardly surprising that Central should have been the only solid Conservative seat in Glasgow.[45]

Table 2: Enfranchisement rates, Glasgow Municipal Wards, 1911.

Wards	Proportion of adult males enfranchised
No. 1 Dalmarnock	46.9
No. 2 Calton	38.9
No. 3 Mile End	46.7
No. 4 Whitevale	50.9
No. 5 Dennistoun	67.5
No. 6 Springburn*	48.1 (50.2)
No. 7 Cowlairs*	57.5 (57.5)
No. 8 Townhead	54.2
No. 9 Blackfriars	51.6
No. 10 Exchange+	282.9
No. 11 Blythswood+	272.0
No. 12 Broomielaw+	67.3
No. 13 Anderston	53.4
No. 14 Sandyford	57.3
No. 15 Park	65.0
No. 16 Cowcaddens	36.8
No. 17 Woodside	58.6
No. 18 Hutchesontown	47.1
No. 19 Gorbals	46.6
No. 20 Kingston	55.3
No. 21 Govanhill*	66.4 (49.2)
No. 22 Langside**	86.7
No. 23 Pollokshields**	85.2
No. 24 Kelvinside**	83.9
No. 25 Maryhill**	56.6
No. 26 Kinning Park**	54.0

* = those wards partly outwith Glasgow Parliamentary Burgh. figures in parentheses give the rate for the area within the Parliamentary Burgh.
** = those wards totally outwith Glasgow Parliamentary Burgh
+ = those wards with a particularly high plural voting element.

[44] Glasgow Corporation, *Report of the Medical Officer of Health* (Glasgow, 1913), p. 231.
[45] Between 1885 and 1918 Central returned a Conservative at every election apart from 1885 and 1906. F.W.S. Craig, *British Parliamentary Election Results 1885–1918* (London, 1974), p. 506.

Langside, Pollokshields and Kelvinside all enjoyed enfranchisement levels of over 80% and in these cases this did reflect their social composition. These wards were the residential areas of Glasgow (especially the last two) and were situated outside the boundaries of the Parliamentary Burgh. The first two lay to the south of the city while Kelvinside (which was where the University was relocated to from the High Street) was the new West End of Glasgow. Kelvinside was seen as being the home of the more anglicised, newer wealth, while Pollokshields represented the more douce and respectable Scottish bourgeoisie.[46] These were the districts where the businessmen of the city tended to live, and given that many of them chose to exercise their franchise elsewhere the true enfranchisement rate was likely to be significantly greater than these already high rates.

The other wards which can be categorised as having high levels of enfranchisement were Dennistoun, Park and Govanhill. Park was famed as a rich district, dominated by the great houses overlooking Kelvingrove Park. At the same time it was more mixed than the suburbs since it was bounded on one side by Kelvinside and on the other by the working class areas of Anderston, Sandyford, Woodside and Cowcaddens. Similarly Dennistoun – this 'bourgeois Ward'[47] – had a strong middle class presence in its centre but also had a working class population overlapping with Townhead and Whitevale.

Govanhill is an especially interesting case. Commonly identified as an 'artisan' ward[48] it lay partly within and partly outwith the Parliamentary Burgh and the enfranchisement rates between the two parts are significantly different. To the North Govanhill was bounded by Gorbals and Hutchesontown and was part of the Blackfriars & Hutchesontown Division. This section of the Ward had less than 50% enfranchisement. Govanhill became more residential to the South where it was bounded by Langside and, given the overall rate of over 66%, this part of the Burgh must have had a level of enfranchisement more akin to the suburban wards. Of added interest is that Govanhill was the only Ward with a high level of enfranchisement which returned a Labour candidate before 1914 – in the municipal election of 1911. In none of the others, with the exception of Dennistoun, did Labour even bother to stand.

The remaining wards (two-thirds of the total) were largely working class and situated in all parts of the City: North, South, East and West.[49] The enfranchisement rates for all seventeen were below 60% while seven of these were actually below 50% and two fell under the 40% mark. Though there was no immutable demarcation between these wards we can make a general distinction between 'artisan' and 'poorer' working class areas, which were

[46] J.H. Muir, *Glasgow in 1901* (Glasgow & Edinburgh, 1901) pp 162–3.
[47] *Forward* 9 Nov. 1907.
[48] Glasgow Corporation, *Report Medical Officer*, p. 231.
[49] PP 1908, CVII *Cost of Living of the Working Classes, Report of an Enquiry By the Board of Trade* (1908).

the descriptive categories employed by Glasgow's Medical Officer of Health. Broadly speaking those wards with rates higher than 50% were artisan or skilled areas while those below were poor or unskilled. Thus Sandyford, Woodside, Maryhill, Kingston and Kinning Park were regarded as artisan as were Townhead, Cowlairs and Springburn which were largely dominated by railway engineering. Cowlairs and Springburn were often regarded as one and the same though there was a noticeable difference between their levels of enfranchisement.

Wards which can be categorised as poor or unskilled were Cowcaddens, Calton, Hutchesontown, Dalmarnock, Anderston and Gorbals, and the first two in particular reveal this in their enfranchisement rates. Blackfriars would also fit into this category containing, as it did, some of the worst of Glasgow's housing stock around the High Street, but it was also an area of small businesses and likely had a greater plural voting element than the rest. Whitevale and Mile End together comprised the East End Division of Camlachie and though recognisably 'poor' in many ways also had a more diverse social profile: Whitevale bordered bourgeois Dennistoun and Mile End stretched out further East to the engineering districts of Parkhead and Shettleston which only became part of the Glasgow Municipal Burgh in 1912.

This rough, descriptive guide to the social structure of the Wards is ragged at the edges with a degree of overlap, particularly between working class areas. However, it does confirm a commonsense view of Glasgow and correctly identifies both the extremes and broad trend of enfranchisement rates. Thus the phenomenally high rates in the business wards of Blythswood and Exchange are obviously due to the plural vote and neither they nor the high rates in the middle class, residential wards are unexpected. At the other end of the scale Cowcaddens was renowned as a 'slum area' and its low rate is just as clearly understood. However, it is possible to go beyond mere description and make a more statistically verifiable analysis relating adult male enfranchisement rates in the wards to social indicators such as health and housing conditions. This is detailed in the Appendix and reveals a positive correlation in every instance, supporting the argument that enfranchisement was linked directly to class and status.

Our discussion so far has been at a general level but it is possible to look at the complexion of the working class electorate (or part of it) in a little more human detail through the membership of Glasgow Trades Council. The Trades Council was by no means representative of the whole working class but its delegates do provide a 'sample' of the organised male workforce, precisely that element we would expect to find on the electoral register.

In 1911 the membership of the Trades Council numbered 287, which included five women. Of the 282 men, 205 were traced to addresses within Glasgow Municipal Burgh and, of this figure, only 113 and 114 appeared on the electoral register in each of the two years 1910–11 and 1911–12; an enfranchisement rate of 55%, only slightly greater than the rate for Glasgow as a whole. The proportion of delegates appearing on the register in both years was 45% while the figure for those appearing in either year was 66%. Even taking this higher figure leaves out a significant element of what must have been not only the most organised but also the most politically aware section of the working class.

Even within this group of activists, however, there were variations. If we take the Amalgamated Society of Engineers (ASE) and the Municipal Employees' Association (MEA) as, respectively, a skilled union and a general union, we can see a marked difference in their enfranchisement levels. The ASE had fourteen delegates representing seven branches on the Trades Council, and the MEA had thirty-six delegates representing twenty-two branches. Of the ASE members, eleven lived within the Municipal Burgh and, of these ten were on the electoral register on either of the two years. Of the MEA members twenty-five could be traced of whom sixteen appeared on the register on either year. The difference in enfranchisement rates between the two Unions in the two years were 30% and 18%. These numbers are quite small (though the MEA accounted for an eighth of total Council delegates) but they do indicate a tendency for skilled workers to be more likely to have the vote than the unskilled. In fact the actual gap between skilled and unskilled was likely to have been much more since the greater number of MEA members who appeared on the register actually had some sort of skill, and only four could be regarded as simply unskilled.[50]

Table 3: Glasgow Trades Council Delegates and the Franchise, 1911.

Delegates	No. traced		On electoral register	
	1910–11	1911–12	Both years	Either year
GTC 205	113 (55%)	114 (56%)	93 (45%)	135 (66%)
MEA 25	13 (52%)	16 (64%)	13 (52%)	16 (64%)
ASE 11	9 (82%)	9 (82%)	8 (73%)	10 (91%)

Table 3 summarises this information. By examining the electoral register over two consecutive years we can clearly see the tendency for individuals to move on and off the voters' roll. Given this it could be argued that the number appearing on the register in either of the two years, the higher figure, was the more representative since it indicates the true number of those likely to qualify as electors.[51] However, the fact remains that the number with the vote in any single year was significantly less and this was due

---

[50] Occupations of MEA members included electrician, engineer, plumber, joiner and brassdresser.

[51] It must be remembered that 1911 was a good year for employment. In the previous years of high unemployment the level of enfranchisement was likely to have been considerably less. 'The stress of poverty disfranchised many of our supporters for the time being.' *Forward*, 14 November 1908.

to the requirement to register for the vote and was a problem faced by everyone who otherwise qualified to vote. As Matthew *et al* have commented, 'It is hard to disagree with the Liberal agents . . . that mass disqualification was inherent in the occupation franchise. It is hard, also, to avoid the conclusion that is precisely why it was there.'[52]

Anyone, be they a middle class businessman, shopkeeper, boilermaker or labourer, could lose their vote temporarily through moving house, but it is clear that it was the poorer, unskilled sections of the working class who suffered most from registration difficulties.[53] As with our figures for the Municipal Wards, the above information on the Trades Council shows that different sections of the male population – who can be identified on a class and status basis – experienced significantly different enfranchisement levels. The differential that existed between the middle class and working class was then repeated within the working class itself.

Labour and its Constituency: Respectability versus Residuum

Recognition of this disparity between 'artisan' and 'poorer class' areas brings us directly to the question of Labour's own attitude towards the franchise. At a formal level Labour was committed to full adult suffrage but it is clear that the extension of the franchise did not present itself as a pressing issue. Writing in the mid-1890s on the task confronting the ILP, Keir Hardie remarked, 'There is no need now to fight the battle of the franchise. Our fathers did that and today only the details remain to be adjusted.'[54] Matthew *et al* see in this evidence of Hardie's 'complete naiveté about electoral statistics', yet it seems highly unlikely that Hardie and other Labour leaders were simply ignorant of the operation of the franchise system and its inbuilt biases against the poor. The major reason why the leadership of the movement for independent labour representation could have accepted such an undemocratic arrangement was because they shared sufficiently in the notions of 'citizenship' and 'respectability' around which the reformed order had been created.

Under the pre-1918 franchise system the vote was not a natural right but a mark of citizenship, a trust which had to be earned. As T.H. Marshall, in his classic account of 'Citizenship and Social Class', has put it, '. . . the political franchise was not one of the rights of citizenship. It was the privilege of a limited economic class, whose limits were extended by each successive Reform Act.'[55] It was not the radical, Painite view of the vote which triumphed in Britain but the Whig perspective of gradual, incremental

---

[52] Matthew *et al*, 'The Franchise Factor', p. 734.
[53] J.F. McCaffrey, ''The Irish Vote in Glasgow in the Later Nineteenth Century', *Innes Review*, xxi (1970), pp. 32–3
[54] Keir Hardie, 'The Independent Labour Party', in A. Reid (ed.), *The New Party* (London, 1895), p. 258; quoted in Matthew *et al*, 'The Franchise Factor', p. 724.
[55] T.H. Marshall, *Sociology at the Crossroads and other Essays* (London, 1963), p. 80.

reform whereby the suffrage was granted to various classes or groups in society as each in turn proved themselves capable of exercising the franchise responsibly. As such it was just as important, if not more so, to calculate who would be excluded from the system.[56]

In the campaigning over the Second Reform Act in 1867 it is not the case that the working class Reform League saw itself as being forced into accepting the proposals of the middle class Reform Union in order to secure half a loaf. The Reform League itself was, at best, uncertain about manhood suffrage and much more comfortable with the notion of household reform and continuing exclusion of the poor.[57] Once an independent labour and socialist movement emerged toward the end of the century, this ambivalence towards the vote and the poor remained. Those without the vote did not have sufficient power and influence to create a demand for further reform in their own right; to a great extent the voteless were invisible. Hardie and the proponents of independent labour were in competition with the Liberals for the votes of the respectable working man; both groups were concerned about the lack of political intelligence among the poor and had no interest in further extensions of the franchise.

Respectability was not simply a piece of false consciousness foisted upon the working class but was part of the lived experience of the working population. Respectability had many connotations which affected the whole household and not just the individual male worker. It can be seen as having been particularly onerous on wives and mothers as they were forced to 'keep up appearances' through the unremitting toil of housework and ensuring the physical cleanliness and 'respectability' of the home and family[58]. It was always possible for a labourer and his family to be respectable but it was undoubtedly easier for a skilled tradesman with his better pay and more regular earnings to aspire to and achieve the desired status.

While respectability was not necessarily exclusive it was, nevertheless, defined in relation to something else, to an altogether more parlous state – that of the poor, the lumpen proletariat, the thriftless, the slum-dweller. In the 1900s the generic title of the 'residuum' became common currency but if the label was new the phenomenon to which it referred was not. Similarly, as middle class efforts to draw distinguishing lines between sections of the working class (the deserving and undeserving poor) were not new, neither was it new for the working class itself to draw distinctions, and both resounded in pejorative, moralistic terms. As Smout has pointed out, the

---

[56] Even the 1918 Representation of the People Act was at pains to maintain a predominantly male electorate by keeping out young women. Pugh, *Electoral Reform*, p. 151.

[57] R. Harrison, *Before the Socialists: Studies in Labour and Politics 1861–1881* (London, 1965), pp .80–1; F.B. Smith, *The Making of the Second Reform Bill* (Melbourne, 1966), pp. 4, 229.

[58] E. Roberts, *A Woman's Place: an Oral History of Working Class Women 1890–1914* (London, 1984), p. 38.

reason why, 'Respectability was a divisive element within the working class', was because, 'it gave a moral dimension to the craftsman's feeling that he was a cut above the labourer in more than just his level of skill.' In terms of suffrage reform,

> There is no doubt that most working class radicals and trade union leaders revelled in their reputation for respectability in the third quarter of the nineteenth century, and they were not at all averse to the Gladstonian idea that by their manifestly excellent qualities they had 'won' the vote.[59]

Joan Smith has argued that Liberal values were not simply opinions held by significant individuals but were part and parcel of the 'commonsense' of the industrial working class of Glasgow. This view of the world encompassed beliefs in free trade, democracy, freedom of small nations, and hostility to landlordism and the House of Lords. Intrinsically connected to such beliefs were the societies people joined, 'the friendly society branches, the co-operatives, and the trade union branches.' In Glasgow socialism, and particularly the ILP, had a Liberal inheritance and there was much that was progressive about that tradition. However, the inheritance was not made available to everyone and its implications were ambivalent, to say the least, when applied to the whole of the working class. 'In Glasgow skilled working [men] . . . were Liberals by conviction, but they could also afford to be Liberals.'[60]

In Glasgow the manufacturing sector was dominant, reflecting the City's central position within the wider Clydeside region and its integrated economic structure of shipbuilding, metalworking, steel making and coal mining.[61] In particular the late nineteenth and early twentieth century growth of engineering, tool-making and metalworking – inextricably linked to shipbuilding and marine engineering – with their reliance upon skilled workers, 'explained the male-dominated, craft-based cultural landscape within large areas of Glasgow.'[62] The industrial structure was much broader than this – even after decades of decline, textiles and clothing still accounted for over 18,000 of the occupied male labour force in 1911. Non manual occupations were also significant, with over 12,000 male clerks in the City.[63] However, in comparison with other cities, Glasgow had a very low

[59] T.C. Smout, *A Century of the Scottish People 1830–1950* (London, 1986), pp. 247–51.
[60] Smith, 'Labour Tradition', p. 49, 33–4.
[61] Shipbuilding was the key to this industrial machine with the Clyde yards producing one third of British tonnage and 18 per cent of world output in 1913. W. Knox, A. McKinlay, J. Smyth, 'Industrialisation, Work and Labour Politics: Clydeside, c. 1850–1990', in R. Schulze (ed.), *Industrial Regions in Transformation* (Essen, 1993), pp. 201–2.
[62] R. Rodger, 'The Labour Force', in Fraser & Mavor, *Glasgow*, p. 167. The extension of the City boundaries in 1912 to include Govan and Partick made this pattern even more pronounced. See Smith, 'Labour Tradition'.
[63] *Census of Scotland 1911*, City of Glasgow.

proportion of professional and middle class occupations. It was manufacturing which predominated with almost seven out of ten workers of both
sexes employed in this sector. Furthermore, skilled men were found outwith
the metal working trades, for instance in furniture and printing.[64]

But, if Glasgow was the home of the skilled man, it was also the domicile of
the unskilled and casual worker. Treble has estimated the pre-war unskilled
male workforce as comprising some 27% of the total occupied male
population. It is impossible to be exact since the census list of occupations
contain some with gradations of skill which cannot be disaggregated and a
number of youths would have gone on to other, apprenticed trades. Even if
this figure is something of an overestimate, it still gives us some indication of
the extent of poverty within the working class of Glasgow. Given average
wages in these occupations of between 16s (80 p.) and 24s a week (£1. 20p.)
and, as such, '. . . it is impossible to argue that the majority of the families of
unskilled workers must have lived at or below the poverty line if they
depended solely upon the income of the head of household.'[65] The poverty
line was usually regarded as 'around about a pound a week', and this was the
figure which the Glasgow Presbytery Commission on Housing focused on in
1890.[66] Two decades later there were still many men earning this amount:
wages of women and young people were even less.

Poverty, however, was not just an absolute but a relative matter. The labourer
worked beside, and for, the skilled man and the most immediate reference
point for both were the wages of each other. Wage rates varied widely, even
amongst skilled workers in the same trade, but the major differential lay
between the tradesmen and their labourers. According to figures collated by
the Board of Trade, in 1905 weekly rates for skilled men in engineering ran
between 36s. 1.5d. (£1. 80.5p.) and 41s. 9d. (£2. 8.75p.) while labourers
received a mere 18s. (90p.) Seven years later the wage rates of most workmen,
though not all, had increased but while the skilled trades in engineering had
experienced an average rise of 8%, their labourers had gone up only 6%.[67]
Similar patterns were identified in other industries and it would appear that the
differential had been getting steadily wider for some time; in 1886 the hourly
rate of a carpenter's labourer was equivalent to 63.3 per cent of the carpenter's,
while in 1906 it was equivalent to only 60.5 per cent.[68]

[64] Rodger, 'Labour Force' p. 167.
[65] J.H. Treble, 'The Market for Unskilled Male Labour in Glasgow 1891–1914', in I.
MacDougall (ed.), *Essays in Scottish Labour History* (Edinburgh, 1978), p. 129
[66] 'The Commission restricted their enquiry to the housing and social conditions of
working men and women whose wages are under 20s.' Presbytery of Glasgow,
Report of Commission on the Housing of the Poor in Relation to Their Social Condition
(Glasgow 1891), p. 10
[67] These figures taken from two enquiries undertaken by the Board of Trade, PP
1908, CVII, *Cost of Living of the Working Classes* (1908); PP 1913, LXVI, *Cost of Living
of the Working Classes . . .* (1912)
[68] E.H. Hunt, *Regional Wage Variations in Britain 1850–1914* (Oxford 1973), Table 1–
5, pp. 68–9.

The whole question of the poor in Glasgow was complicated by the existence of a large Irish-Catholic community. While the Irish may not have been concentrated in particular ghettos, as in Liverpool, they were by no means evenly distributed throughout the city. When Russell made his four-fold classification of Glasgow in the 1880s the proportion of Irish-born in the four Groups reflected worsening social conditions. With a City-wide average of 13% Irish born, there were only 7% in Group One but fully 20% in those areas which comprised Group Four which, in Russell's own words, 'will be at once recognised as the worst districts of Glasgow, both morally and physically.'[69] Similarly, the Irish tended to be concentrated in certain, low-paid occupations. Where the unskilled sector identified by Treble accounted for 27% of all male workers, it employed 44% of Irish male workers. Given that this figure refers only to Irish-born and not the overwhelming majority of the 'Irish' population who were actually born in Scotland, it would hardly be overstating the case that particular jobs – all in the unskilled sector – were largely the preserve of Irishmen.[70]

A racial divide did therefore operate within the Glasgow working class, between artisan and labourer. However, the strength of socialist and labour support for Irish Home Rule and the extent of Irish involvement within the labour movement meant that relations, at least before the 1930s, never deteriorated to the sectarian level of Liverpool.[71] At the same time perceptions of the Irish community gave an extra twist to discussion of the residuum who could be identified not only by individual failings but also through cultural and racial stereotyping. For instance the Rev Donald McLeod, a member of the Glasgow Presbytery Commission, drew a distinction between Highland and Irish immigrants and made a clear connection between the latter and 'drunkenness and self-producing poverty.'[72]

The nature of Clydeside's heavy industry – with its reliance upon international export markets – made it particularly vulnerable to peaks and troughs of the trade cycle. Shipbuilding was particularly volatile and the dependant relationship of one industry upon another meant that unemployment and short-time working was a common experience for both skilled and unskilled. In addition the multiplier effect meant that a slump in the heavy, capital goods sector would resonate into all the other sectors of the economy. This, in turn, would further compound the permanent problem of casual and seasonal labour.[73] In the first decade of the twentieth century

---

[69] J.B. Russell, *The Vital Statistics of the City of Glasgow 1881–1885* (published in 3 parts, Glasgow 1885/6), Part II, p. 75.

[70] *Census of Scotland 1911* Vol. 3 Table III. The whole question of the Irish is gone into in much more detail in Chapter Four.

[71] Smith, 'Labour Tradition', pp. 33, 50.

[72] Presbytery of Glasgow, *Report*, p. 183.

[73] J.H. Treble, 'The Seasonal Demand for Adult Labour in Glasgow, 1890–1914', *Social History*, iii (1978) pp. 43–60; Treble, 'Market for unskilled'; Rodger, 'Labour Force'.

Glasgow experienced two cyclical downturns, in 1903–5 and again in 1907–10, the latter being particularly acute. The Trades Council calculated, on the basis of a survey of one third of its own membership, an unemployment rate of 19.3% in 1908. However, given that the Council's information excluded, 'entirely the non-unionists in the skilled trades, and the labourers, who are mostly unorganised', this was likely a gross under-estimate.[74]

For Glasgow Trades Council, 'Unemployment is really the question of the day', a position which reflected the reality not just of one bad year but consistently high levels of unemployment.[75] Both Treble and Smith have drawn attention to the radicalising impact of this experience. For Smith the campaign which brought 35,000 onto the streets of Glasgow in support of an ILP-led 'Right to Work' demonstration directed against a Liberal Government was critical in the politicisation of the working class. The campaign had originated with the Social Democratic Federation (SDF) but the leading role ultimately was taken by the ILP and Trades Council with the latter re-committing itself to electoral work and beginning the process which would result in the formation of the Glasgow Labour Party a few years later.[76]

Significant as this was in resuscitating Labour's local political fortunes, it was not, as we shall see in the following chapter, sufficient to break Liberalism's hegemony. While the unemployment issue is important in reminding us of the common, shared experiences of the working class it could not, on its own, provide a long-term political rallying point and unifying cause. Apart from anything else, the reality of unemployment was felt differently by different workers. The skilled man, with his union and friendly society benefits, was always able to insulate himself to an extent, though a longer-term crisis such as that of 1907–10 and, even more significantly, the long depression of the inter-war years, saw this capacity stretched to breaking point. For the unskilled, the impact was immediate; in the words of the Charity Organisation Society, 'it is the unskilled and casual labour that suffers first in a season of depression.'[77] Once laid off, such workers had little or no organisational support; since, as Treble reminds us, 'levels of unionisation among the unskilled were very low in Scotland.'[78] Moreover, once trade union organisation and membership among the unskilled and even women workers began to expand dramatically during

[74] Glasgow Trades Council, *Annual Report 1908–09*, p. 16.

[75] Glasgow Trades Council, *Annual Report 1908–09*, p. 14; Treble has calculated the mean average unemployment among unionised engineering and metal workers in this period, with a low of 7.5% in 1906 and a high of 24.2% in 1908. J.H. Treble, 'Unemployment in Glasgow 1903–1910: Anatomy of a crisis', *Scottish Labour History Society Journal*, xxv (1990), Table 1, p. 38.

[76] J. Smith, 'Taking the leadership of the labour movement: the ILP in Glasgow, 1906–1914', in McKinlay & Morris, *ILP on Clydeside*, pp. 65–7. Labour's electoral performance is detailed in Chapter One below.

[77] *Organised Help*, November 1908, quoted in Treble, 'Unemployment in Glasgow', p. 20. This was the official organ of the C.O.S. in Glasgow.

[78] Treble, 'Unemployment in Glasgow', p. 36, fn. 45.

the 'labour unrest' of 1910–14, this produced no immediate political benefit to Labour.[79] Of course, it remained the case that under the pre-1918 franchise, neither women workers nor many poorer male workers would have been able to vote Labour even if they had wanted to.

Labour and the Suffrage

If one force could have cut the Gordian knot which so bedevilled the cause of suffrage reform it was the Labour and socialist movement. This is not to say that Labour would have enforced a measure of reform on its own but, had it turned its formal declaration of universal suffrage into a campaigning commitment, it could have significantly altered the balance of forces on this issue and, possibly, many others. The British Labour movement's inactivity is quite remarkable compared to countries such as Sweden or Belgium where series of general strikes were called between 1886 and 1913 in an attempt to win the franchise.[80] Moreover, while Britain has always emphasised its democratic credentials, these, in fact, did not compare very favourably with other capitalist societies. Britain being, 'among the last of the industrial nations to grant unencumbered universal male suffrage.'[81] Rather than give a lead, Labour reacted to the women's suffrage movement.

It was only when women began to agitate forcibly for the vote that Labour rediscovered the inequities of the existing franchise. For instance, at the very first conference of the STUC in 1897 a resolution in support of equal votes for women was passed, only to be reversed the following year in favour of universal adult suffrage.[82] A similar pattern was repeated at both the TUC and the Labour Party; as soon as a women's suffrage resolution was raised, an adult suffrage motion was passed in response. It was clear to women suffragists and their male supporters that this was primarily a blocking manoeuvre rather than a deeply held principle. Indeed, Keir Hardie was moved to threaten his resignation from the Labour Party in 1907, but to no avail.[83] Eva Gore Booth, active among the women textile workers of the North of England, remarked bitterly upon Labour's hypocrisy over adult suffrage:

---

[79] J.J. Smyth, ' "From Industrial Unrest to Industrial Debacle?" ': the labour left and industrial militancy 1910–14', in W. Kenefick & A. McIvor (eds.), *Roots of Red Clydeside 1910–1914? Labour Unrest and Industrial Relations in West Scotland* (Edinburgh, 1996), pp. 240–58.

[80] G. Therborn, 'The Rule of Capital and the Rise of Democracy', *New Left Review*, ciii (1977), pp. 3–41.

[81] H.F. Moorhouse, 'The Marxist Theory of the Labour Aristocracy', *Social History*, iii (1978), p. 52.

[82] E. Gordon, *Women and the Labour Movement in Scotland 1850–1914* (Oxford, 1991), p. 222.

[83] J. Liddington & J. Norris, *One Hand Tied Behind Us: The Rise of the women's Suffrage Movement* (London, 1978), pp. 231–6.

their position is absolutely indefensible. They have built up the whole of the Labour party on what they are pleased to call a property qualification, a qualification that, according to their own often repeated statement, no democratic person could accept or even compromise with as a temporary instalment of justice. . . . In fact they have eaten their cake and enjoyed and digested it; it is only when a hungry beggar asks for a slice that they find it is poisonous.[84]

The logic of Labour's position was that a limited women's franchise would operate against its own interests since those likely to be given the vote would be upper and middle class women. Socialist advocates of women's suffrage argued the contrary and a series of surveys indicated that the majority of women ratepayers (the group who already had the local franchise and would qualify for the parliamentary vote under a women's bill) were in fact working class.[85] However, such statistical evidence was not sufficient to alter the ingrained belief among socialists and trade unionists that votes for women would simply translate into votes for Conservatives. There was some truth to this given the higher levels of female municipal electors in suburban middle class areas but, even more damaging, was the widespread perception that the existing women municipal voters were inherently anti-Labour.[86]

Ultimately the Labour Party and the non-militant women suffragists of the National Union of Women's Suffrage Societies (NUWSS) did come to a political and electoral arrangement before the War. At its Annual Conference in 1912 Labour reiterated its support for adult suffrage but declared unacceptable any Bill that did not include women. This was sufficient for the NUWSS, frustrated by Liberal convolutions and worried by Asquith's proposed manhood suffrage bill, to establish a fund with which to campaign for Labour candidates at by-elections. The Labour conference in 1913 then went further by confirming it would actually oppose a franchise bill that did not include women.[87] Although it has been argued that this decision by Labour made reform inevitable, it is impossible to be certain what Labour might have done had the Liberals been able to put a manhood suffrage bill before parliament. However, the alliance between suffragists and Labour, disrupted by the outbreak of war, came together again in 1916 once the Speakers' Conference to deal with reform was established. The irony for suffragists was that having campaigned tirelessly for votes for women on the same terms as men, they accepted a proposal which clearly discriminated against women, out of fear of losing their chance to secure any reform.

---

[84] E. Gore Booth in Brougham Villiers, *The Case for Women's Suffrage* (London, 1907), pp. 54–5, quoted in S. Holton, *Feminism and Democracy: Women's Suffrage and Reform Politics in Britain 1900–1918* (Cambridge, 1986), p. 59.

[85] P. Hollis, *Ladies Elect: Women in English Local Government 1865–1914* (Oxford 1987), p. 32; Liddington & Norris, *One Hand*, pp. 184–6.

[86] This and the whole issue of women's suffrage is dealt with in detail in Chapter Five.

[87] Liddington & Norris, *One Hand*, p. 247; Holton, *Feminism and Democracy*, pp. 73, 94.

Labour, rather than throwing its weight behind full adult suffrage, went along with the NUWSS.[88]

Writing in 1906 in support of votes for women, Hardie argued that while full universal suffrage would take over twenty years to achieve, adult male suffrage could be achieved more or less for the asking.[89] One can hardly avoid asking why, if it was so easy, nobody ever bothered to ask. In detailing the process of electoral reform, Pugh has pointed out the very limited role played by the Labour Party, both before 1914 and during the War. Contrary to possible expectations, Labour never pressurised the Liberal Governments of 1906 to 1916 over reform, and this mirrored the Party's preoccupation with consolidating its existing areas of support:

> . . . the party's immediate interest lay in the organised, politically aware sections of the working class already on the parliamentary register; nothing was as yet to be expected from domestic servants living with their employers or labourers residing with farmers who bulked large among the unenfranchised, or indeed from many industrial workers in areas in which, in Ramsay MacDonald's words, "poverty and degradation are of the worst type".[90]

But it was this 'type' which gave Labour most cause for concern and was the reason behind its indifference to suffrage reform. The ambivalence if not outright hostility of the politically conscious worker towards the poor can be traced back to the mid-Victorian period. While Glasgow Trades Council supported manhood suffrage it nonetheless welcomed the Second Reform Act. The Council's Secretary, George Newton, wrote to Lord Elcho in 1866, attempting to assuage his fears of the likely consequences of reform:

> I am not aware that any body has proposed enfranchisement without a residential qualification, with this proviso no scum would be entitled at any time, they do not live in any one house long enough to qualify, so there need be no anxiety about them.[91]

Such attitudes continued and were expressed even by the likes of Keir Hardie. Writing in 1895 during his first stint at Westminster as 'member for the unemployed', Hardie referred specifically on the need to discipline the 'loafers' or 'work-shy' who were seen as contaminating the ranks of the genuinely unemployed: 'Treat them as you will and, above all, see that it is

---

[88] Holton, *Feminism and Democracy*, p. 49.

[89] Holton, *Feminism and Democracy*, p. 58.

[90] Despite Pugh's own assertion that the electoral system was 'broadly representative', it appears to be implicit in the above that there was a bias which operated against the poorer working class, '. . . the unenfranchised men tended to include the least organised, least politically conscious and least articulate sections of the population.' Pugh, *Electoral Reform*, p. 30.

[91] Quote in W.H. Fraser, 'Trades Councils in England and Scotland 1858–1897' (unpublished Ph.D. thesis, University of Sussex, 1967), p. 291.

made impossible for them to propagate their species.'[92] It is not the case
that the poor were denied a vote through any sort of caste or apartheid
system – contemporary references to the slum vote are testimony to its
existence.[93] But the slum dwellers were perceived as a problem and, like the
women municipal electors, could often be blamed for poor results. A
municipal defeat in Bradford brought forth this diatribe from the Labour
candidate; '. . . bitter, intolerant, unsympathetic and insolent, prone to live
on charity rather than on the rights of manhood and womanhood . . . not
until the death rate, the insanitation and the horrible mode of life are
changed, shall we ever see the South Ward of Bradford taking an intelligent
interest in the things mostly concerning it.'[94]

Contained within the above is a political perspective whereby the conditions that gave rise to the depravities of the residuum were to be reformed,
but the slum dwellers were not to be part of their own transformation. This
was a common, if not prevalent, attitude within labour and socialist opinion.
Both the Majority and Minority Reports of the Royal Commission on the
Poor Laws in 1909, (the latter drafted by Sidney and Beatrice Webb and
signed by George Lansbury), were 'as one in their support for the forcible
segregation of those inefficient parasitical elements, the so-called residuum,
who were deemed to be incapable of improvement.' [95] Furthermore, when
practical reforms were being formulated, the poor could be simply left out.
Thus George Carson, Secretary of the Trades Council and ILP town
councillor, argued that if Glasgow Corporation was to build houses, it
should not do so for the improvident poor but the 'respectable low wage
earners.'[96] John Wheatley, whose own housing proposals were to play a
major role in galvanising Labour representation in Glasgow before the War,
shared a similar blind spot towards the slum dwellers, who would not have
been eligible as tenants for his citizens' cottages.[97]

All public discussion of poverty made a distinction between the 'deserving' and 'undeserving' poor. Yet, what proportion of the population did the
latter represent? Rowntree's estimate that 27% of the population of York
lived in primary or secondary poverty may be taken as a general indicator of
a national pattern.[98] It certainly seems to fit Treble's figure for the unskilled

[92] *Labour Leader*, 26 January 1895 quoted in F. Reid, *Keir Hardie: the Making of a Socialist* (London, 1978), p. 168.

[93] Tanner, *Political Change*, pp. 110–1.

[94] Quoted in D. Howell, *British Workers and the Independent Labour Party 1888–1906* (Manchester, 1984), p. 334.

[95] D. Englander, *Poverty and Poor Law Reform in 19th. Century Britain, 1834–1914* (London, 1998), p. 75.

[96] Glasgow Municipal Commission on the Housing of the Poor, *Report* (Glasgow, 1904), p. 550.

[97] J. Wheatley, *A Reply to the Critics of the £8 Cottages* (Glasgow, 1913). See Chapter One, pp. 65–9 on Labour's pre-1914 housing policy

[98] H.C.G. Matthew, 'The Liberal Age' in K.O. Morgan (ed.), *The Oxford Illustrated History of Britain* (Oxford, 1986), p. 315.

male population in pre-war Glasgow.[99] But the proportion that made up the 'dissolute and criminal' would have been much less than that, and certainly much less than the 46% of adult males who were not on the electoral register in Glasgow. The investigations of social explorers, such as Booth and Rowntree, were attempting to come to terms with poverty as a social phenomenon and drew attention to the structural causes of poverty and the influence of the life cycle. But just as the basis of a more humanitarian understanding of the poor was developing, so the fear of the social abyss became all the greater. According to Englander:

> As living standards rose at the close of the nineteenth century the gap between the peripheral poor and the respectable working class became wider. The workhouse loomed larger than previously in the imagination of the newly affluent artisan with pauperism and loss of independence becoming the penultimate form of social descent, exceeded only by imprisonment.[100]

It is here that we can locate Labour's inactivity over the franchise. While it may be that by 1913 or 1914 further reform was inevitable, the sticking point was the extent to which the suffrage would have to be granted. It would have been almost impossible to make any further alteration in the system that would not have been based on universal or adult male suffrage at least. None of the political parties were prepared to take that final step. Labour may have been formally in favour but was unwilling to push the matter. It is not simply a question of whether and to what extent the franchise system limited Labour's progress but what Labour's attitude says about it and its own ambition. In seeking to win the respectable working man from Liberalism, Labour had little perception of women or the poor as part of its own constituency.

Towards a More United Working-class Politics

All of this changed due to the impact of the Great War and in Glasgow, as elsewhere, Labour had to come to terms with the new political situation after 1918 and the new electorate. Labour had to adjust from a position of limited challenger to, and junior partner with, the Liberals, to a situation in which it had sufficient support to supplant the Liberal Party. This was an ambition which had been voiced by Labour leaders since the 1880s, but had never before been within the realm of practical politics. The limited electorate, in the main committed to the Liberals, and composed of the respectable, skilled male working class had gone. The Liberal Party in Glasgow had become a very pale a shadow of its former self by the end of the War after alienating that very group.[101] Women and the poorer

[99] See above p. 18.
[100] Englander, *Poverty and Poor Law,* p. 46.
[101] The political impact of the War is discussed in Chapter Two.

working class were now part of the political nation and the social and political chasm between respectable and residuum had narrowed significantly.

Despite initial fears of mass unemployment at the start of the war, military demands for munitions, ships and supplies led to an unprecedented demand for labour, especially on Clydeside. This situation of full employment, going back to 1911–12, and rising living standards in the later years of the war, continued into an immediate post-war boom. Under such conditions, reinforced by the moral sanction of just reward for having won the war (Homes Fit For Heroes!), working class expectations and organisational strength increased dramatically. By 1920 trade union membership in the United Kingdom stood at 8.3 million or 45.2% of the workforce, compared to only 2.6 million and 14.6% in 1910. Within this general expansion it was the general unions catering for the semi-skilled and unskilled, male and female, which grew most rapidly.[102]

Wage differentials, which had grown prior to 1914, narrowed as the unskilled made advances on the tradesmen. Thus, in Glasgow an engineering labourer received 60% of a turner or fitter's rate in 1914 but 80% in 1920; the difference between a bricklayer and his labourer narrowed from 62% in 1914 to 84% in 1920; and over the same period the gap between a shipwright and his labourer fell from 55% to 76%.[103] The war also saw a marked decline in pauperism. The numbers in receipt of relief from Glasgow Parish, both indoor and outdoor, fell as did the number of applicants which more than halved from the second half of 1914 compared to the latter part of 1918. As a contemporary historical account explained, 'Money was more plentiful, and employment was available for all.' Moreover, although 'numerous hasty war-marriages' led to a later increase in applications for relief by women deserted by their husbands, nonetheless, 'After the war the receipt of pensions prevented a rapid recrudescence of pauperism. . . .'[104]

Even with the return of unemployment in the 1920s, the fall in real wages and sharp drop in trade union membership, the overall position of the working class still stood at a higher level than before the War. The experience of the war-economy, with full employment, the virtual disappearance of casual poverty, and Government regulation of much of industry, meant that notions of respectability with their emphasis on individual responses to general problems had become less realistic. The attention of the working class became increasingly focused on the active role

[102] 'The spread of unionisation during the war was more rapid among women than among any group of men . . .' J.E. Cronin, *Labour and Society in Britain 1918–1979* (London, 1984), pp. 31–2, 241.

[103] Hutchison, *Political History*, p. 287, Table 9.3. extracted from *British Labour Statistics, Historical Abstract, 1886–1968* (London, 1971).

[104] W.R. Scott & J. Cunnison, *The Industries of the Clyde Valley During the War* (Oxford, 1924), pp. 170–1.

of the State.[105] Divisions within the working class did not disappear as a result of this experience but the old distinctions based on status and gender could no longer be held with the same certainty.

What then was the political impact of all this? Hutchison has pointed out the correlation in the post-1918 situation of high union density with Labour electoral success. Moreover, the bulk of new members were from the semi and unskilled,

> It was this section of the working class who had been most likely to be excluded from holding the franchise before 1918, and accordingly their mass accession to the electorate under the Fourth Reform Act had a considerable impact on the political balance in constituencies, especially urban seats.[106]

For Matthew *et al* it was precisely this which scuppered the Liberals. While Labour and the Tories could appeal to this new constituency in 'vulgar' ways, more at the level of rhetoric than policies, the Liberal Party needed, 'an informed and intelligent electorate.' Liberalism could only have survived under the nineteenth century franchise system:

> . . . with that electorate, one large enough to be responsive to particular legislative proposals, but not yet swamped by Bright's 'residuum'. The 1918 Act, however, did more than just treble the electorate: it transformed its character by significantly lowering its political awareness. Not only was the new electorate divided by class in a way that increasingly excluded the Liberals but it was less likely to respond to politics that demanded a high level of political intelligence.[107]

This perspective finds an echo in McLean's study of Glasgow politics in the immediate post-war years, in particular his emphasis upon the creation of a Labour Party 'machine', which came to incorporate the Irish 'machine', geared to and successful in turning out the working class electorate.[108] Whether or not these writers consciously attach pejorative meanings to their descriptions of the electorate, they project an image of an ignorant, docile mass, responsive to subliminal appeals to its sense of common identity, which could be herded into polling-booths relatively easily.[109] A more interesting approach is suggested by Hutchison, who comments that 'the very techniques of traditional political debate seemed ill-adjusted to new

---

[105] J. Hinton, *Labour and Socialism: A History of the British Labour Movement 1867–1974* (Sussex, 1983), pp. 96–117.

[106] Hutchison, *Political History*, pp. 285–6.

[107] Matthew et al, 'The Franchise Factor', pp. 747–9.

[108] McLean, *The Legend*, p. 163.

[109] The connection of Liberalism and Liberal supporters with high political intellect has been questioned by Thorpe who points out the Liberals' own simplicities such as the big loaf of free trade versus the small loaf of protectionism. A. Thorpe, *A History of the British Labour Party* (London, 1997), p. 38.

conditions.' However, 'Labour had developed techniques to reach the voters in, so to speak, their natural habitat rather than the artificial context of large meetings.'[110]

Labour candidates and propagandists addressed impromptu gatherings both at home and at the workplace, making it easier for people to actually hear what was being said and to ask questions in such a normal environment. For women in particular, being spoken to in the security of their everyday surroundings and amongst their neighbours would have been much more likely to give them the confidence to express their own opinions than in the intimidating atmosphere of a public hall. Rather than regard women and the poor as 'ignorant', it should be understood that having been denied a say in the political life of the country for so long, they were hardly likely to share the established views of how proper political debate should be conducted.[111]

Although Labour clearly benefited most from the extension of the franchise, it still had to overcome its own ambivalence towards the new voters. While some, like James Maxton, were enthusiastic in their recognition of the new levels of support that now existed, others, such as Tom Johnston, remained reluctant to accept the slum dweller as part of Labour's constituency. Even in 1921 Johnston continued to regard Labour's support as being located in the better-off artisan wards while claiming, 'the slum areas are represented by Capitalists on public bodies.'[112] As an analysis, however, this was partial at best and was more revealing about Johnston's own disdain towards the slumdweller. In fact, there was plenty of evidence available to Johnston that support in the slum areas was there if Labour was prepared to act on it. For instance, just one month previously Labour had won a seat in the Cowcaddens ward. More spectacularly, in 1920 when all municipal seats were contested, Labour secured a clean sweep in Gorbals, a ward it had never enjoyed success in before.

Housing conditions provide a good indicator of the class composition of an area and of political loyalties. As Chris Cook showed some time ago, for Glasgow and most other large towns in the 1920s, Labour dominated 'areas of severely overcrowded housing'.[113] Utilising figures in the 1921 Census giving the numbers of people per room by municipal wards Cook constructed a three-fold categorisation of wards, from (A) the most overcrowded, to (B) overcrowded 'but with less poverty and deprivation', and (C) 'relatively good housing and . . . residential development'. While Cook's designations are broadly accurate, housing does not, on its own, give the complete picture of an area's social basis. It is very good at the suburban extreme (C) where good housing and wealth went together, and

---

[110] Hutchison, *Political History,* p. 289

[111] See Chapter Five, pp. 178–9 on women and politics in the immediate post-war period.

[112] *Forward* 31 Dec. 1921, quoted in McLean, *The Legend,* p. 177.

[113] C. Cook, *The Age of Alignment: Electoral Politics in Britain 1922–29* (London, 1975), p. 82–87.

in the fifteen best-housed wards in Glasgow Labour was more or less permanently defeated, in very many instances not even contesting the seats.

However, housing statistics are not 100% accurate in distinguishing between working class areas. Cook does not include Gorbals and Anderston in his Group A but to contemporaries (certainly Thomas Johnston) they were among the worst of the slum wards. Likewise, Shettleston and Cowlairs which are in Group A were not slum areas. Similarly housing on its own cannot explain everything about the political loyalties of an area. For instance, Maryhill and Fairfield had almost exactly the same housing conditions (if anything the former was marginally worse), yet while Fairfield was solidly Labour throughout the 1920s, Maryhill was just as definitely pro Moderate. It was not until the advent of the Scottish Protestant League in Glasgow's municipal politics in the 1930s that Maryhill would eventually go Labour.[114]

The categories made by Cook are much more mixed than he realised and the political loyalties of the wards much more fluid. It is not the case that Labour's support at any time was located solely in either artisan or poorer working class areas. Most of the areas where Labour was successful in the immediate post-war years were areas in which it had a prior record of some representation and in 1914 it had sitting councillors in wards as different as Mile End and Hutchesontown contrasted to Springburn and Kinning Park.[115] Nonetheless, there was still a definite relationship between housing and Labour. Housing was the issue on which Labour had built its partial, though real, success in the years leading up to the War and would continue to be of major significance thereafter. Had Labour been able to rid itself of its fear of the residuum and women voters earlier, it might well have enjoyed greater success before 1914.

After the War the franchise was no longer an issue. Although women did not receive the vote on the same terms as men, there was no major campaign to secure full adult suffrage.[116] Nonetheless, there were still class biases operating at both the parliamentary and municipal level. Most of the new voters in 1918 were women but the nature of qualification, i.e. women over thirty who would have qualified for the local government vote, or whose husbands would have, meant that the female electorate was disproportionately middle class. As Turner has pointed out, the correlation of female voters and Conservative support is not necessarily a gender question but a matter of class; high female electorates were a clear signifier of middle class areas.[117] This can be seen in Glasgow where the new electoral roll in 1918 revealed that of the thirty-seven wards, eleven had female majorities; with few exceptions these were all middle class.[118] Moreover, the retention of

---

[114] See Chapter Six for the SPL.
[115] This matter is discussed in more detail in Chapter Three pp. 95–8.
[116] M. Pugh, *Women and the Women's Movement in Britain 1914–1959* (London, 1992), p. 43.
[117] Turner, *British Politics*, pp. 412–4.
[118] *Glasgow Herald*, 1 Nov. 1918.

occupation as the qualification for the municipal franchise meant that young working class men who were not householders in their own right had the same difficulties with registration experienced by young workers before 1914.[119]

With the achievement of adult male suffrage and a majority female suffrage for Parliamentary elections the significance of the *Representation of the People Act* remains massive.[120] Yet, given the points made above and the retention of plural voting and the extension of University seats, the un-democratic, if not anti-democratic elements of the new system were actually quite numerous. Labour's failure to secure straightforward adult suffrage for national and local elections did have detrimental consequences; in Glasgow the majority which Labour secured in parliamentary contests by 1922 was not replicated in local elections until 1933.[121]

Housing and Unemployment

Just as the beginning of the War had raised fears about unemployment so too did the end of the War, and this explains the movement for a shorter working week which, on Clydeside, led to the famous Forty Hour Strike of January 1919.[122] However, the prosperity of the war years continued for a short but critical period after the Armistice as industry experienced an intense re-stocking boom. By the end of 1920, however, it was clear that unemployment had returned.[123] Thereafter, the impact of the dislocation of world trade and the collapse in demand for capital goods saw unemployment established as a permanent feature of the economic landscape. It has been estimated that unemployment in the inter-war years was more than twice as severe as it had been before the war, that the majority of the workforce experienced unemployment at some point and that increasing numbers suffered long-term unemployment.[124] If the 1920s were bad, the 1930s were even worse. The nadir was reached in January 1933 when over 30% of the insured population of Scotland were registered as out of work. In Glasgow the proportion was over 33% with almost 41% of adult men unemployed. In that month fully 136,331

[119] Pugh, *Electoral Reform*, p. 112.

[120] '. . . the Fourth Reform Act stands apart from its predecessors, and deserves a status at least equal to the legislation of 1832.' Dyer, *Capable Citizens*, p. 112.

[121] Full adult suffrage was being called for by the Labour Party in Scotland as early as 1918 because it could see the likely adverse effects. This is discussed in Chapter Three pp. 121–2.

[122] H. McShane & J. Smith, *No Mean Fighter* (London, 1978), p. 101.

[123] The increasing rate of unemployment in late 1920 led Glasgow Corporation to establish a Special Committee on Unemployment with John Wheatley as its Convenor. *Glasgow Herald*, 29 Dec. 1920.

[124] E. Kibblewhite, 'The Impact of Unemployment on the Development of Trade Unions in Scotland, 1918–1939: some aspects', (unpublished Ph.D. thesis, University of Aberdeen, 1979), pp. 68–9.

people were signing on for the dole in the City's labour exchanges with 114,113 persons on poor relief. The improvement thereafter was real but very gradual; at the end of 1938 there were still over 82,000 people unemployed in Glasgow.[125]

This was an era of depression. The West of Scotland economy grew at a substantially lesser rate than that of the UK as a whole and its level of unemployment was always considerably higher. The response of many was simply to leave and the decade from 1921 to 1931 saw a net out migration of 20,000 people, and the total number of emigrants amounted to more than 9% of the population in 1921.[126] By the early 1930s it was clear that the region's industry could not support the existing population but by then emigration was no longer an option.[127] There was an increasing awareness that diversification and the attraction of new industries was necessary. New jobs were created in services, construction and local government, 'but the shift was scarcely significant and the industrial structure of the region remained largely unchanged.'[128]

Mass unemployment shifted bargaining power towards the employers, as evidenced in the engineers' defeat in 1922. However, the employers did not take the opportunity to reorganise work methods as their response to market conditions was to broaden their product base and for this they remained reliant upon the skills and flexibility of their existing labour force.[129] This, in turn, allowed skilled workers to retain both their traditional craftsman's outlook towards the unskilled and their relative advantage in job security. However, the extent of the inter-war depression meant even for skilled workers unemployment was 'at unprecedented levels'.[130] Though skilled men retained their distinction from unskilled, the wage differential did, nonetheless, narrow. Moreover, the increasing role of the state in providing insurance and benefits to most workers saw the old association of skill, union membership and friendly society – upon which had been founded so much of the skilled worker's notion of independence and respectability – lose a great deal of its resonance.

The sustained impact of the depression meant that the political focus had to be upon the State. Trade unions, facing a financial meltdown, could not sustain open-ended commitments to their members. Local authorities were confronted with a vicious circle of unemployment leading to greater

[125] A. Slaven, *The Development of the West of Scotland: 1750–1960* (London, 1975), p. 199; J. Cunnison & J.B.S. Gilfillan (eds.), *Glasgow: The Third Statistical Account of Scotland* (Glasgow, 1958), p. 923; Ministry of Labour, *Local Unemployment Index*.

[126] Board of Trade, *An Industrial Survey of the South-West of Scotland* (London, 1932), p. 8.

[127] Scotland has always had a high rate of emigration but it fell dramatically in the 1930s. Harvie, *No Gods*, p. 47.

[128] Slaven, *West of Scotland*, p. 200

[129] A. McKinlay, 'Employers and Skilled Workers in the Inter-War Depression: engineering and shipbuilding on Clydeside 1919–1939' (unpublished D. Phil. thesis, Oxford 1986), pp. 332–57.

demands on their resources while, at the same time, reducing their capacity
to generate their own income. Glasgow Labour's belief in the power of the
independent municipality and in Scottish Home Rule suffered as a consequence.[131] As early as 1921 Patrick Dollan was calling for unemployment
to become the full financial responsibility of the Westminster Government
since the cost to the local authorities, 'was a burden the ratepayers could not
undertake'. In addition, State funds ought to be made available to the
Corporation to allow it to tackle unemployment through local utility
schemes and house building programmes.[132] Nonetheless, the municipality
could still play a significant role and Labour still held to its policies of direct
labour and a municipal bank as ways of saving money, relieving the pressure
on the rates, and thereby building more council houses at affordable
rents.[133]

Housing had been the issue behind Labour's local success before 1914
and the war-time rent strikes catapulted housing onto the national political
agenda. The Government's emergency response in passing the Rent Restriction Act during the war was followed by a commitment to actually build
houses. At the same time rents remained a political battleground, especially
with the passing of the 1920 Rent Act which ended the rent freeze imposed
in 1915. This provoked another rent strike which, though unsuccessful, did
help solidify Labour's electoral support.[134] Rising rents in the early 1920s
occurred in a situation of falling money wages and the return of unemployment. The position between the wars was, therefore, similar to what it had
been before 1914: low wages and insecurity of employment meant that
people could not afford higher rents for better-quality housing and conse-
quently there had been more or less no private building of working-class
housing for rent since 1904.[135] What was different after 1918 was the direct
involvement of the State in housing provision, but the construction of
council houses did not resolve the issues of housing supply and affordable
rents.

In 1919, in response to the Addison Act, Glasgow Corporation submitted
to the Scottish Department of Health an estimate that it required to build
57,000 houses to meet the City's needs. By 1939 the Corporation had
managed to construct 50,277, yet in 1935 its own overcrowding survey

[130] Kibblewhite, 'Impact of Unemployment', p. 144; McKinlay, 'Employers and
Skilled Workers', pp. 338–9.
[131] D. Howell, *A Lost Left: Three Studies in Socialism and Nationalism* (Manchester,
1986), pp. 240, 244; W. Knox, *Scottish Labour Leaders 1918–1939: A biographical
dictionary* (Edinburgh, 1984), pp. 41–6.
[132] *Glasgow Herald* 26 Sept. 1921.
[133] For instances of this see articles by Patrick Dollan in *Forward*, 29 Oct. 1927, 29 Oct.
1932.
[134] Labour was landed an extra bonus on the eve of the 1922 general election when a
House of Lords' decision in a case pursued by the Labour Housing Association
declared that rent increases imposed by landlords were technically illegal and
could be reclaimed by tenants. See McLean, *The Legend*, pp. 167–73.

revealed an immediate need for 100,000 additional houses.[136] What Glasgow had achieved can be seen as a massive change compared to the 2,199 Corporation houses in 1914 but, on the eve of World War Two, it was still nowhere near solving its housing problem.

What spurred the national Government at the end of the war to commit itself to not just the slogan but the actual commitment of 'homes fit for heroes' was the fear of possible revolution being embraced by five million discharged soldiers and sailors. At the Cabinet meeting in March 1919 to discuss the proposed Housing Bill, Lloyd George urged its acceptance as a form of political insurance, 'Even if it cost a hundred million pounds, what was that compared to the stability of the State?'[137] By the autumn of 1921 with the onset of depression, rising unemployment and the trade unions in retreat, that commitment was abandoned as retrenchment became the order of the day. But the genie could not be put back in the bottle and, one way or another, Government, including Conservative Governments, found they could not ignore housing or disengage the State from direct involvement in the housing market.[138] The Conservatives sought to promote the private sector in the hope of stimulating it to provide working class housing and concentrated direct subsidy at slum clearance, whereas Labour emphasised good quality housing to be provided for the bulk of the working class through local authority provision.

A raft of legislation throughout the inter-war years provided the local authorities with different levels of subsidy and different priorities as regards who council houses were to be built for. In itself this multiplicity of controls and directives can be seen as a constraint upon the municipality, but the new partnership of national and local government was the only way for a city such as Glasgow to build working class houses.[139] The Corporation's strategy was definitely open to criticism. The early council houses, which were of very high quality, were let at rents which the vast majority of workers could not afford. The Corporation's logical desire to have tenants who could certainly pay their rent led to a the highest grades of skilled men, foremen, white collar workers and even professionals inhabiting these houses, not the

[135] R. Rodger, 'Crisis and confrontation in Scottish housing 1880–1914', in Rodger (ed.) *Scottish Housing in the Twentieth Century* (Leicester, 1989), pp. 44–6.

[136] N.J. Morgan, ' "£8 cottages for Glasgow citizens": Innovations in municipal house-building in Glasgow in the inter-war years', in Rodger, *Scottish Housing*, pp. 125–6.

[137] Quoted in M. Swenarton, *Homes Fit For Heroes: The Politics and Architecture in early State Housing in Britain* (London, 1981), p. 78.

[138] 'the government found itself caught up in the momentum of the legitimatory process that it had itself set in motion . . .' Swenarton, *Homes for Heroes*, p. 193.

[139] It was fitting that John Wheatley, the leading propagandist for municipal houses in Glasgow before the War should provide the means, as the First Labour Government's Minister of Health, for the actual construction of so many council houses in the inter-war period. Almost 42 per cent of Glasgow's council houses built between 1919–39 were constructed under the terms of the 1924 Wheatley

people who were meant to be provided for; eventually Glasgow had to introduce a means test whereby council houses were not available to people earning above a certain income level. At the same time the decision to build two and three apartment houses meant that overcrowding continued in many of the new houses. And the construction of slum clearance schemes en bloc and with fewer internal amenities led to a charge that the Corporation was simply building new slums.[140]

If the unskilled and poorer working class were left at the back of the queue, it is not the case that they were simply being ignored or dealt with the penal severity directed towards the residuum before 1914. Labour's own campaign to abolish the slums is testimony to the change in approach. The insistent efforts over the twin issues of house building and rents gave Labour a constant political rallying cry attractive to skilled and poorer workers, employed and unemployed, men and women. The popularity of the housing issue meant that even the Moderate controlled Corporation had to respond by building council houses. The Moderates may have avoided the use of direct labour and preferred to concentrate on slum clearance but the political reality was that they had to respond to a working class electorate; control of the middle class and suburban wards was not sufficient on its own to secure a majority in George Square.

When Labour eventually took control of the Corporation in 1933 it was due to the impact of the Scottish Protestant League splitting the Moderate vote. However, it is tempting to explain Labour's ultimate victory, and more or less permanent majority ever since, as due to the housing issue and in particular the gradual domination of the electorate by the Council tenant. As middle class voters deserted the City for suburbs outwith the municipal boundaries so the thousands of new council households, committed to Labour as the housing party, came to exercise increasing sway in the political balance. Such a pat sociological explanation, however, may disguise as much as it illuminates.

It is logical to identify council tenants as pro-Labour given Labour's belief in council houses and pressure to get more built. Nonetheless, until 1934 no council houses were actually built by Labour. They were built by a Moderate Corporation just as the expansion of Corporation employees occurred under the Moderates. The loss of control in 1933 caused the Moderates, or the predominant Unionist element at least, to focus on the role of both these groups in essentially negative terms. Corporation employees comprised a 'vast army' and the new housing areas of subsidised housing were 'hotbeds of Socialism.'[141]

Yet it is not all that clear that council housing automatically translated into

Act. J. Butt, 'Working Class Housing in Glasgow 1900–1939', in MacDougall, *Scottish Labour History*, p. 162.

[140] See J. McKee, 'Glasgow Working Class Housing Between the Wars 1919–1939' (unpublished M. Litt. thesis, University of Strathclyde, 1977).

[141] NLS Acc 10424, Scottish Conservative and Unionist Association, General Com-

support for Labour. The two wards with the highest level of Corporation housing were Yoker & Knightswood (created in 1932) and Pollokshields with 8155 and 7500 such houses respectively.[142] In Knightswood Labour quickly emerged as the major political force but proved unable to completely dominate as the Moderates won and retained one of the three seats. In Pollokshields the new council electorate made no difference as Moderate domination remained unbroken throughout the twenties and thirties. The neighbouring wards of Ruchill (6646 council houses) and Maryhill (2037) both became solidly Labour in the early 1930s. But if these shifts can be explained by Corporation housing, it had no lasting impact in Pollokshaws (2946) or Whiteinch (2580) where Labour's sole successes occurred in 1933 and were due directly to the intervention of the Scottish Protestant League. Furthermore, a high level of Corporation housing in Shettleston cannot explain its solidly pro-Labour record stretching before 1914. And similarly the complete absence of council housing in Gorbals made no difference in what remained a solidly Labour ward from 1920 to 1939.

From the 1890s and the forces of the democracy under the de facto leadership of John Ferguson, through the immediate pre-war years and Wheatley's campaign for £8 cottages, the war-time rent strikes, to the post-war years of council building programmes, housing was certainly the key issue providing a continuous thread behind Labour's electoral progress. Yet, as well as unifying working class opinion, housing could also be divisive as evidenced by pre-war disinterest in the slum-dweller, and the post-war social distinctions between different types of council housing.[143] Nonetheless, the truly desperate state of Glasgow's housing – in 1931 there were still nearly 600,000, or 55%, of the City's population living in one- or two-roomed houses[144] – meant that the need and desire for better housing at a price people could afford remained a common and a constant feature determining much of the City's political outlook and loyalties. Yet, as we have indicated above and as will be detailed in the following chapters, Labour's progress was not an unbroken line of ascent and Glasgow politics were about more than just housing.

It took Labour until 1933 to win control of the City corporation. In part this could be explained – as it was by the Tories – as due to the increase of

mittee, minutes, 26 November 1934. See Chapter Six, pp 202–3 for more discussion on this.

[142] Corporation of Glasgow, *Review of Operations 1919–1947* (Glasgow, 1948), p. 87. These figures relate to the whole period 1919–47 but almost 90% of the total 57,443 houses were built between 1919 and 1939.

[143] 'Like the poor, the slumdweller we will always have with us . . .' These were the words of labour councillor Jean Mann, attempting to direct attention away from the 'commendable' efforts at slum clearance to the 'urgent, clamant need of the City . . . to reduce overcrowding.' *Forward*, 4 Nov. 1933.

[144] Though a lower proportion this was actually a higher number than in 1911 when there were 471,156 persons or 62% of the population in one or two roomed

council employees and tenants. There was a shift in housing tenure and a drift by the middle class out of the city.[145] But this is only part of the picture. The drama of the sudden transformation in fortunes in 1933 was all down to the SPL and the split in the Moderate ranks. And this was a reaction to the long depression of the Clydeside economy and the lack of confidence which the great depression only accentuated. Despite the division in its own camp as the ILP departed there was sufficient class solidarity among Glasgow working class voters which allowed Labour to see off the direct challenge of the SPL, exploit the temporary disablement of the Moderates and secure a majority at last.

houses. *Census 1911,* Vol. 1 Part 2, City of Glasgow, p. 78; *Census 1931,* Vol. 1 Part 2, City of Glasgow, p. 76.
[145] Cunnison & Gilfillan, *Glasgow,* pp. 60, 65.

CHAPTER ONE

From the Forces of Democracy to Labour Party, 1896–1914

It was not until the last decade of the nineteenth century that an organised, independent labour presence became a feature of the political landscape. All previous efforts at building a labour party, independent of the two major parties, had foundered completely or ended up in accommodation with the Liberals. But the successful return of three Labour men to parliament in the general election of 1892 and the formation of the Independent Labour Party (ILP) the following year suggested that a radical new development was at hand. However, the hopes of pioneers such as Keir Hardie that a new party of labour would displace the Liberals proved illusory.[1] In the general election of 1895 the ILP stood twenty-eight candidates and lost in every single contest, including Hardie's constituency of West Ham. Nevertheless, this defeat did not result in the collapse of the ILP and the cause it represented. Rather, the party found the strength within certain localities to sustain itself and even make some real, if limited, progress.[2]

Of the areas where independent labour emerged, one might have expected Scotland, and particularly Glasgow, to be among the more successful. Keir Hardie had first raised the banner of independent labour at the Mid-Lanark by election of 1888 and, even prior to this, the general election of 1885 had seen the Scottish Land Restoration League (SLRL) stand five candidates against Liberals in and around Glasgow. Hardie's famous campaign, though heavily defeated, gave birth to the Scottish Labour Party (SLP) which was based largely in Glasgow and contested the 1892 election before becoming one of the foundation stones of the ILP in 1893. This activity, however, realised little in terms of a sizeable labour

---

[1] Hardie had been arguing since 1887 that the Liberal Party was, historically, finished. See *The Miner*, Aug. 1887. However, this long-term view co-existed alongside a strategy of trying to win terms from the Liberals.

[2] It has been remarked that 'The ILP did best in small towns with stable populations.' M. Savage & A. Miles, *The Remaking of the British Working Class 1840–1940* (London, 1994), p. 79. However, detailed local studies of ILP strongholds suggest that crucial determinant of success was the level of concentration of industrial employment. For instance Leicester's population grew by 350% between 1860 to 1906 but almost two thirds of its industrial workforce was located in hosiery and footwear. B. Lancaster, *Radicalism, Co-operation and Socialism: Leicester Working Class Politics 1860–1906* (Leicester, 1987). For Bradford and Halifax see K. Laybourn & J. Reynolds, *Liberalism and the Rise of Labour 1890–1918* (London, 1984).

vote and nothing in terms of actual electoral victories. In both the number of candidates put forward and share of the vote secured labour in Scotland performed less well than it in England.[3]

In the 1892 election seven labour candidates stood – four put forward by the SLP and three by the short-lived Scottish United Trades Councils Labour Party (SUTCLP) – and all were heavily defeated. Disappointing as the results were, some consolation could still be taken from them. Speaking at the SLP conference the following January, Hardie made the point that this was the first time 'the Labour Party was . . . in evidence as an organised movement' and went on to claim that the 14% of the poll their candidates had secured in these contests, 'would hold good all over the country, a fact which proves the strength of the labour vote and its power for good if properly directed.'[4] The basis of Hardie's optimism (apart from his own triumph in West Ham) realistically could only have been based upon hoping to force concessions from the Liberals, since in two Glasgow constituencies (Tradeston and Camlachie) the SLP intervention had been sufficient to deprive the Liberals of victory.

However, no arrangements were made with the Liberals and the general election of 1895 saw the ILP's ambitions shattered. Eight candidates were put forward in Scotland, five of whom stood in Glasgow constituencies and one in neighbouring Govan.[5] The average poll in these Clydeside constituencies was under 500 votes or just over 7%; only the miners' leader Bob Smillie in Camlachie managed to get over 10% of the vote. No progress had been made since 1892 and the extent of the failure can be gauged by the fact that Shaw Maxwell, the candidate in Blackfriars and Hutchesontown, managed only half the share of the vote he had secured ten years previously when he had stood for the SLRL in the same constituency. No positive spin could be put on these results and even the *Labour Leader* had to admit the Glasgow polls were 'disgracefully small'.[6] After this debacle Labour's parliamentary ambitions in Glasgow became much more circumspect; only after the Great War would a similar number of seats be contested. And yet it was in that same year, 1895, that labour secured its first significant electoral success in the city when two ILP candidates were returned to the town council.[7]

---

[3] I.G.C. Hutchison, *A Political History of Scotland 1832–1924: Parties, Elections and Issues* (Edinburgh, 1986), p. 183.

[4] *Labour Leader*, Feb. 1893.

[5] The other two candidates were run in Aberdeen and Dundee. F.W.S. Craig, *British Parliamentary Election Results 1885–1918* (London, 1974), pp. 491, 495, 503–9, 546.

[6] Quoted in D. Howell, *British Workers and the Independent Labour Party 1888–1906* (Manchester, 1984), p. 161.

[7] *Labour Leader* 2, 11 Nov. 1895; *Glasgow Herald* 6 Nov. 1895. The Labour forces had enjoyed some success the previous year with two candidates returned for both the School Board and the Town Council. W.H. Fraser, 'The Working Class', in W.H. Fraser & I. (eds.), *Glasgow Volume II 1830–1912* (Manchester, 1996), p. 337. Welcome as these results were to the advocates of independent labour, they were

The background to this achievement was the extension of the city boundaries which had taken place in 1891.[8] Under this it had been stipulated that the municipal wards for the whole city would have to be re-organised in 1896 and in that year all municipal seats (not just the usual third) would have to be contested. So, while the attention of most individuals and organisations were focused on the forthcoming municipal 'general' election (those who won seats in 1895 would only sit for one year instead of the usual three), the ILP took the opportunity of securing at least some sitting councillors.

The 'Stalwarts'

However, Labour forces were being organised on a much wider scale than just the ILP with the trades council planning a substantial intervention in the 'general' poll in 1896. As we will see later, while the ILP could sustain an electoral presence on its own, success at the polls relied upon the involvement of the Trades Council. While both remained distinct and separate organisations, the relationship between them was close with ILP delegates always keen to encourage the council to undertake direct political activity. At the beginning of 1893 an SLP delegate to the annual conference could claim of Glasgow Trades Council that, '[it] was theirs and they would keep it'.[9] During 1895, encouraged by the forthcoming 're-arrangement of the Wards' the trades council appointed a Standing Committee, 'to keep in touch with the Ward Committees and other bodies of workers, so as to be able to increase the numbers and thus strengthen the position of the Labour members of the Town Council'.[10]

This led to the creation of an effective alliance to contest the municipal election, comprising delegates from the trades council, individual union branches, the ILP, the Glasgow Federation of Co-operative Societies and the Irish National League (INL). This body became known as the Workers' Election Committee (WEC) and the councillors returned under its auspices were dubbed the 'Stalwarts'. The WEC ran eleven official candidates in eight wards and saw five returned in what was regarded as a great success.[11] The contrast with the abject failure of the ILP's candidates at the parliamentary polls the previous year is pronounced and indicates that national and local

seriously limited. The Parish Council candidates only secured the last two places out of fifteen and labour did not return another candidate until 1904. Those successful at the November municipal poll appear to have identified themselves as temperance candidates as much, if not more than labour. One presented himself as, 'the Liberal and Trades Council, the social reform, the temperance, and the working man's candidate.' *Glasgow Herald* 7 Nov. 1894; 2 Apr. 1894.

[8] I. Maver, 'Glasgow's Civic Government', in Fraser & Maver *Glasgow*, pp. 466–7.

[9] *Labour Leader*, Feb. 1893.

[10] Glasgow Trades Council, *Annual Report 1895–6*.

[11] Glasgow Trades Council, *Annual Report 1895–6*.

politics had their own agendas and distinct trajectories. A number of factors were operating in Glasgow in 1896 which allowed this strategic alliance to be pursued to some advantage.

There already existed a labour presence or party in the Town council which comprised John Battersby and A.J. Hunter, both trade unionists and closely involved with the trades council; Battersby had been a past President and a member of the Parliamentary Committee, while Hunter was the Secretary of the trades council, a position he held until 1902.[12] These men represented an older Lib-Lab tradition, which had never been very strong and was in the process of being superseded by the younger socialists who were now making the running on the trades council; both Battersby and Hunter became regarded as Stalwarts although they had not run as WEC candidates in 1896.[13]

A much more dynamic role was played by John Ferguson, the de facto leader of Irish nationalist opinion within Glasgow. While remaining both an Irish nationalist and a Liberal, Ferguson had always a close sympathy to the cause of labour. In 1885, against Parnell's injunction that the Irish should vote Conservative, Ferguson, along with Michael Davitt, gave his support to Shaw Maxwell the SLRL candidate in Blackfriars & Hutcheson-town.[14] In 1888 Ferguson was one of Keir Hardie's more prominent (though pessimistic) supporters at Mid Lanark and was an honorary vice president of the SLP until expelled for supporting Liberal candidates in seats the SLP was contesting at the general election of 1892.[15] Ferguson stood for a political alliance between the working class and the middle class and his strategy was outlined in a letter to Hardie shortly after the Mid Lanark contest when it was clear that the intention was to establish the SLP as a permanent body:

> I'm delighted to know the Labour Party is for action. My opinion is still it shd [sic] enter the Liberal Association and work through it. There is certainly an element of danger in two political organisations holding the same principles coming into collision. . . . If you cannot induce the Labourers to join the Liberal Association and push their claims through

[12] *Labour Leader*, 17 Sept. 1898; W.H. Fraser, 'Trades Councils in the Labour Movement in Nineteenth Century Scotland', in I. MacDougall (ed.), *Essays in Scottish Labour History* (Edinburgh, 1978), p. 5.

[13] The first 'labour' success was the election of Henry Tait, Secretary of the Scottish Railway Servants' Union, to the Town Council in 1889. Tait was backed by the Trades Council and, like Battersby and Hunter, was an active Liberal. W.H. Fraser, 'The Working Class' in Fraser & Maver, *Glasgow*, p. 337.

[14] I.S. Wood, 'Irish Immigrants and Scottish Radicalism, in MacDougall, *Scottish Labour History*, p. 72; J.H. Handley, *The Irish in Modern Scotland* (Cork, 1948), p. 276. Although censured by the INL Executive Ferguson's status in Scotland encouraged them to let the matter lie.

[15] D. Lowe, *Souvenirs of Scottish Labour* (Glasgow, 1919) pp 112–3; J.G. Kellas, 'The Mid Lanark By-Election (1888) and the Scottish Labour Party (1888–1894)', *Parliamentary Affairs*, xviii (1965), p. 327.

it by all means organise Labour by itself. Better that than nothing. I'll try all I can in the Liberal Association to support Labour claims . . .[16]

This was hardly a ringing endorsement of independent labour, nonetheless it was an approach Ferguson was able to promote in local if not national politics since the estrangement caused by Home Rule did not operate at the level of the municipality. Furthermore, though an Irish Nationalist, Ferguson was a Protestant and a successful businessman without links to the drinks trade which protected him from any anti-Catholic prejudices. The year after his breach with the SLP Ferguson was returned to Glasgow town council for the Calton Ward in the East End and, although the choice of the local Liberal Association, he became the focus of leadership for the small labour interest.[17] In fact, at this point Ferguson's stamp of approval seems to have been crucial in getting labour candidates returned. After the ILP's success in 1895 the party's national journal commented triumphantly that, 'Our men fought on a pure Socialist programme, and won on the merits of that programme'.[18] This was not how the matter was viewed locally as, according to the *Glasgow Herald*, P.G. Stewart, the successful ILP candidate in Hutchesontown, 'came forward as a disciple of Councillor John Ferguson, whose lead on labour questions, and indeed generally, he is prepared to follow'.[19]

This association became even closer at the 1896 election when the return of the WEC candidates was seen as strengthening Ferguson's position and policy within the Council, not least by Ferguson himself. Speaking on the night of the poll:

He had now at his back, he said, Mr. Brown, Mr. Shaw Maxwell, Councillor Mitchell, and Mr. Cronin, gentlemen who would support him in his programme which he had fought so vigorously during his past tenure of office.[20]

Speaking at the same meeting Boyd Brown 'said he would follow in the footsteps of Councillor Ferguson'.[21] Since this meeting was being held in the INL hall and Brown had just come third in the same ward where Ferguson had topped the poll, he may just have been politically tactful, yet there is no indication that the successful candidates mentioned above, all members of the ILP, had any disagreements either with Ferguson's policies or being identified as his supporters. Ferguson's views on promoting reform as the means of preserving the social fabric and finding inspiration in the new

[16] Francis Johnston Correspondence, John Ferguson to Keir Hardie 17 May 1888, ILP Archive, 1888/87, (Harvester Press microform, original held in London School of Economics).
[17] *Glasgow Herald*, 8 Nov. 1893.
[18] *Labour Leader*, 9 Nov. 1895.
[19] *Glasgow Herald*, 6 Nov. 1895.
[20] *Glasgow Observer*, 7 Nov. 1896.
[21] *Glasgow Observer*, 7 Nov. 1896.

testament were similar to that of many in the ILP and, on certain issues such as the level of a minimum wage he was even more advanced than some of his socialist allies.

The election of 1896, therefore, saw two inter-related issues at work. One was the alliance of 'labour' or 'democratic' forces which came together in the WEC and substantially promoted the cause of independent representation. The other was the question of political leadership where the role played by Ferguson was crucial. It was Ferguson to whom the 'labour' members deferred and it was Ferguson who gave the labour cause a distinct policy. The WEC fought the 1896 election on a nine point programme, the first and most important of which was the taxation of land values.[22] Given that socialists had been criticising the followers of Henry George for almost a decade over this precise issue,[23] the WEC programme could hardly be called socialist but it did contain precise demands of the sort most socialists supported: setting of maximum rents, work or support for the unemployed, and minimum wages and conditions for local authority employees. These were the sorts of issues that were seen to be part of a labour or new democratic agenda. Commenting on the municipal election of 1894, the *Glasgow Herald* bemoaned how 'incongruous' the old, familiar mottoes of 'retrenchment and reform' and 'economy and efficiency' had become:

> especially at this time, when the new democracy is asking that the Corporation shall become a sort of universal employer of labour, which is to be remunerated at trade union rates and is to go on only for eight hours a day. However this may be, it is the fact that in several of the wards in which there were contests many votes were given on the understanding that the candidates for whom they were recorded were 'sound' on the labour and eight hours question.[24]

The policy that would be pursued by the Stalwarts had already been given shape by John Ferguson. In 1894 he introduced two motions: firstly that land values become the basis of local taxation, and secondly, that male employees of the council be paid a minimum of 21s (£1.05) for a six day week. Both motions were heavily defeated but were subsequently passed after the 1896 election.[25] Due to Ferguson the taxation of land values became a sort of test question at local elections and it was only after his death, in 1906, that the ILP in Glasgow could even begin to question its validity and seek to remove it

---

[22] *Glasgow Commonweal,* Nov. 1896.

[23] Most famously at the public debate between George and H.M. Hyndman at the St. James's Hall, London in July 1889, a verbatim report of which was then published by the SDF as, *The Single Tax v. Social Democracy: Which will most benefit the people?* (London, 1889).

[24] *Glasgow Herald,* 7 Nov. 1894.

[25] Also passed were motions to permit a limited Corporation fire insurance and a proposal in favour of Corporation banking, a hardy perennial of municipal socialism. *Labour Leader,* 22 Oct. 1898, interview with John Ferguson, also 17 Sept. & 1 Oct. 1898.

from their municipal programme.[26] Ferguson spent the rest of his life
pursuing the land tax shibboleth and even managed to get a majority of the
Town Council to support a Parliamentary Bill which was still going through
the House of Commons in 1906 after his death. At first sight it is difficult to
see the attraction of the land tax. John Cronin, a WEC candidate, argued in
1896 that what was needed was a programme, 'that will appeal to the
commonsense of the workers', and likely be realised in a few years.[27]

And yet the land tax was a popular rallying cry. It was presented by
Ferguson as the means to pay for further reforms such as those in the WEC
programme and was also identified as a just tax, in that it was directed
against those who were not contributing to the general good of society but
benefiting from the efforts of society. The actual wording of Ferguson's
successful motion was, 'That the land values of the city, not being the
creation of any individual, but the whole community, should be appro-
priated to the service of the city' and he argued that £2 million per annum
was being paid to the ground landlords for the use of the land on which
Glasgow was built. A later ILP commentator wrote that Ferguson was not
really qualified to make such a judgement but through it, 'he managed to
draw so much support to his side. The figure of £2,000,000 became as
popular as John Ferguson himself'.[28] This was not populist posturing. It was
the continuation of a long-standing radicalism that divided society into
producers and non-producers (or workers and drones) and, as such, it
appealed directly to the 'commonsense' of the Glasgow working class.[29]

Ferguson's de facto leadership of the labour or democratic forces indicates the still tenuous grip that labour had on Glasgow's working class
electors; after all Ferguson was associated with but not actually of labour. At
the same time the role Ferguson played helped to establish labour as an
electoral force, as the return of WEC candidates illustrates. Ferguson also
contributed to the growing organisation behind labour through the active
involvement of the INL, five branches of which were affiliated to the WEC.[30]
This involvement was not unproblematic and was criticised by some socialists in Glasgow who regarded the Irish as among the most hostile opponents
of socialism and denied that they had any right to representation as Irishmen. This was part of an argument which opposed the whole strategy of a
'Workers' Party', as the WEC was often referred to, and argued for the

---

[26] See series of articles in very first issues of *Forward* – 'Popular Fallacies – Henry
Georgism exposed' – 13 Oct. 1906, etc.

[27] *Glasgow Commonweal*, Jun. 1896.

[28] *Forward*, 13 Oct. 1906.

[29] See Joan Smith, 'Labour Tradition in Glasgow and Liverpool', *History Workshop*,
xviii (Spring 1984), for a discussion of the Gramscian concept of 'commonsense'
applied to Glasgow. 'Glasgow working men's 'commonsense' was dominated by
strands of a Radical Liberal and Reform tradition which working men had
participated in for three-quarters of a century.' p. 44.

[30] *Glasgow Commonweal*, Oct. 1896.

straightforward promotion of socialism rather than the return of 'two or three Socialists to the Council'. While operating in a workers' alliance with trade unionists and co-operators was also criticised, it was accepted that there was still some implicit connection between these organisations and socialism. Most of the fire was directed at the Irish Nationalists, 'they are so shifty that no party can depend for any length of time upon their support . . . the nationalist party, as a party, in and out of the House of Commons, are among the bitterest opponents of Socialism'.[31]

The Irish also presented a difficulty because of their involvement in the drink trade and 'municipalisation of the liquor traffic' was one of the items in the WEC programme. The INL did try to get this dropped from the programme in 1898 but, though defeated, they did not on that account leave the Committee.[32] The identification of the Irish as part of the democratic forces and the INL's active participation in the WEC qualifies the standard view of the Irish as an impediment to the cause of labour representation prior to the First World War.[33] The association with labour was easier to sustain at the municipal level since Home Rule was not an issue but this local involvement in the WEC does indicate a strong tendency within the Irish community to identify with the cause of labour. This followed from the (poorer) working class composition of the Catholic-Irish who were by no means fully represented by labour organisations, either trade unions or co-operative societies. As Bruce Glasier commented about the United Irish League (as the INL became), despite all its shortcomings it was, nonetheless, 'a democratic party acting for the poor'.[34]

At the other end of the working class spectrum were the ultra-respectable Co-operative societies who also threw their weight behind the WEC in 1896. However, their strict anti-drink stance led them to refuse to endorse one of the WEC candidates (a member of the INL) because, 'he was engaged in the wine and spirit business'.[35] The Scottish Co-operative movement played a more prominent role in labour politics than its counterpart in England, though this was due to the relative weakness of trade unionism in Scotland rather than a consistent commitment to the cause of independent labour.[36]

---

[31] *Glasgow Commonweal,* Aug. 1896. Article by George Neil, 'Socialism or Dishonour'.

[32] *Labour Leader,* 27 Aug.1898.

[33] For instance see J.G. Kellas, *Modern Scotland* (2nd. Ed., London ,1980) p. 140. This issue is dealt with in detail in Chapter Four.

[34] Quoted in Howell, *British Workers and the ILP*, p. 370.

[35] *Scottish Co-operator,* Nov. 1896.

[36] Scottish trade unions have been described as 'small and frequently ineffective' and only experienced steady and consistent growth from the turn of the century. In contrast the co-operative societies enjoyed 'virtually uninterrupted' expansion in the later nineteenth century. The Webbs estimated the number of trade union members in Scotland in 1892 as 147,000, whereas membership of the co-operative societies in 1897 was over 267,000. R.H. Campbell, *Scotland since 1707* (Edinburgh, 1985), pp. 235–9; J.A. Kinloch & J. Butt, *History of the Scottish Co-operative Wholesale Society Limited* (Manchester, 1981), p. 248.

The Co-operators had a particular grievance in 1896 which led them into the labour alliance. This was an attempted boycott by private butchers to prevent Co-op Societies buying directly in the meat and cattle market. Essentially this was an attack by small traders on what they perceived as the unfair competition from the rapidly expanding Co-ops. In 1888 a Scottish Traders' Defence Association had been established in Glasgow which not only attempted boycotts against Co-op societies but also sought to victimise individual co-operators at their place of employment.[37] When the butchers re-activated this campaign in 1896 they did so in a situation which was very likely to lead the Co-ops into direct political involvement. Not only were the labour forces offering to defend the Societies' right to buy in the meat markets, but the whole question of access could only be decided by the City Corporation which actually owned the markets.

One view of the 1896 boycott is that it led Scottish Co-operators into a sustained political involvement.[38] Certainly, the Co-operative movement was represented at the founding of the Scottish Workers' Representation Committee (SWRC) in 1899 and 1900 but the Glasgow societies had by then left the WEC. According to the *Labour Leader*, the non-involvement of the Co-ops in the 1899 election campaign was due to the WEC having changed its secretary who had been a Co-op nominee.[39] However, given that even as early as 1897 the WEC comprised only delegates of the trades council, ILP and INL, the most likely explanation is that, having secured their victory over the private traders, the Co-operators saw no need to continue their political activity.[40] Nonetheless, even their temporary involvement had been important and the election of 1896 was hailed as a great success by the labour forces.

The WEC stood eleven candidates in eight wards in 1896, five of whom were returned.[41] This number does not include candidates given belated recognition, such as P.G. Stewart of the ILP who won in Hutchesontown and went on to become one of the leading figures of the Stalwarts.[42] With the

---

[37] Kinloch & Butt, *Scottish Co-operative Wholesale Society* pp 246–8; J.A. Kinloch, 'The Scottish Co-operative Wholesale Society 1868–1918' (unpublished Ph.D. thesis, University of Strathclyde, 1976), pp. 337–49; W. Maxwell, *The History of Co-operation in Scotland – its Inception and Leaders* (Glasgow, 1910), pp. 329–45; J.A. Flanagan, *Wholesale Co-operation in Scotland: the Fruits of Fifty Years Efforts* (Glasgow, 1920), pp. 133–4, 150–5.

[38] Kinloch & Butt, *Scottish Co-operative Wholesale Society*, p. 254; Kinloch, 'Scottish Co-operative Wholesale Society' p. 355.

[39] *Labour Leader*, 7 Oct. 1899.

[40] *Labour Leader*, 23 Oct. 1897.

[41] Glasgow Trades Council *Annual Report 1895–96*.

[42] The ILP branch in Hutchesontown was the only branch not to affiliate to the WEC. However, Stewart was selected by the Ward Committee and he defeated an Irish candidate who was not on the WEC list either. This confusion indicates what was still a complicated situation. *Glasgow Commonweal*, Oct. 1896; *Glasgow Observer*, 7 Nov. 1896.

association of the 'old labour' figures, Hunter and Battersby, with the WEC (they stood on later occasions as official nominees) and additional gains made in 1897, the Stalwarts soon had eleven councillors, six of whom were members of the ILP and, of these six, three were office bearers on the trades council. One contemporary publication states there were ten Stalwarts in 1898, while a later account refers to a maximum of fourteen.[43] This was nowhere near a majority of the 77 strong Council but it did represent a distinct bloc of votes which could get certain proposals passed.

While Ferguson's long term perspective focused on a land tax he remained interested, nevertheless, in further raising the wages of corporation employees. Having, as he put it, 'secured' the 21s wage, with 'the help of my sterling friend and colleague, P.G. Stewart . . . The real living wage will be my next consideration.' Oddly enough, this led to some disagreement within the ranks of the Stalwarts themselves. According to Ferguson a living wage had to be at a level 'which will afford a proper, moral, intellectual, and physical life'.[44] Presumably what this meant in practice was the 30s figure which had been in the original programme put forward by the WEC. However, George Mitchell, ILP and trades council, opposed any further increase (on the 21s) 'at present' and, instead, favoured an eight hour day, 'which, as every intelligent man knows, must ultimately result in an increase of wages'. Mitchell was infuriated by the actions of the tramway men (municipal employees since the Corporation took over the privately owned tram system in 1894) who, in spite of having their hours reduced and spread over six days, and their wages increased by 1s. 6d., were still willing to work overtime on Sundays. In a disparaging comment, which reveals something of the skilled tradesman's prejudice against the unskilled and unorganised, Mitchell said of the 12,000 municipal employees, 'there are not more than 3,000 worth fighting for. An even smaller number than that belong to trade unions'.[45]

Other concerns given prominence by the Stalwarts were free libraries, proposals to establish council workshops and municipal control of the drink trade.[46] P.G. Stewart was particularly active over housing with proposals to utilise and extend the terms of the Glasgow City Improvement Acts of 1866 and 1897 to clear the worst slums and provide an amount of Council-built housing. However, the advocates of municipal socialism were left with a major problem in Glasgow as the century neared its end: what was left to municipalise? As Stewart put it:

And with regard to the future. Glasgow is in the happy position of having already municipalised everything that even the most advanced

[43] J. Connell, *Glasgow Municipal Enterprise* (Glasgow & London, 1899), pp. 80–1; Labour Party 13th. Annual Conference, Glasgow 1914, *Souvenir*, (Published by the Glasgow Labour Party), p. 35.

[44] *Labour Leader*, 22 Oct. 1898.

[45] *Labour Leader*,17 Sept. 1898, interview with George Mitchell.

[46] *Labour Leader*, 24 Sept. and 1 Oct. 1898.

among other towns contemplates municipalising. We must therefore look for fresh fields to conquer.[47]

Disintegration of the 'Forces of the Democracy'

The emergence of the Stalwarts occurred at a period when the Liberal Party, both in Scotland and Glasgow, was in a weakened position. From having held all seven Glasgow parliamentary constituencies in 1885, the split of 1886 over Home Rule for Ireland had seriously weakened the Liberal grip on the city. In the elections of 1886 and 1892 the Liberals held a bare majority of four seats over two Liberal Unionists and one Conservative. In 1895 the combined unionist forces triumphed as the Conservatives won three seats, the Liberal Unionists two and the Liberal Party held only two; the first time since 1832 that the Liberals had been a minority in Glasgow. Worse was to follow as the Khaki election of 1900 witnessed a Liberal wipe out.[48]

Yet, Labour was unable to capitalise on Liberalism's misfortunes. The ILP's performance in 1895 had been had been derisory and in 1900 there was only a single Labour candidate in the whole of Scotland: A.E. Fletcher who stood in Camlachie under the auspices of the SWRC.[49] It was the ILP which was principally behind this candidature and they were able to mobilise a significant coalition behind Fletcher: the SDF, the Clarion Scouts, the United Irish League (UIL), the trades council and, most significantly, the local Liberal Association.[50] The key to this unity was the Boer War with the Liberals failing to stand a candidate of their own and Fletcher's anti-war stance making him acceptable to the socialists. The result was certainly creditable, 42% of the poll was the best labour had ever achieved in a parliamentary contest, but the unique circumstances of the election reduces its significance.

At the local level, the formation of the WEC and the success of establishing the Stalwart group on the Corporation made Glasgow appear an example which labour should copy on the national stage. In 1901 the *Labour Leader* opened up a debate on electoral strategy under the heading, 'Wanted. A Stalwart Party in Parliament. Can the Forces of Democracy be United:

> The subject for discussion is not the need for a Labour Party or even for its being independent, but whether it is possible for Labour to unite with other advanced sections of politicians so as to secure joint action in

[47] *Labour Leader*, 1 Oct. 1898.
[48] J.F. McCaffrey, 'Political Issues and Developments', in Fraser & Maver, *Glasgow*, pp. 214–5.
[49] SWRC, mss notes of Meeting of Committee, 28 April 1900. National Library of Scotland, microfilm mss 141, part of Scottish Trades Union Congress collection.
[50] Howell, *British Workers and the ILP*, p. 163.

and out of Parliament, and if so, upon what terms and conditions is such joint action to be secured, and what are its likely effects upon the Labour movement'.[51]

Put this way it is clear what outcome the editors desired but, ironically, it was at just this moment that the 'forces of democracy' were disintegrating in Glasgow. Far from establishing labour representation at a secure and constantly growing level, the achievement of the WEC proved to be short lived. At the 1902 municipal poll the *Glasgow Herald* commented upon, 'the almost entire disappearance of the word 'Stalwart' from the vocabulary of the candidates and their supporters. It has for some time been a term of reproach, and has been regarded by various extreme partisans as synonymous with broken pledges and empty promises'.[52]

The WEC was not a political party as such and had little notion of, nor ability to, impose a party discipline on its representatives. Candidates simply had to accept the programme and declare the sources of any funds beyond the election contributions made by the WEC. In the early, heady days of electoral success this was not perceived as a problem, indeed quite the opposite. One contemporary account of the Stalwarts commented approvingly of how they might retain the 'fads and influences of old associations . . . [but] never disagree on essentials. Indeed the constitution of the Committee is more in the nature of an honourable understanding than a set of hard and fast rules which people are punished for breaking'.[53] This was written in 1899 which, ironically, was to be the last good year for the WEC when four out of seven candidates were returned.[54] Over the next couple of years most of the Stalwarts would be removed from their seats in a backlash against the increasing cost and scale of municipal provision.[55]

The emergence of the Stalwarts coincided with (and was partly promoted by) the physical expansion of Glasgow which saw a concomitant expansion of the Corporation's powers and finances.[56] Glasgow's pioneering social provision had been most famously expressed in the Loch Katrine water supply in 1860 after the municipality decided to take over the private water companies, with control of gas following in 1867.[57] After a period of relative inactivity, municipal socialism regained the initiative in the 1880s and reached its apex with the decisions to take over the trams and electricity supply in the early 1890s.[58] While there was more or less complete unanimity over these acquisitions, new political faultlines soon opened up.

---

[51] *Labour Leader*, 19 Oct. 1901.
[52] *Glasgow Herald*, 5 Nov. 1902.
[53] Connell, *Municipal Enterprise*, pp. 83–4.
[54] *Glasgow Herald*, 8 Nov. 1899.
[55] W.H. Fraser, 'Municipal Socialism and Social Policy', in R.J. Morris & R. Rodger (eds.), *The Victorian City: a Reader in Urban History, 1920–1914* (London, 1993), p. 274.
[56] Maver, 'Civic Government', p. 467.
[57] Fraser, 'Municipal Socialism', pp. 260–1.
[58] Maver, 'Civic Government', p. 468.

The desire to continue the process of municipalisation after the trams had been taken over was most clearly expressed by the Liberal element on the non-political town council and a Progressive Union, strongly evangelical and pro-temperance, was set up in 1896 to promote Liberal candidates.[59] The main figure was Samuel Chisholm, a wholesale grocer, who would have become the MP for Camlachie in 1895 had it not been for the intervention of the ILP. This defeat left Chisholm with an abiding hostility towards Labour and, unlike in London, the Glasgow Progressives did not encompass labour or socialism within their ranks.[60]

Municipal socialism predated Labour and, from a Liberal viewpoint which regarded municipal socialism as a manifestation of 'civic spirit', Labour councillors could be regarded as the most enthusiastic proponents of what was a long-established policy.[61] The successes of Ferguson and the Stalwarts within the Corporation were, in a sense, swimming with the tide. However, when the tide of municipalisation began to turn Labour found itself isolated and unable to dictate events. For instance, in spite of protests by the ILP, John Ferguson led the Stalwarts in providing crucial support for Chisholm's' successful bid for the Lord Provostship in 1899. This was in spite of Chisholm's attacks on the Stalwarts, such as claiming they were secretly in the pay of the drinks trade, and the hostility of the Citizens' Union, a pressure group formed in 1898 to combat socialism. While the Citizens' Union was founded in part by supporters of Chisholm and gave its support to pro-Chisholm candidates standing against Stalwarts, it was also opposed to further schemes of municipalisation. This meant that the Citizens' Union was formally in favour of Chisholm being elected but was actually opposed to his policies.[62] The struggle against Labour representation was occurring alongside a more general movement against further municipal provision which, in turn, was overlaid with the perennial engagement between the temperance lobby and the drinks trade.

Chisholm was ardently pro temperance and pro municipalisation. He had no time for Labour generally or the WEC policy of municipal control of the drinks trade, but his determination to proceed with an active municipal programme saw Labour with little option but to give him their qualified

[59] Maver, 'Civic Government', p. 471.

[60] At the 1892 London County Council (LCC) elections the Progressive Party arranged with the London trades council and the labour party for straight fights for labour candidates. Of the twelve labour members of the LCC seven were socialists. P. Thompson, *Socialists, Liberals and Labour: the struggle for London 1885–1914* (London, 1967), pp. 104–5.

[61] See *Municipal Glasgow: Its Evolution and Enterprises* (Glasgow, 1914), 'Preface' by the Lord Provost D.M. Stevenson, p. 2. Stevenson had been a sympathiser of the Socialist League in the 1880s and was close to the Fabians. Unlike his fellow Liberal, Chisholm, Stevenson had no antipathy towards Labour.

[62] Fraser, 'Municipal Socialism', pp. 274–5; I. Maver (Sweeney), 'Local Party Politics and the Temperance Crusade: Glasgow 1890–1902', *Scottish Labour History Society Journal*, xxvii (1992), p. 53

support; the WEC had approved of Chisholm in 1896 because of his defence of the City Improvement Bill which was regarded as a means of providing working class housing.[63] As 'trade' influence began to mobilise against Chisholm so did other private business interests as he pushed ahead with a municipal telephone service and, more significantly, with larger plans for the provision of Council houses. Chisholm had successfully barred licensed premises from all municipal property and planned greater restrictions on licensing generally while, at the same time, his housing project necessitated raising a loan of £750,000.[64] All of the simmering discontent provoked by these issues came to a head in the local election of 1902 when Chisholm defied convention by attempting to secure a second successive term as Lord Provost. However, Chisholm, and the cause of Council housing, met their nemesis in the unlikely shape of 'a presumptuous youth,' one Andrew Scott Gibson.[65]

Gibson made his first appearance on the political stage in 1901 when he won a seat in Springburn. This was a bad year for the Stalwarts whose only success was the unopposed return of P.G. Stewart in Hutchesontown, and the overall result was regarded as a triumph for the Citizens' Union and a check on the ambitions of the Progressive party generally.[66] The one contest which went against this trend was Springburn where there was the highest turnout of voters, almost 70%, and the largest majority, nearly 2,000. At first Gibson was identified as a Stalwart and a Socialist, both by the *Glasgow Herald* and the *Labour Leader*, though the latter soon came to regard him as a 'reactionary' adventurer.[67] Although nothing was ever formally proven there appears to be little doubt that Gibson was, if not in the pocket of, certainly supported by the drinks lobby, and the determination to stop the more stringent licensing restrictions explains Gibson's assault on Chisholm.[68]

The result of the contest in Woodside was a crushing blow to Chisholm and the Progressive cause; on a massive turnout of 83%, Gibson secured a majority over the incumbent Lord Provost of over 1,000 votes. This was immediately interpreted by the *Glasgow Herald*, as 'a declaration in favour of some immediate action toward the restriction of municipal expenditure', while at the same time describing the overall poll as 'a victory of no mean character for the extreme party'.[69] Partly this confusion can be explained by

[63] *Glasgow Commonweal*, Nov. 1896.
[64] Fraser, 'Municipal Socialism', pp. 274–5. The ban on licences in municipal premises had a much longer term effect in making Glasgow's later housing estates 'dry', the ban not being revoked until the 1970s. See Maver, 'Temperance Crusade', p. 48.
[65] *Glasgow Herald*, 5 Nov. 1902.
[66] *Glasgow Herald*, 6 Nov. 1901.
[67] *Glasgow Herald*, 6 Nov. 1901; *Labour Leader*, 9 Nov. 1901, 31 Oct. 1903.
[68] See Maver, 'Temperance Crusade' for details on Gibson and the 'trade'.
[69] *Glasgow Herald*, 5 Nov. 1902.

the mistake in continuing to identify Gibson as a socialist. Yet, at the same time the labour candidates did well; including John Ferguson they successfully contested five wards. Labour, albeit with scant enthusiasm, had supported Chisholm because of the housing issue, while the Citizens' Union also supported him, because they suspected Gibson of even worse.

Gibson's popularity was based on a populist campaign backed by considerable powers of oratory. Harry McShane recalled of him:

> He attacked the Town Council fearlessly and criticised all kinds of corrupt practices; he protested and exploded against all the people at the top and got himself thrown out of the Corporation on a number of occasions. He was nowhere near the Labour point of view, but he was one of the best speakers I ever heard.[70]

Gibson's target was the Liberal and temperance 'establishment' of Glasgow and he delighted in publicising stories of councillors indulging themselves in Corporation hospitality. Gibson successfully tapped into public resentment of Corporation 'extravagance' and this became associated with a rising rates bill and hostility to any further plans of municipalisation, especially the plans for building houses. But more than this Gibson made an appeal to part of the electorate not normally addressed by candidates for municipal office. The self-appointed advocate of the 'claims of the poorer classes', Gibson had, in his own words, been first elected by the 'poorer class of men who lived in Springburn'.[71] The unprecedentedly high turnouts in all of Gibson's election contests tend to support these claims, and his successful shift to the highly respectable Woodside ward in 1902 indicates an ability to appeal to a better off electorate as well. Gibson was and remained a maverick but at times his cult of personality threatened to erupt into a political movement. In 1904, the *Glasgow Herald*, protested against the success of two 'Scott Gibsonites' and even drew a distinction between this 'type' and the 'earnest Socialist'.[72]

Although Gibson had claimed to be a member of the ILP at some point in the past he was never a formal labour or WEC candidate and, after the 1902 election, his relations with Labour were openly hostile. From his perspective labour councillors could be seen as part of the municipal establishment and in particular Gibson clashed with Joseph Burgess, ex-editor of the *Workman's Times,* now based in Glasgow who won a seat in Townhead in 1902. Gibson dubbed Burgess ' the Cockney Columbus who discovered Glasgow', claimed that he had misused Corporation funds on a trip to London and that he had 'intrigued' with the Liberal-Temperance caucus in Woodside against Gibson in 1905.[73] There was little doubt that Gibson was a thorn in Labour's side,

[70] H. McShane & J. Smith, *No Mean Fighter* (London, 1978), p. 14.
[71] *Glasgow Herald,* 5 Nov. 1902.
[72] *Glasgow Herald,* 2 Nov. 1904.
[73] *Star,* 28 Oct. 1905, 27 Jan. 1906.

indirectly in that he was an instrument in encouraging opposition to municipal provision and directly when he once again upped sticks and won Dalmarnock in 1906, a ward the ILP had been trying hard to regain.[74] For the ILP the success of Gibson was at the expense of labour. He represented 'the emergence of a type of free-lance candidate which, by claiming affinity with Labour, does nothing but harm to the Labour cause'. What permitted this phenomenon, it was argued, was, 'The absence of a well-organised Labour party outside the Town Council, with a well-defined municipal policy'.[75] The loose, ill-defined nature of the coalition that had created the Stalwarts was no longer seen as a virtue but a hindrance.

The absence of any central authority not only encouraged the rise of the maverick Scott Gibson but also permitted personality clashes to threaten and seriously weaken Labour's position. As the very particular concerns of municipal politics re-asserted themselves, with candidates operating more or less independently, it was becoming rapidly apparent that the WEC was no more than a mere shell. The loss of the Co-operators seriously depleted the funds of the WEC, which fell by a third as a direct consequence.[76] At the same time the rate payers' reaction was getting underway and eating into Labour's support. One revealing contest occurred in Calton, John Ferguson's constituency, in 1900. The victorious candidate was one Roderick Scott, a butcher who had been a prominent force in the Co-operative boycott. An unsuccessful candidate in 1896, Scott now defeated Boyd S. Brown, one of the original Stalwarts though no longer an official WEC nominee.[77] Nonetheless, it was significant that a figure such as Scott could win so easily in a Ward such as Calton (a majority of over one thousand), and two years later Ferguson only held his own seat by sixty votes.[78]

The Irish were the next element of the democratic forces to drop out. In spite of the hostility of the *Glasgow Observer* (the newspaper catering for Irish nationalist opinion in the city) to the association with labour, Irish involvement in the WEC was very pronounced. Particularly active was the Home Government Branch (HGB), the largest, wealthiest and most-independent minded of the INL branches in Scotland. Alongside John Ferguson was Hugh Murphy, the President of the HGB, who was especially active in promoting labour candidates. Murphy supported the official line by supporting the Liberals at the 1895 general election, though he made no direct criticism of the Labour candidates. Shortly after he was working assiduously for ILP candidates at the local polls, and it was Murphy who proposed

[74] *Glasgow Herald*, 7 Nov. 1906.
[75] *Labour Leader*, 10 Nov. 1904.
[76] Glasgow Trades Council, *Annual Report 1898–99*. The co-op withdrawal saw the WEC finances drop by £50.
[77] *Glasgow Herald*, 7 Nov. 1900.
[78] *Glasgow Herald*, 5 Nov. 1902; Scott remained a councillor for Calton until 1918, Kinloch & Butt, *Scottish Co-operative Wholesale Society*, p. 265.

George Mitchell of the ILP to the Second Ward Committee.[79] With the formation of the WEC this relationship was strengthened and Murphy himself was a candidate in 1898 in Calton, albeit unsuccessful.[80]

Relations between the Irish and Labour seemed to have been consolidated at the general election of 1900 when both the HGB and the *Observer* could support the candidature of Fletcher in Camlachie. Yet, once again local politics were to march to a different tune. Trouble emerged at the municipal polls in 1901 when the WEC candidate, the veteran Shaw Maxwell, blamed his defeat in Mile End at the hands of 'an extraordinary combination of Tories, Liberals, Unionists, Orangemen and Catholics', and bitterly remarked that his advocacy of Home Rule for Ireland for the past twenty-one years deserved, 'a little more gratitude'. The *Observer* was jubilant about this defeat, for which it claimed the credit, arguing that Maxwell had sacrificed the candidature of Hugh Murphy in an attempt to appease the local Tories and prevent them opposing his own re-election. The *Observer* was still hostile to Murphy but chose to regard this as a slight on the whole Irish community and advised its readers to vote for Maxwell's opponent. Other defeated ILP candidates made the effort not to indulge in recriminations and P.G. Stewart, the one Stalwart success, explicitly countered Shaw Maxwell by saying that, 'He would consider himself a traitor to his party if he uttered a single word there which would prevent the advanced forces coming together'.[81] Hostilities simmered on, however, with Shaw Maxwell regaining Mile End at a by election in 1903 – defeating the official WEC candidate, none other than Hugh Murphy – and then retaining the seat at the November poll, this time standing as the WEC nominee.[82] None of this was likely to improve relations with the Irish nationalists.

Oddly enough, in spite of its hostility to Shaw Maxwell, the *Observer* was now looking more favourably on labour representation, and even advised the Stalwarts to sustain a year round campaign and to copy the organisational methods, though not the substance, of Scott Gibson.[83] Adding to the confusion, at the same time the HGB was becoming estranged from the ILP over the former's support for Gibson. To the staunchly pro-temperance *Observer* this was just more proof of the HGB's cosy relations with the drinks lobby, a claim it had been making for some time and which it had even associated the ILP with.[84] Irish involvement with the drinks trade was an

[79] *Glasgow Observer*, 26 Oct. 1895.

[80] *Glasgow Herald*, 2 Nov. 1898.

[81] *Glasgow Observer*, 9 Nov. 1901.

[82] Glasgow Trades Council, *Annual Report 1902–3*; *Labour Leader*, 31 Oct., 7 Nov. 1903.

[83] *Glasgow Observer*, 9 Nov. 1901.

[84] *Glasgow Observer*, 2 Nov. 1895. In 1898 the *Observer* claimed that Murphy and the HMG only spoke for, ' a very narrow circle of Glasgow publicans and Glasgow ILP men who happen to be Irish in nationality and anxious to use the Irish movement to further their own purposes'. Quoted in Handley, *Irish in Modern Scotland*, p. 285.

undeniable fact. Murphy and others in the HGB were employed in the trade but, as we have seen, they were able to accept their failure to get municipal control dropped from the WEC programme.

The Irish, and particularly the HGB's, connections with the drinks trade had long been a cause of comment in Glasgow politics and it may well have been the case that their support for Gibson was merely a marriage of convenience useful to the business careers of certain local politicians. Associating with Gibson certainly paid off for M.J. Connell. Defeated in 1896, when he had been a Liberal and Ward Committee nominee, and again in 1899 when a candidate for the WEC, Connell eventually won a seat in Cowlairs as a supporter of Gibson. One candidate, defeated by a Scott Gibsonite in 1904, was incensed by the role played by the *Star* newspaper (owned by the HGB) and set out to prove that it was 'Mr Scott Gibson's party organ'. The evidence for this was that of forty 'Scottish shareholders' in the paper, over thirty were 'publicans or brewers' travellers, and one a retired publican'. Connell, a lawyer, was also a shareholder and he was Gibson's closest associate on the Town Council, as well as being an office bearer in the HGB.[85]

But, in addition to the hidden machinations of the 'trade', there is also the undeniable fact of Gibson's popular appeal to consider. Gibson's ability to motivate the poorer working class voter was perhaps what upset his critics most. The *Star* commented on the superior attitude displayed by his opponents to the 'type' of people who voted for Gibson. It reported one such, a sausage manufacturer, in Woodside in 1904, as saying, 'He believed the better class were in favour of Baillie Martin. There was a great many of the unthinking, maybe the unwashed, whose support they could not hope to get. They had not the power or sense of thinking'.[86] Given that the Irish community was comprised largely of the poorer working class and likely the target of such comments, it is not difficult to see how they might sympathise with Gibson.

Yet, the Irish alliance with Gibson did not last very long. It was broken in 1906 when Gibson decided to stand as an independent Unionist in Mid-Lanark at the general election, and then resigned his seat at Woodside in order to challenge in Dalmarnock at the municipal polls. The HGB was in no doubt, in spite of their 'fullest support' for Gibson in municipal affairs, that in Mid-Lanark, 'The Irish electors had to give him A SOUND THRASH-ING'.[87] Gibson's decision to contest Dalmarnock was to directly challenge the incumbent, Hugh Alexander, whom he claimed had, as Chairman of the Licensing Bench, obstructed Gibson's elevation to magistrate.[88] Once again Gibson won a huge majority on a massive turnout, but for the HGB this was

[85] *Glasgow Observer*, 5 Nov. 1904.
[86] *Star*, 19 Oct. 1904. The *Star's* comment was that this was a 'gratuitously insulting reference to the working class electors of the ward'.
[87] *Star*, 6 Jan. 1906.
[88] *Glasgow Herald*, 7 Nov. 1906.

egotism gone too far, 'He has . . . left his record behind in the mud of Dalmarnock. Instead of making himself the rallying centre of the advanced forces in the Council, he is completely isolated from the small body of men who have hitherto been associated with him'. Moreover, pointing out how badly the labour candidates had fared – the WEC nominee in Dalmarnock polled less than Gibson's majority over Alexander – it was further commented that 'such freaks' as Gibson were only permitted by, 'the present contemptible condition of the Labour organisation throughout the city'.[89]

And yet 1906 had started well for Labour, both in re-cementing its alliance with Irish nationalists at the general election, and in the triumph of returning its first ever MP for Glasgow. By 1906, of course, there was now a national labour party in existence or, rather, there were two such bodies: the Labour Representation Committee (LRC) which was about to become the Labour Party, and the Scottish Workers' Representation Committee (SWRC). Indeed the SWRC had been established prior to the formation of the London based LRC, further evidence of Scottish Labour's 'organisational precocity'.[90] Moreover, unlike the LRC, the Scottish body also included the Co-operators as well as trade unionists and socialists, an achievement the English body eyed jealously.[91] The formation of the Scottish Trade Union Congress (STUC) in 1897 as a conscious response to the TUC's decision to bar delegates from trades councils, essentially directed against the growing socialist influence at Congress, also indicated a more class conscious and politically motivated labour movement north of the border.[92]

The SWRC appeared to have a bright future. It was established in January 1900 at a founding conference with delegates from trade unions, trades councils, Co-operative societies, the ILP and the SDF.[93] In 1901 it ran Robert Smillie as a candidate at a by-election in North East Lanark and gained almost 3,000 votes or 22% of the poll. This was enough to deprive the Liberals of a seat they had held continuously since 1885 and this result may well have encouraged the agreement reached between Ramsay MacDonald and Herbert Gladstone in 1903.[94] This secret deal, or Lib-Lab pact, intended to avoid Labour and the Liberals clashing in three-cornered contests did not, however, operate in Scotland. The consequences of this were that electoral contests in Scotland would be fought more intensely in the absence of a progressive alliance and, crucially, that labour representation in Scotland would remain at a very low level.

[89] *Star*, 10 Nov. 1906.
[90] D. Howell, *British Workers and the ILP*, pp. 133–44.
[91] Hutchison, *Political History*, p. 250.
[92] A. Tuckett, *The Scottish Trades Union Congress: the First 80 Years, 1897–1977* (Edinburgh, 1986), pp. 19–32
[93] Hutchison, *Political History*, p. 250.
[94] C. Harvie, 'Before the Breakthrough, 1886–1922', in I.Donnachie, C.Harvie & I.Wood (eds.), *Forward! Labour Politics in Scotland 1888–1988* (Edinburgh, 1989), p. 13.

A further by-election in North East Lanark in 1904 (after the Scottish Liberals had rejected any pact) saw Labour increase its vote by over 1000 (securing 28% of the poll) yet still come third and fail to stop the Liberals regaining the seat.[95] The Liberal revival was now underway and would return the party to its leading position in Scotland and Glasgow at the 1906 General Election.

Yet, Labour did make its parliamentary breakthrough in 1906 when out of nine candidates, George Barnes won Glasgow Hutchesontown and Alex Wilkie secured one of the two Dundee seats, both against Liberal opposition. In addition Joseph Burgess, like Barnes the recipient of Irish support, performed creditably in Camlachie, gaining thirty per cent of the poll and depriving the Liberals of victory.[96] Labour's overall success in returning twenty-nine of its candidates throughout Britain enthused the membership of the ILP which, even in Scotland, could share in the general euphoria and even claim to have made a distinctive contribution. Joseph Duncan, then organiser of the Scottish District of the ILP, wrote to his fiancee, 'And so the Revolution is started at last'.

> We have done much better in Scotland than I expected. . . . This is not a big proportion but then it must be remembered that in Scotland we have not a clear fight anywhere. In every constituency we have to fight both Liberal & Tory. Although this makes harder fighting it is much more satisfactory. When we get our men in it means that they go in on our own votes. It declares the open war. . . . It is the clear trumpet call of the revolution.[97]

Such exhilaration about future prospects was widely shared.[98] But in Scotland the cause of labour representation stubbornly refused to move. In the general election of December 1910 William Adamson, the miners' leader, won a further seat in West Fife, giving a grand total of three Scottish Labour MPs. Even this may exaggerate the strength of Labour's 'own votes'. While Barnes and Wilkie originally won their seats against Liberals they did not subsequently have to face Liberal opposition. Adamson's victory was achieved against a Liberal but he appears to have benefited from the decision of the Conservatives not to contest after coming third at the January 1910 election. The crucial factor, as regards Labour's performance in Scotland compared with England, was the failure of the Lib-Lab pact to operate north of the border. The Liberal acceptance of both Barnes and Wilkie after 1906 was simply the acceptance of a *fait accompli*, made easier by the 'loyalty' of the Parliamentary Labour Party to the Liberal Government.

[95] Craig, *Results 1885–1918*, p. 548.
[96] Election results from Craig, *Results 1885–1918*, pp. 495, 503, 505. See Chapter Four for further discussion of these election contests.
[97] National Library of Scotland, Duncan MSS, Acc 5490/2 Joseph Duncan, letter 17 January 1906.
[98] C. Benn, *Keir Hardie* (London, 1992), p. 210.

Elsewhere Labour was not strong enough to force the issue and the Liberals in Camlachie were prepared to lose the seat to the Unionists (as happened in all three elections of 1906 and 1910) rather than cede their claim to Labour. Even if the non-existence of the pact in Scotland was partly due to timing – the Scottish Liberals only considered it after Chamberlain had launched his tariff reform campaign, allowing the Liberal Party to place itself firmly at the head of the progressive forces – Labour's failure to force concessions reflects both its own weakness and the continuing strength of Scottish Liberalism.[99]

At the beginning of 1906 Labour in Glasgow had the Hutchesontown victory to celebrate but the November municipal polls brought only further disappointment. In fact this was Labour's worst performance since it began contesting local elections; it contested eight seats, lost in every one, and received its lowest share of the poll in contested wards. As the *Star* commented, with more than a hint of *schadenfreude*, the Labour candidates were 'completely wiped out'.[100] Relations between the Irish and the ILP, in spite of the co-operation at the general election, had gone from bad to worse. John Ferguson had died earlier in the year and the ILP infuriated Irish opinion by identifying his Calton seat as Labour and running a candidate at the subsequent by-election without any consultation. As a result the Irish electors were advised to vote against Labour and the seat was lost. Further damage occurred in November when the ILP and the nationalists competed against each other in Springburn, and both lost to a candidate the *Forward* identified as receiving the 'Orange vote'.[101]

The Need for Organisation

With the Co-operators long gone, the Irish not only departed but hostile, the WEC was no longer the positive example it had seemed only a few years before. Indeed, after the 1905 municipal polls, when a further two seats were lost, the *Labour Leader* had acidly remarked, 'Perhaps there are reasons for this which the party in Glasgow will have to take into serious considera-tion'.[102] The need for organisation was the cry on everyone's lips, but this was easier said than done. With even the trades council losing interest the WEC had become a shell containing, more or less, only the ILP. But the ILP's own ambitions were also a source of antagonism to its erstwhile allies. As a later account of the break-up of the Stalwarts put it: 'As the Socialists element grew in strength on the WEC its programme and policy became

[99] Hutchison, *Political History*, pp. 259–60; Howell, *British Workers and the ILP*, pp. 171–2.
[100] *Star*, 10 Nov. 1906. The *Forward* (10 Nov.) attempted to claim the victory of J.W. Pratt in Woodside as a victory since Pratt was a Fabian, but he had not stood as either a WEC or ILP candidate and was not regarded as Labour councillor.
[101] *Forward*, 3 Nov. 1906; *Star*, 10 Nov. 1906.
[102] *Labour Leader*, 10. Nov. 1905.

more exclusively "Socialist". This was not to the liking of the UIL, nor the Co-operators, and as a consequence they seceded'.[103]

An opportunity to construct a Labour Party on the ground and provide the political organisation so many were calling for had been offered by the formation of the SWRC At its first annual conference a resolution was passed in favour of the establishment of local committees which would undertake all electoral work – both parliamentary and municipal. This was opposed by the ILP in Glasgow which moved an amendment, 'that local committees only deal with Parliamentary work and leave municipal elections to others'.[104] Whether the ILP opposed this resolution in order to maintain its local dominance or even at that time to maintain its alliance with the Irish (who were not part of or eligible to join the SWRC) is unclear. But what *is* clear is that Labour organisation in Glasgow was in serious decline.

In spite of the optimism surrounding its formation, the SWRC had a short and inglorious history and in 1909 it voted to dissolve itself and was swallowed up by the Labour Party. In terms of selecting candidates, encouraging the formation of local associations, and disseminating propaganda the SWRC was basically 'a failure'.[105] In addition to its own internal lack of dynamism, it had to struggle under the burden of critical underfunding. This was because, although established under the aegis of the STUC, trade unions in Scotland tended on the whole to send their affiliation fees to the London-based Labour Party. The SWRC constantly tried to have it established that, like the STUC, it should have a right to the proportion of monies produced from the Scottish members, but to no avail.[106] Behind this dispute, and the eventual disbandment of the SWRC, was the determination of the Labour Party, and its Secretary Ramsay MacDonald, to maintain all union contributions and to displace the SWRC. As one executive member stated, 'the aim of the Labour Party was to extinguish the Scottish Committee, and proposals to that effect had been made to the Committee during his term of office'.[107] However, the ending of the confusion caused by having two 'labour parties' did nothing to improve matters on the ground, as London essentially neglected Scottish affairs and organisation prior to 1914.[108] What improvements did take place were promoted locally.

In 1908, in the run-up to the November municipal polls, one local ILP activist gave vent to his frustrations about the WEC and 'the same old

---

[103] Labour Party, *Souvenir*, p.35

[104] SWRC, *First Annual Report 1901*, p. 14.

[105] Hutchison, *Political History*, p. 250; also I.G.C. Hutchison, 'Glasgow Working Class Politics', in R.A. Cage (ed.), *The Working Class in Glasgow 1750–1914* (London, 1987), p. 117, 'its efforts were characterised by poor organisation and lack of drive.'

[106] SWRC, *Sixth Annual Report 1906*, p. 9.

[107] SWRC, *Eighth Annual Report 1908*, p. 16. The speaker was Robert Allan, a previous Secretary of the SWRC. See also Hutchison, *Political History*, pp. 252–3 on the machinations of MacDonald.

[108] Hutchison, *Political History*, p. 254. 'Organisation lagged substantially behind the levels attained at this time in England.'

wrangle over trifles, the same old higgle-de-piggledy way of doing things'. Too many seats were being contested without sufficient preparation, more or less guaranteeing failure; 'The Trades Council has withdrawn their delegates [from the WEC]. Isn't it about time the ILP was doing the same, and uniting with the Trades Council to form an LRC?'[109]

In fact some progress was being made along these lines. In Springburn, 'a great Trade union stronghold', a local LRC had selected the Labour candidate.[110] This still was not enough to win the seat and all eight labour candidates went down to defeat in 1908. However, the following year the Trades Council decided to take a more active role and appointed a new Election Committee, at which point Labour's electoral fortunes began to recover.[111] The ILP, the Trades Council and the Fabian Society initiated a series of protracted discussions with the purpose of establishing a Glasgow Labour Party which aim was eventually realised in 1912. The Party comprised delegates from the Trades Council, the Glasgow ILP Federation, the seven divisional LRCs, the Fabian Society and the Women's Labour League. 'It takes the place of the Workers' Municipal Elections Committee (now defunct) and is the controlling body in all matters appertaining to Parliamentary, Municipal, Parish Council and School Board candidatures, and has a deciding voice on questions of policy and discipline, such questions being submitted to a conference of members and public representatives'.[112]

The contrast with the WEC and the Stalwarts is clear. Labour's re-emergence was not to be based upon an attempt to re-activate the 'forces of the democracy' but was a development of Labour's own organisational strength. Moreover, just as the WEC in its heyday had not simply been a centralist shell, but had gathered within it a multiplicity of local organisations, so too did the Glasgow Labour Party. The significant difference is that it did so not as 'a composite body' (which the WEC had been) but as a 'controlling body'. The seven LRCs corresponded to the seven Glasgow Parliamentary Divisions and had responsibility for selecting candidates for local and national elections. The LRCs were themselves delegate bodies, having no individual membership structure, but it was the affiliated organisations that were the evidence of Labour's strength.

For instance the Blackfriars and Hutchesontown LRC during the First World War included delegates from trade union branches, ILP branches, the British Socialist Party (BSP), the Women's Labour League, the Housing Association, the Co-operative Women's Guild, the Food Protest Association, Kinning Park Co-operative Society and the United Baking Co-operative Society.[113] A number

[109] *Forward*, 12 Sept. 1908. The letter was signed 'Disgusted'.

[110] *Forward*, 7 Nov. 1908.

[111] Glasgow Trades Council, *Annual Report 1909–10*.

[112] Labour Party, *Souvenir*, p. 38

[113] *Rules of the Blackfriars and Hutchesontown Labour Representation Committee* (n.d.) Though undated the involvement of the BSP and Food Protest Association indicates the document's provenance as during war time.

of issues are apparent from this list. One is the organised presence of women, whose increasing public role had been in evidence in the years before 1914 but which developed rapidly during the war. There is the very pronounced involvement of the Co-operators. And there is the inclusion of single issue campaigning bodies, the Housing and the Food Protest Associations, indicative of Labour's appeal beyond formal party structures, a process also greatly accelerated during wartime. The one noticeable absence compared with the WEC was the Irish who simply had no basis for affiliation. This created resentment within Irish political opinion, yet the lack of an organised presence did not mean a total absence of Irish input, since even more Irishmen than before were taking active roles in the labour movement. A final point was the continuing significance of the ILP which provided the LRC with eight delegates from four branches. The ILP's ambition to control local elections proved to be unsustainable but, whether acting independently or as part of a broader framework, 'the ILP was the "Labour party" on the ground and in constituency wards around Clydeside'.[114]

While improved organisation was critical to Labour's improved electoral performance, it was not on its own sufficient to turn the tide; organisation and changes in the political climate went together. As we have seen, the democratic alliance behind the WEC was more or less defunct by the early 1900s and between 1904 and 1909 labour won only two seats in the November municipal polls. In 1908 labour representation had fallen to a single seat in Mile End.[115] The break-up of the Stalwarts meant that the WEC took on a more definite socialist identity; all candidates were ILP members and were reliant upon ILP branches for their campaigns. The programme candidates fought under had changed little from the original document of 1896, but the loss of the Co-operators, then the Irish and the growing disinterest of the trades council left 'labour' more exposed to the middle class reaction against the increasing demands being placed upon the rates. The ILP might claim that the labour vote now represented the solid 'bedrock' of confirmed socialist support, but this was little comfort for the loss of seats.[116] In effect, while Labour's policies had not changed the political climate had.

Labour's poor performances were thrown into sharper relief by the successes enjoyed by Scott Gibson, but the problem went deeper than a single maverick opponent. Behind the reaction to any further proposals of municipalisation lay the increasing importance of the rates issue. There had always been opposition to the growth of public services provided by the municipality which found its most faithful expression in the leader columns of the *Glasgow Herald*. At the first election of John Ferguson in 1893 the *Herald* warned its readers against, 'his overwhelming schemes of municipalisation

---

[114] J. Melling, *Rent Strikes: People's Struggles for Housing in West Scotland 1890–1916* (Edinburgh, 1983), p. 39.
[115] *Forward*, 7 Nov. 1908.
[116] *Labour Leader*, 7 Nov. 1908.

and confiscation', thereby drawing the connection between public ownership and the threat to private property.[117] However, this did not deflect the
Corporation which continued with the Scottish practice of operating municipal services at the lowest possible cost, rather than adopting the English
custom of using public profits to subsidise the rates.[118] Nevertheless, groups
of 'concerned ratepayers' began increasingly to organise objections to the
policies of the Corporation and make interventions at the polls.

Moreover, from around 1900 the rates issue became much more pronounced and significant. This was due to particularly large increases in
Glasgow's rates due to municipal reforms, improved amenities and the
increasing cost of building and maintaining the urban environment. National reforms and improvements, as in education, which began to place
more demands upon local authorities generally, also contributed. Glasgow's
local rate increased from 11.4p in the £ in 1890–91 to 18.7p in the £ in 1913/
14 and average tax payments per head of population rose from 71p to 134p.
over the same period, with the consequence that, 'by the 1900s . . . rising
rate poundages became an increasingly controversial issue.'[119] As the ratepayers' pressure groups began to take the initiative, so labour began to run
out of steam. Part of the problem was that Glasgow did not appear to have
much left to municipalise. Further schemes were mooted, such as coal
supplies, milk, banking, housing, but none aroused much enthusiasm, and
suggestions over coal and milk also managed to estrange the co-operative
societies which already provided such services.

As Labour's electoral fortunes steadily declined explanations were offered
to explain away the poor results. Foremost among these were the perceived
hostility of temperance voters and women electors, often regarded as the
same thing. The role of the female electorate is perhaps analogous to the Irish
vote in this instance in that women could qualify for the local vote but only
under very restricted circumstances and accounted for a fraction of the total
electorate. We shall examine the question of women and the vote in more
detail in a later chapter, but for the moment it is sufficient to comment that
explanations of defeat that claimed, 'In reality, we did win on the men's vote',
are not very convincing.[120] The hostility of the temperance lobby to labour
candidates was a more or less constant opposition. Labour challenged the
temperance lobby with their own solution of municipal control of the drink

---

[117] *Glasgow Herald*, 8 Nov. 1893.

[118] Fraser, 'Municipal Socialism', p. 262.

[119] T. Hart, 'Urban Growth and Municipal Government: Glasgow in a Comparative
Context, 1846–1914', in A. Slaven & D.H. Aldcroft (eds.), *Business, Banking and
Urban History* (Edinburgh, 1982), pp. 200–1. Other areas of local taxation saw even
greater proportional increases; for instance, between 1900 and 1906 the Glasgow
Poor Rate more than doubled, from 10.25d. in the £ to over 20d PP 1901, XXVII,
PP1907, XXXVII *Annual Reports of the Local Government Board for Scotland.*

[120] This was the claim made by William Stewart in 1904 after his defeat in Dalmarnock. *Labour Leader*, 11 Nov. 1904. See Chapter Five for discussion of Labour's
attitude to the local female electorate.

trade and also by directly refuting the claim that drink was the cause of poverty.[121] However, labour was itself imbued with temperance sympathies and it is difficult to avoid the conclusion that a public declaration of such was regarded as a necessary part of electioneering. In 1906 of nine 'Forward' candidates, no fewer than eight claimed to be life long abstainers and one was even described as a 'Labour and Temperance nominee'.[122] Yet, while temperance remained significant it was not the issue it had been and, moreover, it had not prevented the labour successes of the later 1890s.[123]

The nadir of Labour's electoral fortunes appeared to be the election of 1908, when all eight candidates were defeated. This meant that in four years of municipal elections Labour had managed to win a single contest. Yet, 1908 saw the return of mass unemployment to Glasgow with the Trades Council estimating '20,000 skilled workers going idle' plus a similar number of labourers and 'several thousands' of women workers.[124] In response to this there developed a socialist led movement of protest, as the ILP and the SDF worked together in organising meetings and demonstrations to demand relief. In addition a Glasgow Unemployed Committee was formed by the ILP and Trades Council which operated at a city-wide level, organising massive demonstrations and pressurising the corporation's official Distress Committee to greater urgency. As the unemployment continued it bit hard into the funds of the skilled unions who then found themselves, like their labourers, applying for relief to the Corporation and the Charity Organisation Society.[125]

This period of unemployment has been identified as critical in 'the growth of the labour movement in Glasgow'. As Labour was galvanised by the impact of unemployment – the 1909 May Day march numbered 30,000 – so it was the ILP which was best placed to provide the political leadership of the Glasgow labour movement.[126] The plight of the unemployed, especially the skilled, respectable working man, allowed Labour to focus demands upon both the national and local state and to make public provision a more popular issue once again. For the Trades Council, 'Unemployment is really the question of the day' and it proposed that all trade unionists should make a Right to Work Bill a test question at the next election.[127] At the same time a decision taken by the Town Council to exploit the tramway surplus as a means of lowering the rates stung the Trades Council into action to try and defend the principle that, as the working class were the main users of the trams, they should get the

---

[121] For instance see J. O'Connor Kessack, *Is Drink the Cause of Poverty? A Reply to the Temperance Party* (Glasgow, 1907).
[122] This was Ben Shaw in Kinning Park who was standing against a publican. *Forward*, 3 Nov. 17 November 1906
[123] Maver, 'Temperance Crusade', pp.44–63.
[124] Glasgow Trades Council, *Annual Report 1907–08*, p. 27.
[125] J. Smith, 'Taking the Leadership of the labour movement: the ILP in Glasgow, 1906–1914', in A. McKinlay & R.J. Morris (eds.), *The ILP on Clydeside 1893–1932: from foundation to disintegration* (Manchester, 1991), p. 66.
[126] Smith, 'Taking the Leadership', pp. 65–70.
[127] Glasgow Trades Council, *Annual Report 1908–09*, pp. 13–4

major benefit directly by way of low fares. It is hardly surprising that the municipal elections in 1909 saw the Trades Council take a more active role again in establishing an Election Committee.[128]

At the November polls only a handful of seats were contested but this more circumspect campaign paid dividends with an increase in the share of the vote and one victory.[129] The success was in Townhead where the candidate was nominated by the Trades Council's election committee, and a further seat was gained in the same ward in a subsequent by-election.[130] From this moment on Labour once again began to enjoy electoral success and rebuilt a presence on the Corporation but it was only in retrospect that 1909 appeared as a turning point. There was no rejoicing at having won a single seat; the disappointments of the previous years had cut too deep to allow that. As the *Forward* put it; 'For the present, Municipal Socialism is in the lean and dry stage. It stands in need of new ideas and a new inspiration'.[131]

Labour's Re-emergence, 1910–14: the Housing Question

If the tramways had been the big topic in municipal politics in the early 1890s, the single most important concern after 1910 was housing. Housing, of course, was not a new issue, it was a deep seated problem in urban Scotland. In working class areas, even non-socialist candidates could make housing and anti-landlordism a plank of their programme as, for instance, a 'temperance and working-man's candidate' in the Gorbals in 1891 who appealed to the electors, 'to vote down the landlord and house factor clique'.[132] In 1894 an ILP candidate called for the City to build houses alongside a proposal for direct labour to be employed in their construction.[133] The original WEC programme of 1896 had included the demands for legally fixed maximum rents and the direct building of houses by the Corporation; two years later it specifically called for the 'erection of artisan dwellings', via the city Improvement Trust, 'to be let at rents sufficient to cover the cost of construction and maintenance'.[134]

Once again, Labour's priorities had been set out by John Ferguson in his original election manifesto of 1893. This brief programme called for the appropriation of 'Ground values' and the formation of a labour opinion in the Council which would use existing powers, while seeking yet greater powers, in order to improve the condition of the working class, 'by means of a living wage, natural hours of labour, comfortable

[128] Glasgow Trades Council, *Annual Report 1908–09*, p. 15.
[129] *Forward*, 6 Nov. 1909.
[130] Glasgow Trades Council, *Annual Report 1909–10*, p. 16
[131] *Forward*, 13 Nov. 1909.
[132] *Glasgow Herald*, 4 Nov. 1891.
[133] *Glasgow Herald*, 7 Nov. 1894.
[134] *Labour Leader*, 27 Aug. 1898.

healthy homes, and proper places of recreation'.[135] As we have seen, the Stalwarts had some success with the first two items. Although not without some ambivalence within its own ranks, Labour was able to make hours and conditions of municipal workers a test question for candidates in working class wards. Housing, however, did not become such a test question and this was partly because the Corporation did not have direct responsibility for and control over the provision of housing as it did have over the wages and conditions of its own employees. Although demands could be formulated for the Corporation to actually do something it had first to acquire the necessary powers from Parliament, a protracted process that held little promise of any immediate progress. Furthermore, the attempts to get such powers helped create the ratepayers' backlash against municipal provision.

With Chisholm's defeat in 1902 so the ambitious housing plans fell by the wayside. Instead of raising £750,000 to construct thousands of workman's dwellings, the Corporation was authorised to spend only £150,000 to complete projects already started.[136] The debate over expenditure was also a debate over who the Corporation should make provision for: the respectable low wage earner or the dissipated poor.

Opponents of the housing plans argued that it was not or should not be a function of the municipality to build for the ordinary, 'decent' poor but should concentrate solely on the 'improvident and destructive'. Professor Smart of Glasgow University stipulated that any houses built should, 'given the destructive habits of this class', be made of concrete, with only the most basic amenities, and have no removable fittings; essentially indestructible cells.[137] The logic behind this position was the expense involved but also included concerns over waste, the deterrent impact upon private provision, and fears over the political impact upon voters who were also tenants. The Glasgow Municipal Commission on the Housing of the Poor, which was set up in 1902, essentially agreed with the views of Smart and the Citizens' Union.[138] Diametrically opposed to such opinions, however, was George Carson, Secretary of the Trades Council, who, in his evidence to the Municipal Commission, stated, 'If the Corporation are to build houses at all, it must be for the thrifty, industrious and sober working classes . . .'.[139]

Ironically, 1902 had been one of Labour's better performances at the local polls but it was overshadowed by the consequences of Scott Gibson's

---

[135] Reprinted in *Labour Leader,* 22 Oct. 1898.

[136] *Municipal Glasgow,* pp. 64–7; W.H. Fraser, 'Labour and the Changing City', in G. Gordon (ed.), *Perspectives of the Scottish City* (Aberdeen, 1985), p. 170.

[137] W. Smart, *The Housing Problem and the Municipality* (Glasgow, 1902), quoted in Fraser, 'Municipal Socialism', pp. 274–5.

[138] Fraser, 'Changing City', pp. 170–1. Smart had been a supporter of municipal provision in the past but had joined the Citizens' Union.

[139] *Glasgow Municipal Commission on the Housing of the Poor* (Glasgow, 1904), p. 550.

defeat of the Lord Provost and Labour proved incapable of resisting the opposition to municipal provision. Yet, 1902 had important consequences for the future of Labour's position. Labour began to articulate much more clearly its ideas on housing and the role of the state in providing good quality housing for the 'respectable' working class. Joseph Burgess in his evidence to the Municipal Commission argued the case for garden cities of cottage type houses as opposed to tenements, an approach which John Wheatley basically reactivated, with much more political effect, in the years immediately before the War.[140]

Another stimulus to labour representation was the further expansion of the City boundaries in 1912 which brought in Partick, Govan and Tollcross. The existing boundaries had been rendered obsolete and confusing by rapid urban development and the case for extension was unanswerable; the whole area was effectively one city and had been so for some time.[141] The price demanded by the outlying burghs, however, was exemption from Glasgow rates for a considerable period.[142] As in 1891 and in the case of Kinning Park (incorporated in 1906), the most vociferous advocates of inclusion were the local labour organisations and Labour candidates were well to the fore in the 1911 elections which were dominated by the boundary issue.[143]

Among the new generation of Labour leaders emerging in Clydeside at this time was John Wheatley. Already a sitting councillor for Shettleston in Lanark County Council, Wheatley came top of the poll for the new Glasgow ward of Shettleston and Tollcross in 1912, establishing the beginning of the ILP's dominance, both municipal and parliamentary, in the East End. In a sense, Wheatley was to take over the mantle of John Ferguson in that he provided a simple but effective housing programme that Labour could campaign for and attract votes behind. The major difference being that while Ferguson was a semi-detached supporter of Labour, Wheatley was a member of the ILP and loyal to the cause of labour only.

Wheatley had been a member of the UIL before joining the ILP and before 1914 he was best known for his role in establishing the Catholic Socialist Society and his (largely successful) campaign to establish that Catholics could also be socialists. Wheatley was by no means the first Irish Catholic in Scotland to embrace socialism but what made him so prominent was his public role in arguing the essential compatibility of Christianity and socialism and in attempting to convince the Irish Catholic population generally that their future lay with Labour. To this end Wheatley established the Catholic Socialist Society (CSS) which was in turn promoted by the *Forward* which provided a regular column, 'Catholic

---

140 *Glasgow Municipal Commission*, p. 254.
141 See the case argued by the *Glasgow Herald*, 2 Nov. 1911.
142 Melling, *Rent Strikes*, p.19.
143 Labour made two gains in Govan. *Glasgow Herald*, 8 Nov. 1911; *Forward*, 11 Nov. 1911.

Notes', to publicise the arguments and activities of Wheatley and the CSS.[144]

Although Wheatley at times faced hostility from within the Church, including having his effigy burned outside his home by a crowd from his own parish, his arguments were given a tacit consent by the Catholic hierarchy in Glasgow, unlike Leeds where a CSS rapidly collapsed after being condemned by the Bishop. Both the *Glasgow Observer* and Archbishop Maquire of Glasgow took a relatively open attitude to the Labour Party and could talk of how it would eventually replace the Liberals, and how Irish voters could vote Labour, at least at the local level.[145] While the *Observer* was by now largely in favour of Labour in municipal elections, it remained concerned at the level of Catholic representation on the Corporation. With the advent of the Glasgow Labour Party there was no scope for a distinct Irish presence as there had been under the WEC, and for this reason the *Observer*, reluctantly, opposed Labour at the polls in 1912 declaring this, 'a deplorable necessity . . . we are willing to be allies, we decline to be slaves'.[146] This injunction, which included Shettleston, did not stop Wheatley triumphing at the top of the poll, a result Tom Johnston saw as particularly gratifying and of no little significance. The 'official' Irish opposition, Johnston claimed, was partly because they, 'knew that if [Wheatley] was elected they could no longer tell the Irish working man that the Labour Party was anti-Irish'.[147] This was a simplification of the *Observer's* argument but, nonetheless, Wheatley's status as the only Catholic on Glasgow Corporation must have itself provided a powerful argument in support of his case that the Irish working class should embrace Labour.

With the successful reaction against municipalisation after 1902 and the Corporation's decision in 1908 to use the tramway surplus to offset the rates, there was something of a re-appraisal of municipal socialism. Joseph Burgess, who had a decade ago eulogised the achievements of the Stalwarts, now pointed out 'the inherent capitalism' of municipal services.[148] Yet, although there was a greater emphasis placed upon the national state, e.g. over unemployment, the ILP still focused attention upon the locality and a belief in what democratic communities could achieve by way of public services. Municipal socialism was not rejected but the effort made to inject it with a fresh perspective and credibility. The Glasgow Labour Party programme

---

[144] Perhaps the best source on Wheatley remains S. Cooper, 'John Wheatley: A Study in Labour History (Unpublished Ph.D. thesis, University of Glasgow, 1973); D. Howell, *A Lost Left: Three Studies in Socialism and Nationalism* (Manchester, 1986), provides a valuable analysis of Wheatley's political ideas and their development. See also I. S. Wood, *John Wheatley* (Manchester, 1990).

[145] B. Purdie, 'Outside the Chapel Door: the Glasgow Catholic Socialist Society 1906–22' (Unpublished thesis, Ruskin College, 1976), pp. 23–6.

[146] *Glasgow Observe*, 7 Nov. 1912, quoted in Wood, *Wheatley*, p. 34

[147] *Forward*, 9 Nov. 1912.

[148] *Forward*, 8, 15 Oct. 1910. Quoted in Fraser, 'Municipal Socialism', p. 278.

retained the taxation of land values and municipal control of the drinks trade, and called for a municipal works department, as well as municipal supply of coal, bread and milk, municipal laundries, a municipal bank and the construction of corporation houses.[149] The issue which stimulated most interest was housing and it was here that Wheatley played a critical role.

As we have seen, housing was not a new issue in Glasgow but in the years after 1902 the objective situation steadily deteriorated. For the decade preceding 1914 Glasgow experienced almost no additions to its stock of working class housing; the state of the housing market was so disorganised that there were large numbers of houses standing empty, thus exacerbating the shortage of appropriate housing at affordable rents. The problem was essentially one of poverty: people could not afford the houses that were available, while the returns on low rent properties were such as to make building unprofitable. In 1913 the Labour Party Housing Committee (LPHC) was formed in Glasgow, in a situation described by its chief organiser, Andrew McBride, as 'in easy reach of a famine in housing'.[150]

The LPHC was a campaigning body for Wheatley's housing scheme, the so called 'artisan' or 'eight pound cottages'. The essence of Wheatley's plan – as outlined in his pamphlet, *Eight Pound Cottages for Glasgow Citizens* – was that the Corporation should build cottage-style houses for working class families which could be let at a rent of only £8 per annum, the funds for which were not to come from the rates but from the surplus generated by the trams.[151] Wheatley identified precisely the sort of houses that should be built; four-apartments plus kitchen and bathroom and 'an average garden area for each house of 130 square feet'. Such plans were not original but Wheatley's major contribution lay in publicising his scheme and galvanising public opinion in support. Like George Carson in 1902 Wheatley's main concern lay with the respectable working class; the 'slumdweller' would have to wait. Moreover, only around one thousand houses per annum could have been built and Wheatley admitted this was not sufficient for the City's needs. However, he argued that should the experiment prove itself then the Corporation would find other ways of extending the scale of this type of house building.[152]

In its simplicity and popularity, Wheatley's scheme was similar to John Ferguson's proposal to tax land values with its magical figure of £2m. Labour had found its 'new inspiration'. A sizeable and self-confident Labour presence was now established in George Square but, for all that, it remained a minority. A fundamental transformation in Labour's fortunes would only come about due to the political upheavals caused by the coming war.

[149] Fraser, 'Changing City', p. 175.
[150] Quoted in Melling, *Rent Strikes*, p. 40.
[151] J. Wheatley, *Eight Pound Cottages for Glasgow Citizens* (Glasgow, 1913).
[152] J. Wheatley, *A Reply to the Critics of £8 Cottages* (Glasgow, 1913).

CHAPTER TWO

War and Labour's Transformation, 1912–1922

The First World War marks a watershed in the rise of the Labour Party. It was only after the war that Labour appeared as a truly national party with realistic ambitions of taking office at Westminster, or George Square for that matter. This may have been obscured by Labour's disappointing results at the General Election of 1918 but it was, nonetheless, true. In the 1918 election Labour won fifty-seven seats, hardly a marked improvement on the previous general election of December 1910 when it had returned forty MPs. However, a much more significant contrast can be seen in the number of candidates. Where Labour had stood in fifty-six seats in December 1910 (itself a reduction from the seventy-eight contested in January), in 1918 Labour's challenge had increased over six-fold to 361 candidates. In Scotland the expansion was even more impressive; the five candidates of 1910 had become forty-six in 1918. That only seven MPs were returned in Scotland (and only one in Glasgow) was a shock to Labour's expectations and appears to negate the view that the War had any significant radical impact, but so long as Labour's position in 1910 is kept in mind, the contrast in 1918 remained marked: after all Labour did more than double its representation and, perhaps more significantly, came second in another thirty-six seats, establishing a firm base for its future advance.[1]

Labour's Electoral Position in 1914

By 1914 Labour held only three of Scotland's seventy constituencies. Labour's limited campaign in the December 1910 election was not followed by any marked improvement in subsequent by elections; in five contests the

[1] There is some confusion over the candidates and results of this election. F.W.S. Craig, *British Electoral Facts, 1885–1975* (London, 1976), is the source relied upon by most historians, but it would appear that he underestimates Labour's performance in 1918. D. Butler & G. Butler, *British Political Facts 1900–1985* (London, 1986), give the number of Labour candidates in the UK in 1918 as 388 and the number of Labour MPs as 63. Also Craig lists only 6 Labour MPs in Scotland, whereas Labour won seven seats: Aberdeen North, Ayrshire South, Dundee, Edinburgh Central, Glasgow Govan, Hamilton, and West Fife. Craig identifies as Labour only those candidates formally labelled as 'Labour Party', but it is clear that the small number of 'independent labour', Co-operative and BSP nominees were to all intents and purposes Labour candidates.

Labour candidates came last in every one. There was some consolation that Labour's intervention in three of those seats cost the Liberals victory, but there was little evidence of a growing Labour vote.[2] In England, Labour's by-election performance was better in terms of share of the vote though, even here, no gains were made. These results have been interpreted as evidence that the Liberals were withstanding the challenge of Labour nationally, at least up to 1914.[3] At the same time they cast doubt on how extensive or independent Labour's campaign would be at the following general election, widely expected to be in 1915. Although the Labour Party was officially opposed to continuing the electoral pact with the Liberals, this did not necessarily mean that the Progressive Alliance was at an end, rather it appears likely that it would be continued on a more informal basis.[4] In Scotland, Labour appeared even less likely to step outwith the shadow of the Liberal Party. At the very most Labour would have contested seventeen seats in a general election in 1914 or 1915 and, as far as Glasgow was concerned, the ILP was proposing a deal with the Liberals whereby, if Labour was given a straight run in Hutchesontown and Camlachie, it would not contest any other seats in the city.[5]

If Labour's efforts were circumscribed at the parliamentary level, municipal elections tell a different tale. Although housing provided the big municipal issue Labour had been seeking, the improvement in its local electoral performance had begun before the housing campaign took off. The single victory in 1909 was followed by two by-election victories and Labour representation now steadily increased. Prior to the city extension in 1912 the number of Labour councillors had reached twelve and with the elections for the newly extended Glasgow in 1912 there was an infusion of new blood from outlying burghs with victories in Fairfield (Govan), and Shettleston & Tollcross so that by mid 1914 there were seventeen Labour councillors in eleven wards.[6] The significance that the housing question quickly achieved can be seen in the results of the 1913 poll where the Labour campaign – 'prosecuted . . . with greater vigour than at any previous election in Glasgow' – was built around Wheatley's housing scheme and gave Labour one of its best ever results with victories in six wards.[7]

By 1914 Labour in Glasgow had left the dark days of 1905–08 far behind. Once again it had established a sizeable group on the Corporation, its level of representation was on an upward trajectory and it had a stronger

---

[2] I.G.C. Hutchison, *A Political History of Scotland 1932–1924* (Edinburgh, 1986), pp. 256–9.

[3] P.F. Clarke, 'The electoral position of the Liberal and Labour parties, 1910–1914', *English Historical Review*, xc (1975), pp. 828–36.

[4] D. Tanner, *Political Change and the Labour Party 1900–1918* (Cambridge, 1990), pp. 318–9.

[5] Hutchison, *Political History*, p. 265.

[6] Glasgow Trades Council, *Annual Reports 1911–12, 1912–13–14*

[7] *Glasgow Herald*, 5 Nov. 1913.

organisational base to sustain its electoral efforts. Partial evidence of this is given by the fact that Labour actually defeated Scott Gibson in 1914.[8] However, to get a true picture of Labour's position, these successes have to be seen in relation to the full representation of the Corporation.

After the expansion of 1912 the number of wards in the City increased from twenty-six to thirty-seven, giving a total elected membership of 111. In 1913 Labour candidates stood in thirteen of the seventeen contested wards, gaining just under 50% per cent of the votes cast in those thirteen wards and returning six councillors. Labour representation, therefore, seemed to match its popular vote. After the polls in 1914, the last elections to be held for the duration of the War, the total number of Labour councillors was nineteen, an all-time high. Yet, at around 17% of the total Corporation, this remained much the same level of representation enjoyed by the Stalwarts at their most successful[9]. Furthermore, Labour never contested a majority of seats – there were huge areas of the city where it never stood at all – and was only successful in around one third of the City Wards. This still left room for further progress if Labour could dominate all three seats in the wards where it had at least one member. However, it is significant that Labour was, apart from a very few occasions, unable to monopolise any single ward and, even had it done so, it would still have been well short of a majority. Most wards were not contested, the sitting members being returned unopposed or a new candidate selected by the ward committee, a practice made easier by the 'non-partisan system' in Scottish municipal elections.[10] This non-partisanship, which meant that Liberals and Conservatives did not contest elections directly, i.e. under party colours, was of course challenged by Labour which was, under that convention, regarded as a 'sectional' interest.[11]

Labour's re-emergence in the pre-war years was part of a process in which local politics were becoming more sharply polarised. After 1902 and the defeat of the municipal housing programme, Liberals, Unionists and Conservatives had began to co-operate more closely together in a more economy minded Corporation. Furthermore, in response to Labour's electoral gains and the formation of the Glasgow Labour Party, these 'hitherto disparate groups' had, by 1913, formed an anti-Socialist 'Moderate' alliance to fight local elections.[12] Such a polarisation was something many Labour activists

[8] *Glasgow Herald*, 4 Nov. 1914. Scott Gibson had shifted seats again, this time to Plantation in Govan. However, he was obviously no longer the force he had once been, indicated by a very low poll.

[9] *Glasgow Herald*, 4 Nov. 1914. Labour Party, *Souvenir* (1914), gives a possibly exaggerated figure of 14 Stalwarts which would have accounted for just under 19% of the total Corporation.

[10] *Glasgow Herald*, 8 Nov. 1911.

[11] *Glasgow Herald*, 5 Nov. 1913.

[12] I. Maver, 'Local Party Politics and the Temperance Crusade: Glasgow, 1890–1902', *The Journal of the Scottish Labour History Society*, xxvii (1992), p. 58. Liberal and Tory alliances were also evident in municipal contests in England and Wales. See M.G. Sheppard & J.L. Halstead, 'Labour's Municipal Election Performance

had long desired as a means of simplifying the political issues and electoral choices into a clear pro- versus anti-labour dichotomy.[13] While this had been achieved to an extent in municipal affairs, in national elections the main contest still lay firmly between Liberal and Conservative.[14]

Industrial Unrest and Politics

Labour's re-emergence as a force in Glasgow's municipal politics was linked to the distress caused by the slump of 1908–09 and the attendant mass unemployment.[15] Labour's continuing local success thereafter occurred at the same time as the explosion of industrial unrest which rocked Britain in the immediate pre-war years. Yet it is not at all clear that the two phenomena were directly related; many Labour activists had begun to despair at the perceived failure of the Parliamentary Labour Party (PLP) and were looking for alternative strategies. Moreover, the Labour Party was ambivalent towards the unrest, at first welcoming it but, as it continued, Labour's national leadership lost patience and denounced what it saw as essentially anarchic behaviour.[16]

The background to the strike wave was a decade of stagnant or declining real wages for many workers. Associated with this was the increasing pressure on the work effort provoked by the application of new machinery and management techniques and the 'speeding up' of the labour process. As unemployment abated by the end of 1910 and workers began to regain some confidence in their bargaining strength, so there was a massive backlog of resentments waiting to burst through. Describing events in late 1911, George Carson, Secretary of the Glasgow Trades Council, wrote: 'It is no exaggeration to say that in number and magnitude the labour disputes . . .

in Provincial England and Wales 1901–13', *Bulletin of the Society for the Study of Labour History*, xxxix (1979), p. 42. For more detail on such local anti-socialist arrangements in London, Leicester and West Yorkshire see P. Thompson, *Socialists, Liberals and Labour: the struggle for London 1885–1914* (London, 1967); B. Lancaster, *Radicalism, Co-operation and Socialism: Leicester Working Class Politics 1860–1906* (Leicester, 1987); K. Laybourn & J. Reynolds, *Liberalism and the Rise of Labour 1890–1918* (London, 1984).

[13] D. Howell, *British Workers and the Independent Labour Party, 1888–1906* (Manchester, 1984), p. 281.

[14] The Conservatives and Liberal Unionists merged to form the Scottish Unionist Association in 1912, though they had always co-operated closely at elections. For the growth in Conservative electoral support during this period, see D. Urwin, 'The Development of the Conservative Party Organisation in Scotland until 1912', *Scottish Historical Review*, xliv (1965), pp. 89–111.

[15] J.H. Treble, 'Unemployment in Glasgow 1903–1910: Anatomy of a Crisis', *Scottish Labour History Society Journal*, xxv (1990), pp 8–39.

[16] Labour' response to the industrial unrest is discussed in more detail in J. J. Smyth, ' "From Industrial Unrest to Industrial Debacle"?: The Labour left and industrial militancy, 1910–1914', in W. Kenefick & A. McIvor (eds.), *Roots of Red Clydeside 1910–1914: Labour Unrest and Industrial Relations in West Scotland* (Edinburgh, 1996), pp. 240–58.

have largely exceeded that of any previous year, and never in the history of the movement has such an upheaval taken place'.[17] It was this sudden burst of industrial militancy and direct action which led John MacLean to speculate about living in 'the rapids of revolution'.[18]

It is some time since historians have given much credence to George Dangerfield's famous thesis, in his *The Strange Death of Liberal England*, that a social cataclysm was averted only by the outbreak of War in August 1914.[19] One of the strongest arguments against the view of revolution avoided is that the industrial unrest declined between 1912 and 1914.[20] However, recent research has seriously questioned this view, at least for the Clydeside area. By examining local sources, rather than relying on official national figures, it has been shown that strike activity was sustained throughout 1913 and 1914.[21] While the disputes in 1913 and 1914 were more likely to be short and unofficial, they were also more likely to involve unskilled workers, male and female, and include demands for union recognition.[22] It was this which lay behind the national flood of new members into the trade unions whose membership grew from around 2.5 million in 1909 to 4.1 million in 1913, a rate of expansion greater than that experienced during the War and immediately after.[23]

There was little or no immediate political benefit from all this activity for the socialist left. While there is no doubting the extent of syndicalist involvement in the strike wave, there is little evidence to show that syndicalism as a movement made significant inroads into the working class.[24] On Clydeside the main proponent of industrial unionism was the Socialist Labour Party (SocLP), a breakaway from the SDF which was heavily influenced by the American socialist Daniel De Leon.[25] However, while

[17] Glasgow Trades Council, *Annual Report 1911–12*, p. 15.

[18] 'The times we are living in are so stirring and full of change that it is not impossible to believe that we are living in the rapids of revolution'. Speech to Renfrewshire Co-operative Conference, 25 Nov. 1911. N. Milton (ed.), *John MacLean: In the Rapids of Revolution* (London, 1978), p. 62.

[19] G. Dangerfield, *The Strange Death of Liberal England* (London, 1966, first published 1935).

[20] H. Pelling, *A History of British Trade Unionism* (Middlesex,1976), p. 138.

[21] The Board of Trade identified six strikes in the whole of Scotland in 1914, whereas there were actually 55 strikes in the West of Scotland alone. Glasgow Labour History Workshop, 'The Labour Unrest in West Scotland, 1910–14', in Kenefick & McIvor, *Roots of Red Clydeside*, p. 24.

[22] Glasgow Labour History Workshop, 'Labour Unrest', p. 24; E. Gordon, *Women and the Labour Movement in Scotland 1850–1914* (Oxford, 1991).

[23] E.H. Hunt, *British Labour History 1815–1914* (London, 1985), p. 295; R. McKibbin, *The Evolution of the Labour Party 1910–1924* (London, 1986), p. 86.

[24] Bob Holton, *British Syndicalism 1910–1914: Myths and Realities* (London, 1976), p. 202.

[25] On the role and significance of the SLP see Raymond Challinor, *The Origins of British Bolshevism* (London, 1977); also Walter Kendall, *The Revolutionary Movement in Britain 1900–21: the origins of British Communism* (London, 1969), Chapter Four, 'The British SLP'

the SocLP has often been credited with a leading role in the pre-war unrest and the war-time shop stewards' movement, it was the ILP which was much more consistently and successfully active in the trade union field.[26] Socialists on Clydeside generally did not embrace syndicalism because of its essentially anti-political stance. However, many activists were attracted to the cause of 'Socialist Unity' in contrast to the deadening effect of the 'Labour Alliance'.

The idea of all socialists coming together in a purely socialist party received a great fillip with the dramatic victory of Victor Grayson at the Colne Valley by election in 1907 when he defeated both Conservative and Liberal opponents. In 1910 the new British Socialist Party was formed with Grayson and Robert Blatchford playing prominent roles, alongside the leadership of the SDF. Individual ILP members, such as Harry McShane, were immediately attracted to the new body in which they hoped to combine parliamentary and extra-parliamentary activity. On Clydeside John MacLean continued to report positively on the unrest in his articles for the party paper *Justice*. However, it quickly became apparent that the BSP was more or less the old SDF in another guise, the leadership of which maintained their somewhat superior attitude to mere industrial disputes.[27] It was the ILP which maintained its leading position on the left in Glasgow with large numbers of its members taking an active role in the industrial disputes and in organising unskilled workers into unions.

Yet, for all this the ILP's own brand of politics remained unchanged. It retained the 'separate spheres' approach of political activity and industrial activity. While this approach gave the ILP considerable flexibility and allowed its members to participate in a variety of movements, it also meant that it was unable to politicise the industrial unrest and channel it into support for Labour, at least not directly. As we have seen, the results of parliamentary by elections did not show any surge in support for Labour, though, given the degree of disappointment felt in the PLP, perhaps this was not so surprising. In Glasgow an indication of Labour's lack of progress and confidence is that it did not even stand in the three by elections held in the City during these years.[28] Little wonder that John MacLean had to admit in 1913 that Scottish workers were 'still seething like lions industrially, but lying like lambs politically'.[29]

Labour's performance in municipal elections, however, gave much more

[26] J. Smith, 'Taking the leadership of the labour movement: the ILP in Glasgow, 1906–1914', in A. McKinlay & R.J. Morris (eds.), *The ILP on Clydeside 1893–1932: from foundation to disintegration* (Manchester, 1991), p. 75; Gordon, *Women in Scotland*, pp. 258–9.

[27] Smyth, 'Unrest to Debacle', pp. 248–50.

[28] These were in St. Rollox (1912), Tradeston and Govan (both 1911). F.W.S. Craig, *British Parliamentary Election Results, 1885–1918* (London, 1974), pp. 508, 509, 546. Technically Govan was still a Lanarkshire constituency but it was now part of Glasgow municipality and would become a Glasgow parliamentary seat in 1918.

[29] Quoted in D. Howell, *A Lost Left: three studies in socialism and nationalism* (Manchester, 1986), p. 162.

cause for optimism as the gains in Glasgow were mirrored across Scotland. Seats won and net gains both showed an upward trend, with 1911 and 1913 being particularly good years, though the total numbers involved remained small.[30] This pattern seems to closely replicate that in England and Wales where there was a marked improvement in the number of successful candidates from 1910.[31] The role of industrial unrest in this improvement is difficult to gauge. In the November 1911 polls in Glasgow one of Labour's gains was in Townhead, where Alexander Turner of the ILP took the seat from the sitting councillor. Turner was the Scottish Secretary of the Municipal Employees Association and had led a short, unsuccessful, strike by the Corporation tramwaymen shortly before the election.[32] Turner's victory gave Labour a clean sweep of all three seats in Townhead which provides evidence for the view that industrial activity was no hindrance to Labour in the municipal arena.

However, there was little effort made to harness the industrial unrest behind Labour. Wheatley, Labour's main strategist in Glasgow made no mention of it in his writings and appears to have been completely unaffected by it.[33] In the years leading up to the First World War the Glasgow Labour Party never once discussed the unrest. In contrast it discussed housing almost endlessly. The all-consuming nature of the housing question for the Party in Glasgow is indicated in the municipal election results of 1913 where Labour gained six seats but suffered two defeats. However, these defeats were due to the failure of the two sitting Labour councillors to vote for the £8 cottages scheme in the Council; a course of action which led to 'apathy' among local activists.[34]

Labour's local political strategy remained that of increased municipalisation, an approach geared mainly to consumerist issues through the provision of services to the citizens of the City. The only industrial issues which impinged on its approach were the long standing demands for minimum wages and conditions for council employees, and a direct works department. While the unrest strengthened the labour movement generally in terms of encouraging union membership and organisation, it did not provoke any major electoral shift. Labour may well have been able to improve its electoral performance; certainly at the local level it could look forward to gradually increasing its vote and number of councillors. In the parlia-

---

[30] *Forward*, 9 Nov. 1911, 15 Nov. 1913. Labour's net gains of council seats was nineteen in 1911, eight in 1912 and twenty-three in 1913.

[31] Sheppard & Halstead, 'Labour's Municipal Performance', pp. 39–62. There was also a similar downward blip in 1912.

[32] *Forward*, 11 Nov. 1911; *Glasgow Herald*, 6 Nov. 1911. See I. Maver, 'Glasgow's municipal workers and industrial strife', in Kenefick & McIvor, *Roots of Red Clydeside*, pp. 233–6.

[33] See I.S. Wood, *John Wheatley* (Manchester, 1990), where no mention at all is made of the unrest, presumably because it was of no significance to Wheatley.

[34] *Forward*, 8 Nov. 1913. The scheme was only defeated by one vote.

mentary sphere Labour was not effectively challenging the Liberal Party: only a major political upheaval would alter this situation.

Wartime Unrest and the Red Clyde

The initial impact of the War was to smother political differences. Throughout Europe socialists were thrown into confusion and retreated from their principles of internationalism and peace; among the belligerents only the Russian and Serbian socialist parties opposed the war.[35] In Britain, the Labour Party followed the trend and gave its backing to the war effort. Even Ramsay MacDonald, who resigned as chairman of the PLP and was denigrated by the yellow press as a pacifist, was never an opponent of the war effort.[36] Supporters of the war were to be found in all the socialist organisations: ILP, BSP, and SocLP. The most famous Clydeside socialist John MacLean was opposed to the war from the very beginning; but while MacLean would ultimately embrace a revolutionary opposition to the war, his initial stance was not so confrontational, though it was abrasive enough to result in his imprisonment.[37] The initial public response to the declaration of war was overwhelmingly favourable, with Scotland being even more enthusiastic than England in terms of providing voluntary recruits.[38] Anyone speaking out against the war could expect to attract not just official attention but immediate public hostility; Harry McShane has left a graphic account of being chased by a patriotic crowd and beaten unconscious.[39] Nonetheless a socialist anti-war propaganda was maintained in the city throughout the war years and, as the war wore on, so opposition became more voluble and Glasgow was recognised as the main area where opponents of the carnage could gain a sympathetic hearing:

> Despite the sharp tensions of the later war years, however, MacLean remained able to hold open air public meetings. In this Glasgow, and perhaps MacLean, were unique, as in most other cities anti-war orators were in danger of being pulled off their platform, brutally beaten and chased off the streets.[40]

[35] D. Sassoon, *One Hundred years of Socialism: The West European Left in the Twentieth Century* (London, 1997), p. 28.

[36] MacDonald's general view was that Britain should have remained neutral and he found himself caught up in 'tortuous ambiguity' in trying both to not support the war effort but not opposing it either. D. Marquand, *Ramsay MacDonald* (London, 1977), p. 175.

[37] See the discussion of this by W.W. Knox in his biography of *MacLean* in *Scottish Labour Leaders 1918–1939* (Edinburgh, 1984), pp. 183–5; also B.J. Ripley & J. McHugh, *John MacLean* (Manchester, 1989), pp. 88–9.

[38] 'I do not believe that anywhere in the world was the voluntary response so great as in Scotland.' John Buchan, 'The Battle Honours of Scotland', *Glasgow Herald* 15 Nov. 1918; C. Harvie, *No Gods and Precious Few Heroes* (Edinburgh, 1993), pp. 10–11.

[39] H. McShane & J. Smith, *No Mean Fighter* (London, 1978), pp. 85–6.

[40] Kendall, *Revolutionary Movement*, p. 112

Formal politics came to an end with the agreement of a parliamentary truce before the end of August. The municipal polls were held in November, with Labour making another two gains in Glasgow, but the campaigns were muted and in the summer of 1915 even local elections were postponed for the duration of the conflict.[41] Even more dramatic was the more or less immediate and total cessation of industrial disputes; in mid-July there were an estimated 72,000 industrial workers on strike, but by February 1915 there were 'practically nil'. As the official History of the Ministry of Munitions commented, 'The first six months were a time of peace in the labour world, such as had never existed before and has not existed since.'[42]

This peace was rudely shattered by the Clydeside engineers who went out in the middle of February in what became known as the '2d. an hour strike'. The immediate cause was the rapid rise in the cost of food and the employment of American engineers by Weir's of Cathcart on a substantial premium above local wages. However, the strike was really a continuation of a simmering dispute that had been primed before war was declared. The members of the Amalgamated Society of Engineers (ASE) had been bound by a three year agreement signed in early 1912 and the local area had declared its intention of 2d. on the hourly rate as early as July 1914. Frustrated by being unable to exploit the buoyant labour market and high profits during this period, the war-time situation of full employment and guaranteed profits, together with escalating prices and the provocation by Weir, saw 10,000 engineers willing to risk the opprobrium of public opinion and stop work when the employers refused to go above 0.5d. per hour. In mid March the engineers voted to accept Government arbitration and were awarded 1d. and 10% on piece rates.[43]

This was not to be the end of unrest. Over the next twelve months discontent escalated. The local activists who organised the February strike maintained contact and re-emerged later in the year as the Clyde Workers' Committee (CWC). This was the organisation which became infamous as the major opponent of dilution and was demonised as hostile to the war effort. It was in this period that Clydeside's reputation for militancy was first established as the shop stewards imposed their authority over the trade union officials. However much some recent historians may challenge the validity of Clydeside's reputation and the role of the CWC, contemporaries were in little doubt: 'From February, 1915, onwards, the unrest and discontent on the Clyde were, both in degree and in kind, exceptional.'[44] Nonetheless, questions remain about the extent and politicisation of this militancy.

---

[41] *Glasgow Herald*, 24 Jul. 1915.

[42] *History of the Ministry of Munitions* (London, 1920), Vol. I, Pt. II, p. 72. Hereafter *HMM*.

[43] J. Hinton, *The First Shop Stewards' Movement* (London, 1973), pp. 108; I.S. McLean, *The Legend of Red Clydeside* (Edinburgh, 1983), pp. 11–13; *HMM* Vol. IV Pt. II, pp. 36–9.

[44] *HMM*, Vol. I Pt. III, p. 48.

Much of the 'legend' of Red Clydeside has been promoted by the various memoirs and biographies of some of the more famous participants, in particular those relating to Willie Gallacher and John MacLean.[45] In these works, which are essentially celebrations of Clydeside's militancy, the various movements and disparate events of the war and the early 1920s are regarded as parts of a wider whole: there is a constant suggestion that a revolutionary outbreak was an almost tangible possibility. This perspective was expressed most forcibly at the time by MacLean who saw Scotland as uniquely placed to inflict a mortal wound on the British Empire, with Glasgow taking the leading role as, 'a Petrograd, a Revolutionary storm centre second to none.'[46] Gallacher argued much the same (though without the nationalist perspective of MacLean) in his appropriately titled memoirs, *Revolt on the Clyde*, first published in 1936: 'we were carrying on a strike, when we ought to have been making a revolution.'[47]

This argument of a missed revolutionary opportunity may have had more to do with Gallacher's subsequent career in the Communist Party of Great Britain (1935 saw his election to Parliament for West Fife) than with the actual unfolding of events at the time. Yet, for all the romanticism attached to the literature of Red Clyde, such accounts contain a kernel of truth; the experiences of war-time and immediately after were parts of a wider totality, rather than a series of random events. This is not to say that any single group, revolutionary or otherwise, was orchestrating events (even Gallacher did not claim that), but it is to argue that the conflicts on Clydeside were more than, 'episodic and widely separated in time.'[48]

There already exists an extensive literature on this period and on the extent and direction of the industrial militancy and it is unnecessary to go over the same ground again.[49] The emphasis here is on the general politicisation of this unrest. The very fact that there was a war going on and that the Government had armed itself with emergency powers meant that all disputes involved a direct confrontation with the state, whether or not that is what the participants intended. Antagonism between workers and

---

[45] Biographical treatments of Glasgow include: Guy Aldred, *John MacLean: Martyr of the Class Struggle* (Glasgow, 1932); Tom Bell, *John MacLean: a Fighter for Freedom* (Glasgow, 1944); Tom Bell, *Pioneering Days* (London, 1941); William Gallacher, *Revolt on the Clyde* (London, 1936); William Gallacher, *Last Memoirs* (London, 1966); David Kirkwood, *My Life of Revolt* (London, 1935); Thomas Johnston, *Memories* (London, 1952).

[46] *Vanguard*, Nov. 1920.

[47] Gallacher, *Revolt*, p. 221; also quoted in McLean, *Legend*, p. 135.

[48] Harvie, *No Gods*, p. 17.

[49] See Hinton, *Shop Stewards*; McLean, *Legend*; J. Melling, 'Whatever happened to Red Clydeside? Industrial Conflict and the Politics of Skill in the First World War', and J. Foster, 'Strike Action and Working Class Politics on Clydeside 1914–1919', both articles in *International Review of Social History*, xxxv, (1990); also J. Melling, 'Work, culture and politics on 'Red Clydeside': the ILP during the First World War', McKinlay & Morris, *ILP on Clydeside*, pp. 83–122.

employers and between tenants and factors was nothing new on Clydeside, but because of the war that antagonism assumed a new political dimension which had been absent in the pre-war labour unrest. Previously Labour activists could operate a twin track approach to industrial issues on the one hand and electoral activity on the other. Now, with all elections in abeyance, that division was no longer possible; industrial and social unrest became political issues. This can be seen in the prominent role played by leading ILP figures such as James Messer, Harry Hopkins and John Wheatley. As an engineer and active shop steward, Messer's involvement in the CWC was unproblematic (though he has often been overshadowed by the more 'revolutionary' socialists such as Gallacher), but Wheatley's role was a new departure for a political figure who had said little or nothing about the pre-war unrest.[50]

It was widely recognised from a very early stage that in order to meet the massive demand for munitions the production process would have to be streamlined. In essence the work of the skilled engineers would have to be reorganised and simplified to allow for the utilisation of unskilled labour. This was the process of dilution which so worried the engineers, threatening their very status as craftsmen and their future earnings potential. Government attempts to win the support of the unions and the skilled men involved a carrot and stick approach, though with increasing reliance upon the stick. Moves to avert strikes and lockouts for the duration of hostilities began almost as soon as war was declared. Although the Defence of the Realm Act (DORA) gave the Government considerable statutory powers, it tried to follow a largely voluntary process of getting the unions to agree to abandon their restrictive practices. The Treasury Agreement with the skilled unions in early 1915 promised that the status quo would be resumed after the war. The problem was that the union officials had little effective control over their membership and the engineers were less prepared to abandon their traditional rights and were not so sanguine about the likelihood of their restoration.[51]

The Government moved towards increasing compulsion with the Munitions of War Act passed in July 1915.[52] The need for armaments meant that manpower had to be controlled; workers, especially skilled workers, had to

[50] The role of ILP trade union activists in industrial activities and the link they provided to electoral and community politics is analysed in the work of J. Smith, 'Labour Tradition in Glasgow and Liverpool', *History Workshop*, xviii (Spring 1984); Smith, 'Taking the Leadership'; Melling, 'Whatever Happened to Red Clydeside?'; Melling 'Work, culture, politics'; Melling, *Rent Strikes: People's Struggles for Housing in West Scotland 1890–1916* (Edinburgh, 1983).

[51] There was plenty of commentary at the time on how war-time dilution could and should be made permanent as a means of securing cheap labour in the future. *Forward* made sure that such opinions were brought to the attention of the skilled men. See *HMM*, Vol. IV, Part II, pp. 47–8.

[52] C. Wrigley, *David Lloyd George and the British Labour Movement* (Brighton, 1976), Chapter six.

be directed to where they were needed and could not be allowed to move from one job to another. Logical as this may have been in the conditions, it was perceived by the men as a major restriction on their liberty and yet another sacrifice demanded of them, while employers remained free to gather in huge profits. In fact popular resentment at war-profiteering had forced the Government to include certain restrictions and controls on employers in the legislation, but in the first few years of war at any rate, it was the workers who were making the major sacrifices.

The Government-appointed Commission to examine the causes of industrial unrest took its evidence in 1917 and found the main cause to be the increased cost of living. While real wages fell between 1914 and 1916, by the spring of 1917 food prices had almost doubled, amid growing resentment at 'profiteering'.[53] On Clydeside in 1915 the steep rise in food prices occurred alongside sharp rises in rents as the pre-war housing shortage became the expected 'famine'. All of the war-time official reports and commentaries agreed that on Clydeside the housing situation – the generally dreadful conditions, the extra pressure on an already overstretched supply, and the opportunity taken by landlords to push up rents – was one of, if not the, major sources of discontent.[54] In such an environment resentments accumulated and festered, threatening to boil over. As regards the situation in the factories and shipyards, 'The grievances were as a rule trivial, if taken singly, but they were numerous and insistent.'[55] Government officials became increasingly concerned that another strike was 'inevitable' and that a single 'untoward incident' might provide the spark.[56]

There were plenty of sparks flying about in Glasgow in the summer and autumn of 1915. The heavy handed actions of house factors, especially evictions of the most vulnerable of tenants such as soldiers' families, provoked immediate reactions among neighbours which were then channelled by the ILP and the housing campaign bodies into a more structured political response.[57] Housing was an issue more capable of uniting people than the struggle over dilution; the latter was inherently sectional as skilled men sought to guard their privileges against unskilled and female workers. Yet, although the CWC did not lead the rent strike it is not the case that the industrial and housing issues were unrelated. Whether employed in engineering workshops or shipyards, the workers were also tenants. And, as the householder, it was the man's name on the rent book and he who would be summoned to court to face an eviction order. In October the shop stewards

---

[53] Wrigley, *Lloyd George*, pp. 179–80; J. Cronin, *The Politics of State Expansion* (London, 1991). p. 46.

[54] See for instance PP 1917, XIV, *Report of the Royal Commission on the Housing of the Industrial Population of Scotland Rural and Urban*, Ch. XXXIV 'Bad Housing as a Factor in Industrial Unrest'.

[55] *HMM* Vol. IV, Part II, p. 62.

[56] *HMM* Vol. IV, Part II, p. 55.

[57] Melling, *Rent Strikes*, pp. 66–7.

at Parkhead Forge sent a letter to the Corporation with a clear threat of industrial action if the rents issue was not resolved.[58] As the crisis reached its climax, five shipyards and an armaments factory, came out in support of eighteen tenants (mostly shipyard workers) who were being prosecuted by their factor in the small claims court.[59]

At the same time as the rents issue was inflaming passions so too was the Munitions Act which, on the Clyde, soon became known as 'the Slavery Act'.[60] The main problem was section seven of the Act which allowed a workman to leave one job for another only if he was furnished with a certificate from his original employer. Any workman who left without such a certificate had to face a Tribunal or face six weeks of enforced unemployment. However, employers who refused a certificate faced no penalties and already enjoyed a situation where strikes were illegal. It may not have been the intention but the Munitions of War Act gave employers and foremen more powers in their face to face dealings with their workers, and this in an area with a tradition of autocratic management and 'bitter industrial conflicts'.[61] The involvement of the trade unions meant that they too were implicated. When the Chairman of the ASE came to Glasgow in October to explain the Munitions Act to his members, he got short shrift and the meeting quickly became a 'bear garden'.[62]

The rent strike movement ended in success as the Government rushed through Parliament a Bill restricting rent increases on all houses with an annual rent of £30 per annum or less. The Bill became law before Christmas 1915, though it was not a total victory as there was no fair rents tribunal established and landlords and factors retained powers of eviction; powers that continued to be used throughout the war.[63] At the same time there was continuing and growing industrial unrest over dilution and the leaving certificate issue. The efforts of the Ministry of Munitions to promote dilution were being frustrated not only by the CWC but also by the ASE which formally declared itself in favour but dragged its feet over practicalities. In addition, local employers were hardly enthusiastic, partly through their own innate conservatism and inefficiency and partly through frustration at the Government for not taking a more aggressive line against the both the ASE and the shop stewards.[64]

The CWC attempted to turn the demand for dilution into a programme

58 *Forward*, 9 Oct. 1915.
59 Melling, *Rent Strikes*, pp. 92–3.
60 *HMM* Vol. IV, Part II, p. 47
61 A. McKinlay, 'Employers and Skilled Workers in the Inter-War Depression: Engineering and Shipbuilding on Clydeside 1919–1939' (unpublished D. Phil. thesis, University of Oxford, 1986) pp. 48, 58.
62 *HMM* Vol. IV, Part II, p. 55.
63 'The Rent Restriction Act, 1915, restored the peace without bringing the agitation to an end.' D. Englander, *Landlord and Tenant in Urban Britain 1838–1918* (Oxford, 1983), p. 235.; Melling, *Rent Strikes*, pp. 99–103
64 McLean, *Legend*, chapter four.

of workers' control. Therein lay the progressive and socialist element of their strategy, but it also led John MacLean to criticise them for avoiding the other, more awkward question of the war itself.[65] The remit of the CWC did not run in the shipyards, nor in all the engineering factories and, furthermore, there were divisions within the Committee. The most critical was the individual role played by David Kirkwood at Beardmore's factory in Parkhead. Guided to an extent by John Wheatley, Kirkwood arranged a separate dilution agreement covering Beardmore's alone in January 1916 which destroyed the CWC's efforts at presenting a united front to the authorities; shortly afterwards the CWC effectively adopted the Parkhead scheme.[66] The initiative had now swung to the Government which acted with increasing confidence.

In January 1916 Peter Petroff, a Russian socialist and close confidant of MacLean's was arrested, sentenced to two months imprisonment and then interned; the same fate befell his German-born wife.[67] This was the first in a train of arrests, prosecutions and deportations directed at antiwar socialists and the CWC. The latter's newspaper *The Worker* was suppressed in early February (*Forward* and MacLean's *Vanguard* having already been closed down) under the spurious excuse of a supposedly seditious article entitled 'Should the Workers' Arm?, which actually argued that they should not do so. For the same reason Gallacher, Muir and Bell were arrested but an immediate strike secured their release on bail. In March attention shifted back to Beardmore's where Kirkwood found his authority for policing the dilution agreement suddenly removed. While Parkhead went out on strike it was only supported by some factories, a direct response to the Parkhead workers' failure to support the previous month's strike and their readiness to break the CWC's united front. Kirkwood and eight other shop stewards were seized and deported from the Glasgow munitions production area and the strike fizzled out by early April.[68] In that same month, John MacLean was sentenced to three years hard labour, Gallacher, Muir and Bell to one year, as were James Maxton and James MacDougall for anti-war propaganda, and a shop steward at Weirs also received a sentence of eighteenth months for sedition.[69]

Was there a conspiracy against the CWC?[70] Certainly, there were im-

---

[65] John MacLean publicly criticised Willie Gallacher's deliberate myopia. 'How could any man calling himself a socialist come to speak at a meeting and *not* refer to the war that is raging in Europe.' McShane & Smith, *No Mean Fighter*, p. 77.

[66] McKinlay, 'Employers and Skilled Workers', p. 61.

[67] J. Smyth & M. Rodgers, 'Peter Petroff and the Socialist Movement in Britain, 1907–18', *Immigrants and Minorities*, ii (1983), p. 108; McShane & Smith, *No Mean Fighter*, p. 80.

[68] McLean, *Legend*, p. 82.

[69] McShane & Smith, *No Mean Fighter*, pp. 80–1.

portant officials such as Lynden Macassey who believed the CWC was involved in a plot of its own – to sabotage the production of munitions in order to aid Germany. The rumours of German gold financing the Clydeside shop stewards were fantastical but in the heightened reality of wartime they could easily appear convincing or at least be exploited to justify any repressive measures.[71] Certainly the CWC had been identified as a serious nuisance as early as November and the ultimate actions taken against its members, i.e. deportation, had been suggested within Government circles for some time prior to March.[72] Whether this adds up to a consistent and carefully planned assault on the CWC by the Ministry of Munitions is perhaps secondary to the larger issue that under the exigencies of war the CWC did have to be 'smashed', as an internal Admiralty memorandum put it in November 1915.[73] As the national situation became more and more serious, so those responsible for harnessing the productive resources of the country became convinced, 'that curtailment of civil liberties was imperatively required by the pressures of war.'[74] While that was written to describe the attitude of Beveridge it could just as equally be applied to Lloyd George.

Liberties, Lloyd George and the Decline of Liberalism

One of most significant arguments against 'Red Clydeside' is that once the Government had effectively defeated the shop stewards by the Spring of 1916, the area was largely quiet thereafter.[75] However, this perspective has been questioned by more recent studies which argue that the unrest did not begin and end with the CWC; in fact the engineers disputes of 1915 and 1916, 'comprise only a relatively small fragment of the illegal wartime strikes.'[76]

The workers involved (including women) came from a wide range of

[70] The argument that there was a ruthless plot directed against the CWC by the Ministry of Munitions (and William Beveridge in particular) is made by J. Hinton, 'The Clyde Workers Committee and the Dilution Struggle', in A. Briggs & J. Saville (eds.), *Essays in Labour History 1886–1923* (London, 1971); and by T. Brotherstone, 'The Suppression of Forward', *The Journal of the Scottish Labour History Society*, i (1969). The contrary view is taken by McLean, *Legend*, Chapter seven; and J. Harris, *William Beveridge: a biography* (Oxford 1997), pp. 212–23 who point out that the obstruction of the ASE was as much an obstacle if not more so than the CWC. See also R. Davidson, 'War-Time Labour Policy 1914–16: a Reappraisal', *Scottish Labour History Society Journal*, viii (1974), pp. 3–20.

[71] 'Who, on the Government side, believed in the myth that there was a C.W.C. plot? Initially, it seems, everybody . . .' McLean, *Legend*, p. 83

[72] J. Hinton, 'The Suppression of the Forward – a note', *The Journal of the Scottish Labour History Society*, vii (1974).

[73] Quoted in Hinton, 'Suppression of Forward', p. 26.

[74] Harris, *William Beveridge*, p. 223.

[75] See McLean, *Legend*; Harvie, *No Gods*; and also Hinton, *Shop Stewards*, whose own focus falls on the period up to Spring 1916.

[76] Foster, 'Strike Action', p. 40. See also G. Rubin, *War, Law and Labour: the Munitions Acts, State Regulation and the Unions, 1915–1921* (Oxford, 1987),

industries and the strikes were about much more than demarcation, at times being concerned with demands for union recognition. In fact, there was a pattern similar to that of the pre-war unrest on Clydeside where continuing smaller, but nonetheless significant, disputes have been overshadowed in the historical account by the more famous set-piece battles. Given that the war did bring about full employment it would have been surprising had workers not sought to take advantage of the unique circumstances. As the war progressed there was more strike action, concentrated primarily in shipbuilding, coal and steel. The most famous strike of all – the Forty Hours Strike of January 1919 – may have taken place after the armistice, but it was essentially a continuation of the war-time unrest; the intention was to maintain the situation of full employment which was threatened by the end of munitions production and the mass demobilization of the army.[77] While there was no political strike against the war, the one day stoppages in May Day 1918 and 1919 had a definite political edge.

As well as the strikes (all of which were illegal acts under wartime legislation), there was also the continuing war of attrition being carried on at the Munitions Tribunals. These had been established in all the major industrial centres, but the Glasgow Tribunal was 'the busiest and most controversial'.[78] As strikes were outlawed and Government control extended over large parts of industry, some means had to be found of regulating and resolving workplace antagonisms. The Tribunals were presided over by a Chairman who had the power to make a judgement binding on both workers and employers. Formally each party was to be treated equally but essentially the dice were loaded; 'wartime Government policy must be understood as entailing temporary, if relatively mild, restrictions upon employers, as well as severe restrictions upon munitions workers.'[79] However, this did not mean that workers boycotted the tribunals (impossible in any case), but rather used them as a means of ventilating their grievances and pointing out the unreasonable and even unpatriotic conduct of employers.

The tribunals have been likened to a 'carnival' as large numbers attended and pushed the legal processes to the limit with their sheer physical presence, interruptions, funny remarks, and other irreverent tactics. This Clydeside 'charivari' made sense as workers, denounced in the press for supposedly subverting the war effort, sought to defend their own interests and turn the spotlight on their employers; as in the rent strikes, workers would often couch their arguments in patriotic terms. That the tribunals could be utilised in this way indicates that there was no complete breakdown

p. 158, 'In fact, significant industrial unrest continued in spite of the emasculation of the CWC following the shop stewards deportations, and flared up at regular intervals.'

[77] Foster, 'Strike Action', pp. 53–4.
[78] Rubin, *War, Law and Labour*, p. 2.
[79] Rubin, *War Law and Labour*, p. 17.

in authority (the public airing of grievances may well have helped defuse tension) but, nonetheless, the relationships of authority were put under significant strain and criticism. Government and employers were seen to be working in collusion and the law, far from being independent, was yoked to the State's purpose of disciplining labour in order to maximise production.[80]

That industrial issues became political issues, therefore, was as much due to the actions of Government as anything else. Whereas in the past the state could claim to stand aside from industrial disputes, favouring neither one side or the other, that fiction became harder to sustain as the Government's actions clearly tipped the scales in favour of the employers. In the eyes of Government officials, such as William Beveridge, intervention was positively desirable since: 'he was coming to believe that the war had given the workers a position of dominance unparalleled since the time of the Black Death'.[81] As the war continued the Government attempted to play a more even handed role (though with what success is debatable) but it would be difficult for it to undo the damage inflicted upon the reputation of the state and of the Liberal Party as non-partisan and the defender of individual liberty.

It was bad enough that a Liberal Government was abandoning so many of its principles, but it only compounded matters by appearing to be doing so in a clearly partisan manner. Even the leader of the Conservative Party, Bonar Law, speaking in Parliament in early 1915, castigated the Government for allowing profiteering by ship owners, '. . . ships today are making simply enormous profits, and those profits come from the very cause for which the people of this country are making sacrifices in every direction and even giving their lives.'[82] For a Tory to castigate the Liberals in such a way was rather ironic, but it indicated the extent of public disquiet. Even with the formation of the Coalition Government, the removal of Asquith and Bonar Law's appointment as Chancellor, it was still a Liberal Prime Minister who was in charge and even the formal support of the PLP could not shield Lloyd George and the Liberal Party from the suspicion and hostility of the wider labour movement.[83]

If Liberalism was to have a future after the war it needed to maintain its appeal to both middle class and working class voters. But, the actions of the Liberal Government stretched the loyalty of skilled workers (a crucial constituency) to the limits. It was not just declared revolutionaries, such as John MacLean or the anarchist Guy Aldred, who were persecuted by the state, but ordinary tenants had been prosecuted during the rent strike and throughout the war large numbers of workers appeared before munitions

---

[80] Three Tribunal chairmen in Glasgow were removed from office because they were seen as not enforcing the regulations with sufficient vigour. See Rubin, *War, Law and Labour*, chapter four.

[81] Harris, *William Beveridge*, p. 204

[82] Quoted in *HMM*, Vol. IV, Pt. II, p. 38.

[83] Wrigley, *Lloyd George*, p. x.

tribunals. Many working class people had been brought in to direct conflict with the state, had been made criminals, technically, and often labelled as an enemy within, or as shirkers and drunks. In this the role of Lloyd George was paramount and became critical to the future of Liberalism in Glasgow.

Lloyd George's persuasive oratory was famous and was used to good effect in cajoling and encouraging the TUC and Labour Party. However, alongside his skilful mix of patriotic appeal and compliments, he favoured industrial conscription and was prepared to demonize certain groups of workers in order to strengthen his hand in tightening labour discipline. The violent criticisms made about bad time keeping and drunkenness, especially on the Clyde, were part of this strategy.

Allegations of drunkenness among Clydeside workers were first made after the engineer's strike in February 1915 when Lloyd George provocatively commented that, 'Drink is doing more damage in this war than all the German submarines put together.'[84] That there was no substance to this claim was confirmed by the official history of the Ministry of Munitions after the war.[85] But drink was linked to the perceived problem of bad time keeping and general poor work effort which encouraged a 'moral panic' which was sustained throughout the war; graphically expressed in a newspaper headline in the autumn of 1915, 'Shall We Shoot Slackers?'.[86] The fact that time keeping was better during the war than before did not prevent such an atmosphere from developing. Again, Lloyd George was crucially involved, manipulating selective evidence in 'a characteristically duplicitous argument' in order to push through 'the drastic remedy of legal compulsion'.[87] Given this, it is hardly surprising the Lloyd George received such rough treatment at his infamous meeting with the Glasgow engineers on Christmas day 1915.

The background to this meeting was the decision that the Minister should tour the munitions districts to put the case for dilution directly to the men; the assumption being that his persuasive powers and common touch would dissipate any hostility. After an uneventful visit to Tyneside, Lloyd George arrived in Glasgow on 23 December and over the next few days things went from bad to worse: shop stewards at various works refused to meet him; at other meetings he was lectured by socialist militants; Glasgow Trades Council passed a resolution calling for a public protest against his visit; local union officials boycotted his large set-piece meeting in St. Andrew's Halls on Christmas Day morning, thus making it easier for the CWC to pack it with its supporters.[88]

There are two versions of the meeting: the authorised version which was told explicitly not to report any disturbances, and the unofficial version

[84] *Daily Record*, 1 Mar. 1915, quoted in McLean, *Legend*, p. 13.

[85] *HMM*, Vol. IV, Pt. II, pp. 42–3.

[86] Rubin, *War, Law and Labour*, p. 190.

[87] Rubin, *War, Law and Labour*, p. 181.

[88] Wrigley, *Lloyd George*, pp. 153–4; McLean, *Legend*, pp. 49–53.

which appeared in *Forward*. The meeting was something of a shambles with both speakers, Arthur Henderson and Lloyd George, being constantly interrupted and the Chairman more or less forced to abandon proceedings rather than draw matters to a tidy conclusion. What is not so certain is how widely shared was the antagonism. The official view within the Ministry of Munitions at the time was that the disturbances were caused by a minority of between 300 and 500 out of the total audience of 3,000, and that the majority were supportive of Lloyd George.[89] However, a few years later, when compiling the official history of the Ministry, *Forward's* version of events was included as an appendix, 'Since the interruptions afford an instructive commentary upon the attitude of a *considerable* minority'.[90] The same source also states that, 'Many of the men were in a bad humour', and suggests in its discussion of the suppression of *Forward*, 'there is no reason to deny the editor's claim that the reports were accurate.'[91] Almost forty years later, Tom Johnston who as editor was responsible for publishing the report, stood by his original account, 'a more unruly audience surely never gathered in Glasgow.'[92]

The anger was provoked not so much by dilution but by the Munitions of War Act and especially the running sore of leaving certificates. As Davie Kirkwood had put it when introducing Lloyd George to the shop stewards at Parkhead Forge on the 23rd., 'We regard him with suspicion because every act with which his name is associated has the taint of slavery about it.'[93] The long term significance of this Christmas meeting lies not so much with the suppression of *Forward* (an act of pique on the part of the Minister of Munitions) or the assault on the CWC, but as an indicator of the loss of authority and even respect that Lloyd George and the Liberal Party suffered within the organised working class.

The change in mood can be gauged from comparing this meeting with the reception Lloyd George received on his previous visit to Glasgow, in February 1914, when he also spoke at the St. Andrews Halls which was the largest and most prestigious of the City's many public venues. This meeting was on land reform and was the opening of a new campaign in Scotland. This was not simply an old favourite being given another outing but was actually regarded as the key to continued Liberal success, certainly by Lloyd George. By embracing Henry George's old plan for the taxation of land values, the Liberals were able to re-galvanise much of their own support and, once again, wrong foot Labour.[94] The social and economic ills of both rural and urban Scotland could be tackled by raising additional revenue for

---

[89] Wrigley, *Lloyd George*, p. 155.
[90] *HMM*, Vol. IV, Pt. IV, p. 105 my emphasis, plus pp. 176–90 Appendix XIX.
[91] *HMM*, Vol. IV, Pt. IV, pp. 105, 112.
[92] Johnston, *Memories*, p. 37
[93] *HMM*, Vol. IV, Pt. IV, p. 102.
[94] I. Packer, 'The Land Issue and the Future of Scottish Liberalism in 1914', *The Scottish Historical Review*, lxxv (1996), pp. 52–71; M. Tichelar, 'Socialists, Labour

reforms and shifting the rate burden away from business.[95] As the leader of this campaign and the Chancellor behind the 'People's Budget', Lloyd George was the major radical spokesman who could best combine old and new Liberalism in a way that would continue to attract public support among middle class and working class electors.[96]

Enthusiasm and expectations ran high and the St. Andrew's Hall (capacity 5,000) could have been filled 'many times over'. Demand for tickets was so high that an enterprising printer ran off hundreds of forged tickets which delayed the start of the meeting. When he did, eventually, get going, Lloyd George did not disappoint and gave a bravura performance. He spoke at length about the injustices of the clearances and role of the Duke of Sutherland; rural depopulation was a 'great evil' due to low, poverty wages. And this was linked to the towns and cities and the 'outrageous' cost of land whereby 'the energies of the municipalities are completely crippled' by the greed of the landowners. Poverty and the terrible infant mortality rate were directly linked to the high cost of land. Lloyd George illustrated his case by arguing that it had cost the citizens of Glasgow a quarter of a million pounds to clear a six acre area of slums, 'that the owners ought to have been compelled to clear as a nuisance.'[97]

The contrast with the reception Lloyd George received just twenty months later was stark. In 1915 he could hardly make himself heard over barracking from the floor and the heckling recorded in *Forward's* version of events has the ring of truth about it; while Glasgow audiences may have lionised their heroes they could be cruel to performers they considered below par. The city had a reputation as the graveyard of comedians, and Lloyd George and Henderson were treated like a poor double act. One of Lloyd George's favourite ploys when speaking to a labour audience was to stress his own humble origins, 'I want to talk to you in all sincerity as a man brought up in a worker's home.' He had used much the same formulation when speaking to the TUC in September, but in Glasgow it cut no ice whatsoever.[98] Appeals to consider the men in the trenches and plucky little Belgium were given short shrift: 'Oh, heavens, how long do we have to suffer this?', 'No sentiment, we're here for business.' When he spoke of the heavy responsibility he bore as a Minister he was reminded that, 'The money's good.'

The Christmas Day meeting was not just a blow to Lloyd George's ego but

and the Land: the Response of the Labour Party to the Land Campaign of Lloyd George before the First World War', *Twentieth Century British History*, viii (1997), pp. 127–44.

[95] Hutchison, *Political History*, pp. 242–5.

[96] 'It is clear that the great Liberal Showman will fight the next election on Land Reform . . . Mr Lloyd George has chosen his ground well.' *Forward*, 20 Jul. 1912, quoted in Tichelar, 'Socialists, Labour, Land', p. 133.

[97] *Glasgow Herald*, 5 Feb. 1914.

[98] *HMM*, Vol. IV, Pt. I, p. 41 'I beg you as a man brought up in a workman's home . . .'

to Liberalism. The political discourse of 1914, the rallying cries of land
reform and the people versus the aristocracy would never have the same
resonance again. War time appeals to patriotic duty interspersed with
intimidation were hardly the best means of retaining the political loyalties
of the skilled working man. Even though Lloyd George had not repeated the
allegations of drunkenness after the summer of 1915, that insult was not to
be forgotten.

Lloyd George returned to Glasgow and the St. Andrew's Hall one more
time as Prime Minister when he received the freedom of the City in June
1917. Bolstered by the great and the good, he made a joke about being
surrounded by Glasgow men in London, a reference to the large number of
West of Scotland businessmen he had brought into his Government.[99]
There were no hecklers in this carefully vetted audience and Lloyd George
was welcomed into the Hall by a choir of women munitions workers and
'shell girls' waving the flags of the allies. Outside, however, was a 2,000 strong
demonstration against the Prime Minister, singing the red flag. Unfortunately for Lloyd George, shell girls did not get the vote in 1918.

Lloyd George was not universally unpopular, far from it. But much of his
support was from Unionist circles.[100] His actions during the war had
effectively destroyed any hopes of sustaining the alliance between working
class and middle class electors upon which Liberalism depended. Although
invited to speak in Glasgow by the Liberal Council in October 1918, Lloyd
George refused and, indeed, he never appeared in Glasgow during the
election.[101] More than this, however, he effectively sabotaged the Liberal
campaign. As the split with Asquith hardened into two opposing groups so
Lloyd George's decision to call an election and contest it as leader of the
Coalition spelt disaster for Liberalism and nowhere more so than in
Glasgow.

1918–1922: A New Political Configuration

Once it was clear the Coalition would remain in place, it was accepted by
everyone that it would be victorious; during the election Asquith's stated
ambition was to lead the Opposition.[102] Expectations of a sizeable Liberal
presence in the new House were dramatically threatened by Lloyd George's
issuing of the 'coupon' to Government supporters. The Glasgow Liberal
Council immediately issued a protest to the Prime Minister against the

---

[99] *Glasgow Herald*, 30 Jun. 1917.
[100] In Camlachie the Coalition Unionist candidate declared at an election meeting,
'I am here to speak on behalf of Mr. Lloyd George', while his Liberal opponent
attacked the Prime Minister directly for hiding behind the 'coupon'; 'He would
like to know what prevented Mr. Lloyd George facing criticism like an ordinary
man.' *Glasgow Herald*, 3 Dec. 1918.
[101] *Glasgow Herald*, 18, 21 Oct. 1918.
[102] *Glasgow Herald*, 19 Nov. 1918.

'distinctly undemocratic measure', pointing out that the consequence in Scotland would be 'a wholesale transference of Liberal seats to Unionists', and that the position in Glasgow was 'particularly deplorable'.[103] These fears were fully realised as Liberal candidates fell, 'before the verdict of the country like leaves in wintry weather'.[104]

The 'coupon' election devastated the Liberals in Glasgow. It was a disaster from which they never recovered. For the coalition on the other hand, and especially for the Unionists, the election was a triumph. The enlarged parliamentary burgh now comprised fifteen constituencies, compared to seven in 1910, and all but one was secured by Coalition candidates: Coalition Conservatives took ten seats, Coalition Liberals three, Coalition Labour one, and the Labour Party secured the final seat. Not a single independent or 'Asquithian' Liberal won a seat and, to rub salt in a very raw wound, six of their seven candidates lost their deposits.[105] Although the Liberal Party in Scotland staged a recovery in the subsequent elections of 1922 and 1923, before their ultimate rout in 1924, it was removed from Glasgow completely; a single National Liberal success in Partick in 1923 was to be the last ever Liberal MP returned in the City they had dominated for most of the previous century.[106]

In sharp contrast to a divided and traumatised Liberal Party, Labour in Glasgow was increasingly confident and ambitious. Having stood only two candidates in the elections of 1910, Labour now contested all but one of the Glasgow constituencies. Moreover, it launched its challenge as a campaigning movement, embracing labour and socialist activists from a variety of organisations, who, at least for a short time at the end of the war, found common cause against employers, the state and even the national Labour Party.[107] Much to the chagrin of Labour's national executive, the confessed revolutionary John MacLean was run as the Labour candidate in Govan (despite being in prison), and his first lieutenant, James MacDougall, was the de facto Labour candidate in Tradeston.[108] The bulk of the candidates (ten) were ILPers which reflects that Party's leading role in the Glasgow labour movement. It was not just the increase in its own membership, dramatic as that was in the final years of the war, but the linkage which its activists provided through their involvement in the various campaigns and organisations which spanned the industrial, community and electoral

---

[103] *Glasgow Herald*, 28 Nov. 1918.

[104] *Glasgow Herald*, 30 Dec, 1918.

[105] The pro-unionist *Herald* gleefully pointed out that the new £150 deposit had been specifically intended to discourage 'freak' candidates. *Glasgow Herald*, 30 Dec. 1918.

[106] The pattern in Glasgow does not conform to that identified by Tanner in areas of previous Liberal strength whereby Labour made only limited progress and 'the Liberal Party was not eradicated'. Tanner, *Political Change*, pp. 384–5.

[107] See Melling 'Work, culture, politics', p. 111 and 'Whatever Happened to Red Clydeside?', p. 32.

[108] MacDougall was formally a BSP candidate but there was no Labour candidate and local activists supported him.

fields.[109] The latent or suppressed differences between reformists and revolutionaries would become apparent in the early 1920s, particularly with the formation of the Communist Party, but for the moment, the political leadership of a united left lay with the ILP.

Even before the war the ILP had been active in promoting grass-roots campaigns, especially over housing, and in encouraging the direct involvement of women. During the war and under the impact of the rent strike this movement accelerated. The growth of trade unionism, also evident prior to 1914, continued during the war, though under quite different political circumstances. The development and politicisation of working class organizations can be seen in the experience of the Co-operative movement. Between 1914 and 1918 the membership of Co-operative societies in Scotland increased from 467,270 to 590,710.[110] At the same time, the unequal treatment the Co-op stores received over the distribution of food and the treatment of personnel at the hands of the middle class dominated bodies set up by Government to oversee conscription led to demands for direct political activity, culminating in the formation of the Co-operative Party in 1917 which, to all intents and purposes, operated as part of the Labour Party.[111]

The new commitment of such a respectable group as the Co-operators was an undoubted boon to Labour, and yet it occurred at a time when the distinction between respectable and rough was becoming blurred. Indeed, the war-time experience of full employment threw into doubt the whole question of a permanent residuum and, of course, the Representation of the People Act in 1918 extended the vote not just to some women but to all men, including the poorest. Differences and gradations within the working class did not disappear but during the war and because of it, they became less significant. The old fears of some Labour strategists about the reactionary nature of women and the slum-dwellers were still in evidence, but they quickly evaporated in the new post-war situation.[112]

Going into the 1918 General Election Labour in Glasgow was confident, not of victory but of a definite improvement in its position; three seats were generally regarded as winnable and optimists hoped for five.[113] The end result of a single victory in Govan was a major disappointment and has been identified as the major piece of evidence in denying the war-time unrest of

---

[109] See Melling, 'Work, culture, politics' and A. McKinlay, ' "Doubtful wisdom and uncertain promise": strategy, ideology and organisation, 1918–1922', in McKinlay & Morris, *ILP on Clydeside.*

[110] J.A. Kinloch, 'The Scottish Co-operative Wholesale Society 1868–1918' (unpublished Ph.D.thesis, University of Strathclyde, 1976), p. 376; J.A. Kinloch & J. Butt, *History of the Scottish Co-operative Wholesale Society Limited* (Manchester, 1981), p. 269.

[111] Kinloch, 'Scottish Co-operative Wholesale Society', p. 375, and chapter fourteen generally; Kinloch & Butt, *Scottish Co-operative Wholesale Society,* Chapter 12. See also T. Adams, 'The Formation of the Co-operative Party Re-considered', *International Review of Social History,* xxxii (1987), pp. 48–68.

[112] On this see Introduction and Chapter Five, 'Labour's Women'.

[113] *Glasgow Herald,* 30 Dec. 1918; McLean, *Legend,* p. 154.

'Red Clydeside' any role in the subsequent post-war shift in support towards Labour.[114] While the 1918 result is a necessary corrective to any simplistic notion that Labour was about to sweep away all opposition, it should not be allowed to disguise the extent of Labour's progress.

In the General Election of December 1910 Labour stood two candidates in the Clydeside area who polled 5,701 votes between them. In 1918 there were fourteen Labour candidates who polled almost 90,000 votes and averaged over 6,000 each. Although only one MP was returned on each occasion, Labour in 1918 was operating on a completely new level. Its disappointment was testimony to this new ambition. It is likely that the successful outcome of the war would have witnessed a swing towards the Government in any case, and the exploitation of this by Lloyd George and the Coalition in calling a quick election meant a landslide was largely expected, although the creation of a more or less genuinely mass democratic electorate may have been expected to operate more in Labour's favour.

However, the speed of the election meant that the intended enfranchisements of the Fourth Reform Act did not come into effect immediately or completely. There were insufficient arrangements made for allowing soldiers and sailors to vote, and many servicemen and other non-householders 'lost' their votes due to the inadequate preparation of the electoral register.[115] It is revealing that the register under which the 1918 election was fought included over 100,000 men who were on naval or military service, almost one third of the male voters and one fifth of the total electorate.[116] Only in Hillhead, 'a district from which the officer class would be drawn' was there a large soldiers' poll, while *Forward* reckoned that although the majority of soldiers supported Labour only a quarter of them actually got to cast their votes.[117] Certainly the turnout in 1918 was markedly smaller than subsequent general elections; 56% cent compared to 76% in 1922.[118] The 1918 election is not, therefore, of critical importance and Labour, as we shall see, made rapid strides thereafter.

While the Unionists had succeeded beyond their wildest dreams, their victory was by no means absolute. The votes in 1918 had been cast for the Coalition and the Unionists had been fortunate with the distribution of the Coupon. How they would fare fighting on their own as Conservatives was

[114] McLean, *Legend*, pp. 154–7.
[115] These points are made in McLean, *Legend*, p. 155; see also. A. Reid, 'Glasgow Socialism', *Social History*, xi (1986) p. 92 who turns them against McLean's thesis.
[116] *Glasgow Herald*, 31 Oct. 1918 which commented that the total number of servicemen was a 'remarkably large proportion of 102,739'.
[117] *Forward*, 4 Jan. 1919.
[118] It is also revealing that while the Labour share of the electorate increased dramatically between 1918 and 1922, the combined vote of the right wing candidates remained exactly the same. See J. Smyth, 'Labour and Socialism in Glasgow 1880–1914: the electoral challenge prior to democracy' (unpublished Ph.D. thesis, University of Edinburgh, 1987), pp. 326 – 31 for a more detailed discussion and analysis of electoral figures.

likely to be another matter and, recognising how precarious their position actually was, helps explain why the Scottish Unionist MPs argued strongly for maintaining the association with Lloyd George in 1922.[119] Their fears were to be more than justified at the general election following the break up of the coalition in October 1922. In sharp contrast to the situation in England where the Conservatives increased their number of MPs slightly, in Scotland they saw their representation halved and the reversal of their fortunes was nowhere more apparent than in Glasgow where they were swamped by a triumphant Labour Party.[120]

The 1922 Election stands as the greatest single landmark in Glasgow's electoral history; from having only one of the City's MPs, Labour suddenly held ten seats, fully two-thirds of the City's Parliamentary representation. The results of this election and the phenomenal scenes of celebration as the successful candidates boarded their special train for London and Westminster are just as much part of the Red Clydeside legend as the rent strikes and industrial unrest of the war.[121] That the MPs did not live up to the ambitious claims they made on their departure does not deny the significance of the moment itself: Labour had truly arrived as a political force. Although, as we shall see in the next chapter, Labour's victory was not replicated at the municipal level until much later, as regards parliamentary representation Labour was now dominant in Glasgow; apart from the debacle of 1931 Labour held a majority of the City's constituencies throughout the inter-war period.[122]

The change in the political configuration can be seen quite clearly in the impact of three-way contests. The contrast is sharp: prior to the war, it was the Conservatives who benefited from a split between Liberal and Labour, it was now Labour who took advantage in a situation where the other two parties were contesting for essentially the same vote. Recognition of this forced Labour's opponents into co-operation with each other. Furthermore, as we shall see in the following chapter, the anti-labour arrangements which had been evident to an extent in local elections prior to the war, now became the defining feature of municipal contests. So, in both national and city politics Labour stood now in opposition to a combined right-wing which effectively came to mean the Conservatives.

---

[119] Hutchison, *Political History*, p. 314.; C. Cook, *The Age of Alignment: Electoral Politics in Britain 1922–1929* (London, 1975), p. 17.

[120] Whereas in England the number of Conservative MPs returned rose to 307 compared to 295 in 1918, in Scotland the twenty-eight Conservative victories in 1918 shrunk to just thirteen in 1922, as Labour grew from seven to twenty-nine MPs. see F.W. S. Craig, *British Electoral Facts*, pp. 9–11.

[121] See the *Glasgow Herald*, 20 Nov. 1922 for a description of the triumphant departure of the Labour MPs from St. Enoch station. See also Howell, *Lost Left*, p. 252 on the event's significance for Wheatley.

[122] The distinctly ILP successes of the 1930s are here included among 'Labour'.

CHAPTER THREE

Labour's Long Haul:
Local Elections, 1920–1932

Wherever one dates Labour's electoral breakthrough in Glasgow, be it 1918 or 1922, it is clear that the 1920s saw a new political configuration, one in which Labour and the Conservatives faced each other as more or less equal forces. The Liberals were also-rans. In Parliamentary elections, as we have seen, Labour was the predominant party; its single seat in 1918 became ten in 1922 (and 1923) and, although Labour lost two seats in 1924 it still held eight of the city's fifteen constituencies. In the general election of 1929 Labour again won ten seats on 52% of the total poll.[1] However, this success was not replicated at the municipal level where Labour remained in a minority throughout the 1920s and early 1930s. Labour representation on the Town Council was on a much higher level than before the war yet still it remained as an apparently permanent opposition.

After the disappointment of the General election of 1918, Labour did not have to wait long for more favourable signs. In July 1919 there was a by-election in the Lanarkshire mining constituency of Bothwell which Labour took from the Coalition on a 20% swing.[2] This was followed by the November municipal elections where Labour in Glasgow made substantial gains and enjoyed even more success the following year. As a consequence of the extension of the City in 1912 there was to have been a re-drawing of the ward boundaries and an election for all seats in all wards after five years. Because of the war this local general election was postponed until 1920. This presented Labour with an opportunity similar to that of 1895/6. Because all three ward seats would have to be re-contested in 1920, the election of 1919 was not keenly fought. There were only ten contests but Labour candidates stood in them all, winning eight; three sitting councillors were returned and five new seats were won. In addition four sitting Labour members were returned unopposed and this meant that Labour representation now stood at an all-time high of twenty-four councillors.[3] In the 'general' election of 1920, however, Labour took a quantum leap forward.

In this election Labour won seats in eighteen of the City's thirty-seven

---

[1] Electoral information taken from F.W.S. Craig, *British Parliamentary Election Results 1918–1949* (Chichester, 1983), pp. 585–99.

[2] G. Brown, 'The Labour Party and Political Change in Scotland: the Politics of Five Elections', (unpublished Ph.D. thesis, University of Edinburgh, 1982), p 128.

[3] *Glasgow Herald*, 5 Nov. 1919.

wards giving it forty-four councillors out of a total of 111 elected members. Table One tries to give some idea of the change and continuity in Labour's local representation from 1896. This is a difficult exercise because of changes in the franchise, changes in ward boundaries and the greater scope of Labour's electoral performance. Nevertheless, by looking at Labour representation in three key dates, 1896/7, 1914 and 1920 we can chart Labour's electoral progress. There are two significant points that emerge from this tabulation. One is that Labour representation had moved onto a new level post 1918 which had been beyond it before the war. The second is that while Labour made some new conquests in 1920, most of its gains came in wards where it had enjoyed a degree of representation pre-war. For instance, in Hutchesontown, Govan, Shettleston and Springburn where Labour won all three ward seats in 1920 it already held one and usually two seats in 1914. In certain wards there was an even longer tradition of Labour representation going back to the first big effort by the Workers' Election Committee in 1896, e.g. Dalmarnock, Mile End, and (again) Hutchesontown and Springburn.

The secret ballot does not allow for a definite examination of the social background of Labour's supporters, but the variety of wards in which Labour was successful indicate that it garnered votes from both the 're-spectable' and the 'poorer' working class. If the artisan wards of Govan and Springburn proved to be bastions of Labour support in the 1920s, so too did the Gorbals and Mile End. In one account the results of the municipal elections between 1919 and 1922 are evidence of: 'how the labour vote spread from "labour aristocratic" districts to "unskilled" districts to pro-duce a recognisable forerunner of modern voting patterns.'[4] The agency of this spread was the Labour electoral machine which, in the extension into the unskilled areas, eventually encompassed the existing Irish 'machine'.[5] From this perspective Irish support for Labour only really occurred after Labour began to retreat on its anti-drink stance following the prohibition referendum of 1920.[6]

The role and influence of the Irish shall be discussed in a later chapter, but the point to emphasise here is that Labour already enjoyed both latent and actual support among the poorer working class, including the Irish. For some Labour figures, such as Tom Johnston, this may have been difficult to accept since it contradicted his view of Labour's natural constituency being the respectable working man, but it was true nonetheless. Likewise the insistence upon identifying the growth in Labour's vote after 1918 fails to account for the pre-existing spread of support for Labour both geographi-cally and socially within Glasgow. As we have shown previously, Labour already enjoyed electoral success in poorer areas like Hutchesontown and

---

[4] I.S. McLean, *The Legend of Red Clydeside* (Edinburgh, 1983), pp. 177–8.
[5] McLean, *Legend*, p. 201.
[6] McLean, *Legend*, pp. 180–3, 241.

Table 1: Labour representation in Glasgow Wards, 1920, 1914, 1896/7.

Ward	No. of Labour Councillors		
	1920	1914	1896/7
1. Shettleston & Tollcross	***	**	–
2. Parkhead	***	–	–
3. Dalmarnock	***	**	*
4. Calton	*	0	**
5. Mile End	***	**	**
6. Whitevale	0	0	0
7. Dennistoun	0	0	0
8. Provan	*	–	–
9. Cowlairs	***	*	*
10. Springburn	***	*	*
11. Townhead	**	**	*
12. Exchange	0	0	0
13. Blythswood	0	0	0
14. Anderston	*	*	0
15. Sandyford	0	0	0
16. Park	0	0	0
17. Cowcaddens	0	0	0
18. Woodside	***	*	0
19. Ruchill	**	–	–
20. North Kelvin	0	0	0
21. Maryhill	**	0	0
22. Kelvinside	0	0	0
23. Partick West	0	0	0
24. Partick East	0	0	0
25. Whiteinch	0	0	0
26. Hutchesontown	***	**	**
27. Gorbals	***	0	0
28. Kingston	**	0	0
29. Kinning Park	0	*	–
30. Govan	***	**	–
31. Fairfield	***	**	–
32. Pollokshields	0	0	0
33. Camphill	0	0	0
34. Pollokshaws	0	0	0
35. Govanhill	0	0	0
36. Langside	0	0	0
37. Cathcart	0	0	0
TOTAL	44	19	10
	(40%)	(17%)	(13%)

Note: Each * represents one Labour Councillor; '–' indicates that the Ward or an equivalent did not then exist; figures in parentheses give Labour representation as a proportion of the total membership of the Corporation.

the East End generally as well as more artisan areas before the war. The impact of the wartime unrest and the franchise reform of 1918 allowed Labour the opportunity to more fully harvest this support.

Party and Electoral Organisation I: The ILP, 'The People's Party'

The agency which gathered in these votes was the city-wide network of ILP branches. It was the ILP which provided the continuous link between Labour as a minor political force in the 1890s to the electoral triumphs of the 1920s. The inaugural conference of the Scottish Advisory Council of the Labour Party held in 1915 acknowledged the crucial role played by the ILP, 'The [ILP] is the most . . . active element in the movement. . . . There can be no question that Labour Representation would have been a very much smaller affair . . . but for the work of the ILP.'[7]

While other sections of the Labour movement were involved in election campaigns it was the ILP branches – there were no Labour Party branches as such – which provided the engine of the Labour machine. The Scottish Council of the Labour Party, in its Executive Report for 1919, estimated that the members of trade unions affiliated to the party were responsible for 10% of propaganda work and 25% of electoral work, while the individual members of the ILP carried out 90% of propaganda work and 75% of electoral work.[8] Over the following decade this situation did not change materially. As Brown comments on the 1920s, 'It was the Independent Labour Party that was the fulcrum of Labour Party activity within Scotland.'[9] Within Glasgow this was especially so.

The new Labour Party constitution of 1918 and the introduction of individual membership appeared to threaten the ILP's formative position. Within the Glasgow ILP there was a strong movement in favour of disaffiliation from the Labour Party and a special meeting was held in August of 1919 to discuss the issue. The result of the debate was that a resolution to stay in the Labour Party won over an amendment to separate, though only by the relatively close vote of seventy to fifty-one.[10] The following year the debate was taken up at the Scottish Conference where six Clydeside branches voted in favour of separation, though the result this time was more comfortably in favour of remaining in the Labour Party.[11] Throughout the 1920s and indeed up to the ILP's eventual disaffiliation,

---

[7] *Report of the Inaugural Conference of the Scottish Advisory Council of the Labour Party* (1915), p. 20.

[8] *Report of the Fifth Annual Conference of the Labour Party (Scottish Council)*, (1919), p. 21.

[9] Brown, 'Labour and Political Change', p. 400.

[10] Glasgow ILP Federation, *Special Aggregate Meeting of Branch Members*, 29 Aug. 1919.

[11] A. McKinlay, ' "Doubtful wisdom and uncertain promise": strategy, ideology and organisation, 1918–1922', in A. McKinlay & R.J. Morris (eds.), *The ILP on Clydeside 1893–1932: from foundation to disintegration* (Manchester, 1991), p. 128.

individual membership and local branches of the Labour Party remained a dead letter, and the ILP continued to dominate the Labour Party in Scotland. Arthur Woodburn commented that in 1932, 'There was practically no Labour Party in Scotland . . . the real drive was in the Independent Labour Party.'[12] Already dominant in Glasgow prior to 1914 the War only increased the ILP's strength and influence and it continued to grow after 1918. The ILP could, when it chose, be tactically astute and ruthless to get its own way in terms of policy and the selection of candidates.[13] Mainly, however, it was the greater enthusiasm and energy of its members which secured the ILP's predominance. The vast majority of Labour parliamentary candidates in Scotland throughout the 1920s were members of the ILP and in 1920 the executive of the Glasgow Labour Party had fourteen ILPers out of eighteen members.[14] By 1924 the Glasgow Federation could boast that:

> The Glasgow ILP is now the "People's Party". Its influence and usefulness predominates in every phase of public life of the City. We are stronger, numerically, than ever we have been. Our representation on Public Bodies is higher than at any previous period.[15]

This was not mere self-aggrandisement. Even its opponents recognised the ILP's influence, even if they were hardly complimentary about it. The *Glasgow Herald* commented on the eve of the Municipal election of 1923:

> The official 'Labour' candidates are almost, if not entirely composed of members of the Independent Labour Party, a Socialist organisation comparatively small in numbers but active and aggressive, and exerting an influence far out of proportion to its numerical strength.[16]

ILP membership doubled in Glasgow between 1917 and 1920 when it stood at a high point of around 2,600 members. The social composition of the party remained the same as before 1914, i.e. drawn from skilled and clerical grades, but with a significant layer of younger workers whose concerns lay more with the radicalism of wartime industrial struggles rather than with the continuous slog of annual elections. As post-war boom turned to slump so the Glasgow ILP was vulnerable to a loss of membership – due to its predominantly working class character and its relatively high level of subscriptions; by early 1922 party membership receded to 1400.[17] Many of

---

[12] A. Woodburn, unpublished autobiography, p. 66. Quoted in Brown, 'Labour and Political Change', p. 376.

[13] I.G.C. Hutchison, *A Political history of Scotland 1832–1914* (Edinburgh, 1983), pp. 297–303.

[14] See Brown, 'Labour and Political Change', on Labour Party candidates; McKinlay, 'Doubtful Wisdom', p. 129 on Glasgow LP Executive.

[15] Glasgow ILP Federation, *Annual Report 1923–24*, p. 2.

[16] *Glasgow Herald*, 1 Nov. 1923.

[17] Glasgow ILP Federation, *Annual Report 1921–22*.

those who left were the younger workers and women attracted to the party in the euphoria of the later war years and immediately after. As mass unemployment effectively halted industrial militancy, so the ILP re-affirmed its primary function of fighting and winning elections.[18]

As before, the electoral unit – municipal ward – remained the basis of branch organisation. Along with variations in membership, so the number of branches rose and fell. In 1921/2 the number of branches fell from twenty-nine to twenty-five, though in the following years, as membership stabilised so the number of branches increased, thirty-one in 1922/3 and thirty-four in 1923/4. The aim, expressed by the Federation in 1923, was for thirty-seven – 'one for each Municipal Ward.'[19] This ambition was in fact achieved in 1929 when the Federation could boast thirty-nine branches. The connection between Labour electoral success and ILP activity, which was evident in the pre-war years, remained: this was summed up in the official Party comment on the 1923 Municipal polls, 'the Wards in which we have continued success have all strong ILP branches.'[20]

As the ILP's electoral ambitions grew in the post-war years so it formed branches in new areas of the City. The expansion of party organisation into the southern suburbs suggests a possible increase of lower middle class involvement, while the formation of branches in areas such as Gorbals and Cowcaddens suggests that semi- and unskilled workers were also attracted to the ILP. Enthusiasm on its own, however, could not guarantee electoral success. By the early 1920s Partick and Govanhill had emerged as two of the largest branches in the Glasgow Federation (in fact Partick had the biggest membership in 1920), yet both areas remained stubbornly hostile to Labour representation; throughout the 1920s only one Labour candidate was returned at the November polls for the three wards covered by these branches. Similarly, the formation of branches in middle class areas such as Cathcart, Pollokshaws and Shawlands made no difference; Labour never won an election in these areas and very often did not bother to contest the seats. Branch membership in such wards tended to be relatively small, as it did in the 'slum' wards. Yet, if suburban Glasgow remained resolutely opposed to Labour, the poorer working class areas proved much more receptive; Gorbals and Cowcaddens soon became bastions of Labour representation. At the same time the link between ILP activity and Labour representation could be seen clearly in areas such as Bridgeton, Govan and Hutchesontown; continuously strong ILP branches and predominant Labour representation.[21]

[18] McKinlay, 'Doubtful Wisdom', pp. 135–9.
[19] Glasgow ILP Federation, *Annual Report 1922–23*.
[20] Glasgow ILP Federation, *Annual Report 1923–24*.
[21] Glasgow ILP Federation, *Annual Reports*, various. Election information taken from the *Glasgow Herald* 1920–1930.

Party and Electoral Organisation II: the Moderates, 'Non-political but Anti-Socialist'

Labour's success in the general elections of 1922 and 1923 (in winning ten of the city's fifteen seats) was due largely to there being a split right wing vote. In both years Labour won an 'extra' two seats because of this: in 1922 Camlachie and Maryhill, and in 1923 Maryhill and Partick. In 1924 when all fifteen seats were contested as two-party contests, Labour's share of the vote hardly altered, but it fell back to a more representative eight constituencies.[22] As the Liberals and Unionists competed in the post-war years for the middle class vote it was not clear what the ultimate outcome would be – triumph for either party or even their merger into a new 'moderate' or 'right-wing' political force. There was considerable support among Scottish Unionists for a continuation of the Coalition Government and the revival of Scottish Liberalism in 1923, when it won twenty-two seats against the Unionist total of fourteen, showed that some form of continuing co-operation was necessary to defeat Labour.[23] In the 1924 election it was common knowledge that both parties were operating 'secret' pacts in a large number of constituencies.[24]

The balance of forces on the right had clearly and fundamentally shifted to the Unionist camp by 1924, when the Liberals stood in only two of Glasgow's divisions while the Unionists were the anti-Labour standard bearers in the other thirteen. The success of Sir R.J. Collie in Partick in 1922 was the last time any Liberal was returned in Glasgow, a desperate decline in what had just a few years before been a solidly 'Liberal' city. Although Liberal and Unionist differences remained, they were much less significant after 1918. The overriding concern for right wing opinion was the need to contain Labour. Anti-Bolshevism or anti-Socialism was the rallying cry in the post-war years and it operated very successfully in local politics.

The gains made by Labour at the local elections in 1919 and the forthcoming municipal general election in 1920 helped concentrate minds on how to cope with the growing left wing presence. With the advent of the Russian Revolution and industrial discontent at home, a plethora of anti-Socialist organisations, such as the Middle Class Union (MCU) and the Economic League (EL), were formed. In Glasgow the Citizens' Union had been active in the pre-war years in attempting to secure candidates opposed to further municipal undertakings. Almost immediately after the November 1919 local poll the Citizens' Union took the initiative in organising a wider movement, 'to combat the Socialist propaganda in Glasgow.'[25] It was

---

[22] Craig, *Election Results 1918–1949*; Hutchison, *Political History*, pp. 281–2.

[23] Hutchison, *Political History*, p. 322, for the view that Liberal decline was 'not pre-ordained'.

[24] Hutchison, *Political History*, pp. 325–8.; Brown, 'Labour and Political Change', pp. 335–40.

[25] NLS, Acc 10424/73, SCUA archive, Glasgow Unionist Association, minute book, General Committee 22 Dec. 1919.

accepted that the task in hand was beyond the Citizens' Union 'as now constituted' and a provisional committee was formed of three delegates from the Glasgow Unionist Association, the Glasgow Liberal Council and the Women's Citizens' Association.[26] The committee invited delegates from other societies and among those joining were the Rotary Club, the City Business Club, and the Citizens' Vigilance Association, as well as the Citizens' Union.[27] This umbrella organisation was first called the Glasgow Municipal Electors' League but this was dissolved and a new body called the Glasgow Good Government Committee (1920) was established in its place.[28]

This organisation was intended, as its very title suggests, as a temporary initiative to counter Labour's expected assault on the Town Council in 1920.[29] However, it became a permanent feature and, as the Good Government League, was responsible for directing 'moderate' efforts at the municipal polls. This it did with notable success, as the Moderate Party controlled Glasgow Town Council quite comfortably until 1933.[30] The formation of the League was of considerable importance as it allowed Unionists and Liberals to co-operate against Labour while maintaining the tradition of 'no politics' in local government. Had Unionists and Liberals fought under Party labels and competed against each other, Labour would very likely have benefited from a split right-wing vote.

For the Unionists the extension of the franchise in 1918 first began to exercise their minds on the future of municipal politics and how best to deal with the Labour threat. For some, most notably Sir Charles Cleland, Chairman of the Glasgow Unionist Association (GUA), the obvious answer was to put forward Unionist candidates.[31] This was a long-held view by Cleland and was mainly directed against the Liberals whom he considered had long operated an effective, if formally hidden, party political approach to municipal affairs. Liberal Associations had as one of their aims the return of Liberal sympathisers to local bodies, they controlled the selection of candidates through ward committees, and they had the support of pressure groups such as the temperance societies which were effectively Liberal.[32] However, even though Unionist councillors were also elected 'covertly',

[26] NLS Acc. 10424/9 (xii) SCUA Archive, 'Sir Lewis Shedden's file relating to Glasgow municipal elections, 1896–1939', Sir Lewis Shedden, typescript, no title, December 1919, Hereafter 'Shedden . . . Municipal elections'; Brown, 'Labour and Political Change', pp. 190–1.

[27] 'Shedden . . . Municipal elections', 1919; Hutchison, *Political History*, p. 321, also includes the YMCA, the National Council of Women and the Middle Class Union.

[28] NLS, Acc 10424/73, SCUA archive, Glasgow Unionist Association, minute book, General Committee 30 Aug. 1920.

[29] *Glasgow Herald*, 30 Sep. 1920.

[30] 1933 was also the year the Good Government League was dissolved. *Glasgow Herald*, 17 Dec. 1932; See also 'Shedden . . . Municipal elections'.

[31] NLS, Acc 10424/73, SCUA archive, GUA, minutes, General Committee 26 Nov. 1919.

[32] 'Shedden . . . Municipal elections'.

opinion within the party as a whole was against introducing 'imperial' politics into local affairs. The original invitation from the Citizens' Union, therefore, found the Glasgow Unionists in a receptive frame of mind; anxious to combat Labour's threatened advance and happier to do so in a non party political manner.

Rather than fight under their own colours, the Glasgow Unionists enthusiastically embraced the concept of a 'broad front' in municipal politics and submitted the following resolution to the Scottish Conference in October 1920:

> That the time has come when the Unionist Associations throughout the country, should actively concern themselves in Local Government Elections, and that, acting when possible in combination with other non-Socialist Organisations, they should endeavour to secure the return to Town and County Councils, Parish Councils, and Education Authorities of men and women of sound progressive and anti-Socialist opinions.

Both the Western and the Eastern Divisional Councils approved of this resolution and it was subsequently passed.[33] Thus, Glasgow provided a model for the rest of Scotland. It is difficult not to see the Liberals as junior partners. The split in the Liberal Party was formalised in 1920 and their organisation in Glasgow deteriorated rapidly. The only Liberals returned for Glasgow in 1918 were three Coalition Liberals and their organisation, even where they held the seat, 'was regarded as a paper fiction.'[34] Certainly, Liberals were involved in the Good Government League, the original decision 'to form an organisation non-political but anti-Socialist' was taken jointly by the GUA and the Coalition Liberals.[35]

The original constitution of the Municipal Electors' League was regarded by the GUA as too 'nebulous and vague' and insufficiently anti-Socialist. While they were prepared to sacrifice doctrinal clarity for the sake of unity, the Unionists pressed for a more definite statement of opposition to Socialism which, after all, 'was the principal object for which the formation of such a League was originally proposed'.[36] The Unionists held sway – the League agreed to a new, explicitly anti-socialist clause in the constitution – even though it led to the withdrawal of the Citizens' Vigilance Association.[37]

[33] NLS, Acc 10424/73, SCUA archive, GUA, minutes, General Committee; ' Shedden Municipal elections', Ts, n.d. but circa 1937.

[34] Hutchison, *Political History*, p. 321.

[35] Other Liberals also participated but some remained apart since they did not wish to alienate Labour support at the local temperance polls in 1920. 'Shedden . . . Municipal elections', Ts, n.d. but circa 1937.

[36] NLS, Acc 10424/73, SCUA archive, GUA, minutes, General Committee 26 Apr., 3 May 1920.

[37] NLS, Acc 10424/73, SCUA archive, GUA, minutes, General Committee, 31 May 1920. The Unionists regarded the Citizens' Vigilance Association, at least before the war, as a Liberal organisation.

Why the League was dissolved and replaced by the Good Government Committee is not clear as there does not appear to have been any change in policy – which remained that of consolidating the 'moderate' forces in the fight against Labour, in particular trying to avoid too many Moderates standing. Nor was there any change in the wide range of support for it; if anything, support increased. In the month before the election the *Glasgow Herald* described the League as, 'composed of representatives of the leading political parties, Unionist, Liberal and Liberal Coalition, and of commercial, social, educational and religious agencies.'[38]

The municipal general election of 1920 was a success for the Moderates with the Labour assault being firmly repulsed. Commenting on the results, Cleland of the GUA considered that the Good Government Committee 'had worked very well, and he was of opinion that a somewhat similar Organisation would be created for future Elections.'[39] Yet, when the Committee did establish itself permanently as the Good Government League, the Glasgow Unionists decided not to affiliate.[40] This decision did not, however, represent a break in the broad front approach or herald a move to running Unionist candidates. Rather, the GUA, through its own Local Elections Subcommittee co-operated closely with the Good Government League. While at times the Unionists might criticise the League over some minor issue, mostly they did work together. The closeness of the relationship can be seen during the 1925 polls when the two organisations agreed that the GUA issue to its membership (between 20–25,000) its own circular and the manifesto of the League; the recipients 'would be asked to make themselves active in their own and neighbouring Wards, and to assist on polling day.'[41]

Virtually all anti-Labour candidates were designated 'Moderate' but the party as such only existed within the Council Chambers; it had no existence outside of George Square.[42] Neither was the Good Government League a surrogate party, as it had no full time officials and concentrated its activities on the period immediately prior to the polls.[43] Its main function was to select suitable candidates and to ensure that Moderates did not stand against one another. In this it was largely successful and in the 1920s it was Labour which was more likely to suffer a split in its vote (due to the competition from left-wing parties), than the Moderates. After the election of 1920 it was 1926 before rival Moderates faced each other in contests

[38] *Glasgow Herald*, 21 Oct. 1920.
[39] NLS, Acc 10424/73, SCUA archive, GUA, minutes, General Committee 29 Nov. 1920.
[40] NLS, Acc 10424/73, SCUA archive, GUA, minutes, General Committee 30 May 1921.
[41] NLS, Acc 10424/73, SCUA archive, GUA, minutes, General Committee, 25 Oct. 1925.
[42] As the *Glasgow Herald* put it at the time of the 1920 election, 'The name Moderate has been adopted as covering all opponents of the Labour Programme.' 3 Nov. 1920.
[43] 'Shedden . . . Municipal elections', Ts, n.d. but circa 1937.

involving Labour. This was not so significant in Cowcaddens where the Labour vote easily beat that of the combined Moderate poll, but it did matter in Sandyford where Labour won the seat (for the first time) on a minority vote. The *Glasgow Herald* railed against this result especially as the candidate recommended by the Good Government League got 1,000 votes more than his Moderate rival.[44]

The Course of Elections, 1920–1930

It was the strategy outlined above, a sort of non-political politics, which lay behind the Moderate domination of the Town Council. Anti-socialism was its guiding principle, but it was certainly effective. Labour's municipal breakthrough of 1920 did not prove to be harbinger of further success leading inexorably to a Labour controlled council. Rather Labour had reached an apparent plateau and for the next decade or so its representation stayed at much the same level, in stark contrast to the parliamentary representation of the city.

In preparing for the municipal election of 1921 the Glasgow Federation of the ILP categorised the various wards of the City. The wards which were held by Labour had all to be defended. These numbered seventeen, or eighteen if Doherty, the 'unofficial labour' councillor in Cowcaddens was included.[45] Of the other wards, eight were identified as 'ought to be fought': Govanhill, Kinning Park, North Kelvin, Partick East, Pollokshaws, Sandyford, Whitevale and Townhead. Five wards were regarded as 'might be fought': Dennistoun, Cathcart, Partick West, Whiteinch and Camphill. And five wards were written of as 'hopeless': Blythswood, Kelvinside, Langside, Exchange and Pollokshields.[46] In all Labour contested twenty-nine wards but lost five seats and made no gains. The eight wards it did not bother to contest came from the 'might be' and 'hopeless' categories. Three wards among these two groups were contested – Dennistoun, Exchange and Partick West – where Labour secured c. 18%, 33% and 26% of the vote respectively. Of more interest, however, are those wards which the ILP considered 'ought to be fought', since these were the areas where they felt they had some reasonable chance of success and, indeed, would be the key areas for Labour to win if they were ever to gain a majority of the City Council.

---

[44] *Glasgow Herald*, 4 Nov. 1926.

[45] There was some complaint within the ILP that Doherty was supported when he was not a labour candidate. The explanation was that he was recommended by the Trades and Labour Council and that ILP support therefore followed because of its affiliation. Glasgow Federation ILP, Executive Council minutes, 25 Nov. 1921, Mitchell Library, Glasgow.

[46] Glasgow ILP Federation, Executive Council, minutes, 2 Sep. 1921. One ward was unaccounted for, Park, but it seems safe to include this in the "hopeless" category.

The results for Labour were very dispiriting. The Moderates held their
seats comfortably with four figure majorities in all of these wards. In all, the
Labour share of the vote was 36%. Not surprisingly, the following year, 1922,
saw Labour decide not to contest half of these wards. The general elections
of 1922, 1923 and 1924 all took place close to the municipal polling dates
and one would expect the respective elections to have broadly similar
outcomes. In 1922 Labour's performance at the November municipal poll
foreshadowed its spectacular gains in the general election ten days later.[47]
However, in 1922 Labour made only a single gain on the town council and
this after having lost five seats in 1921. In 1923, when Labour again won two
thirds of the City's parliamentary seats, it made no gain locally; winning two
and losing two wards. Finally, in 1924 when Labour lost two parliamentary
divisions, it made three net gains on the City council. In that year, Labour
made a considerable effort by standing in all but six municipal seats, a
relatively high number of contests. Yet, the result left Labour with forty-two
Councillors (two fewer than in 1920) against a Moderate total of sixty-nine.
There was no breakthrough into new areas as the four seats gained,
Anderston, Kingston, Ruchill and Woodside, had all been won in 1920
and lost in 1921; these were wards Labour expected to hold and, with the
exception of Ruchill, Labour did win in most years between 1920 and 1930.

In 1922 Labour only stood in twenty-three of the city's thirty-seven wards.
This was an exceptionally high proportion of uncontested seats, but every
year there were a significant number of candidates returned unopposed and
invariably these were Moderate candidates. Even at the general poll in 1920
there were four uncontested wards; in three of these Moderates were given a
walkover and in the other (Townhead) the representation was split between
one Moderate and two Labour.[48] Just as Labour developed its own strongholds where Moderates were rarely, if ever, returned so there were large
areas of the city where Labour failed to make any inroads. These were the
same areas where there had been no Labour representatives before 1914:
middle class wards like Dennistoun and Park, the business centre, the West
End of Kelvinside and Partick and the suburbs to the South (see Table
One); the 'might be' and 'hopeless' wards. Just how impossible these areas
were for Labour to penetrate can be gauged from the fact that during the
1920s Labour did not win a single seat in any of these wards, with the
exception of a solitary gain in Partick West in 1929.

The political struggle in the 1920s, in municipal elections, was a long war
of attrition; there was the occasional coup for each side but no alteration in
the overall strength of either. The one year in which there appeared to be a
breakthrough was 1926 when Labour made eight clear gains, pushing its

[47] McLean, *Legend*, pp. 162–3. This is done by grouping the municipal wards into
their respective parliamentary constituencies and comparing the two results.
[48] After 1920, the next Labour candidate to be returned unopposed, other than at a
by-election, was in 1929 for Hutchesontown.

representation to an all-time high of fifty-one.[49] This was, of course, the year of the General Strike and the lockout of the miners – events which galvanised the ILP.

The Strike in Glasgow was organised by the Central Strike Co-ordinating Committee (CSCC) which was set up by the Trades Council's Industrial Committee. The CSCC, which 'was a Council of Action in all but name',[50] was composed of twenty-three men, mostly union officials. Communist party influence was strong on the CSCC, providing five of its members and the Chairman, Peter Kerrigan, although they were there as active trade unionists and not as party members; the CSCC had no representatives from any of the political parties or the Co-operative movement. The ILP was represented on the CSCC by Harry Hopkins, but it had no directing role to play in the strike.[51] This, of course, was the norm for the ILP; what involvement, if any, it had in industrial disputes had always been via the action of particular individuals. Prior to the Strike, however, the Glasgow Federation had established its own Industrial Committee which tried to undertake a census of the branches in order to 'group the members according to their industries.'[52] This does not appear to have been an attempt to prepare for the looming confrontation but, rather, an effort to develop some sort of longer term industrial policy for the Party. However, the response of the branches was 'very poor' and the committee seems to have been allowed to wither.[53]

The response to the strike call in Glasgow was overwhelmingly positive. According to a Ministry of Labour Report on Glasgow, written just before the Strike was called off, 'There is not the slightest sign of any break whatever in the strike. In fact many of those now working wish to join in.'[54] The only area of concern were the tramways, but otherwise the workers were solidly behind the CSCC which set up sixteen Area Committees to run the Strike.[55] In turn, however, the strikers met a determined enemy; by the end of the Strike 7,000 volunteers had been enrolled into strike breaking duty, including 300 students.[56] Not surprisingly, there were a series of violent confrontations between strikers and volunteers, with the former suffering a large number of arrests. In fact, although the General Strike is famous for having been conducted with relatively little violence, Glasgow can claim to have been the area where hostilities between the two

---

[49] *Glasgow Herald*, 3 Nov. 1926 gave Labour forty-eight Councillors but the Herald identified two councillors as 'independents' who were effectively Labour members.

[50] S. Bhaumick, 'Glasgow', in M. Morris (ed.), *The General Strike* (London, 1980), p. 401

[51] Bhaumick, 'Glasgow'.

[52] Glasgow ILP Federation, Executive Council, minutes, 12 March 1926.

[53] Glasgow ILP Federation, Executive Council, minutes, 30 July 1926.

[54] Quoted in Bhaumick, 'Glasgow', p. 395, who dates this report as 11 May.

[55] Bhaumick, 'Glasgow', p. 399.

[56] Bhaumick, 'Glasgow', p. 408.

sides were at their most extreme.[57] This and the exemplary solidarity shown by the workers occurred without the real involvement of the most important element of the local industrial workforce; engineering and shipbuilding were among the 'second wave' of strikers, not called out till 12 May (the very day the strike was called off) and so had little direct input to the struggle.

In spite of the defensiveness which was induced in the labour movement as a result of the debacle of the General Strike and the exhausting struggle in defence of the miners, the local elections in 1926 gave Labour its best results since 1920. The reasons for this appear to have been a combination of heightened class consciousness as a result of the Strike, public sympathy for the miners and a new lease of life given to the ILP branches and membership. The ILP's wholehearted support of the mining communities may have given it 'a welcome psychological respite.'[58] The Glasgow ILP Report for 1925 complained of 'the prevalent apathy of poverty' which the Party had to face and critical reaction against the short-lived Labour Government.[59] In sharp contrast, the Report for the following year, referred to 1926 as 'perhaps in many ways the most extraordinary year in its history.'[60] The miners' struggle dominated the life of the ILP branches over the seven months of the lock-out. The ILP ran ten communal kitchens of its own and assisted on another two. The Party raised almost £3,500 for this purpose and its propaganda activity, which was greatly extended, was directed at the miners' cause almost exclusively.[61] The ILP's own members were 'very much affected by unemployment and victimisation consequent on the General Strike' but, nevertheless the Federation's membership did increase by 100 over the year.[62]

The ILP remained committed to its *raison d'être* – winning Labour representation on all public bodies – but it had not yet become purely an electoral 'machine'. In 1926 the ILP could return to what it did best – electioneering combined with a high moral purpose. The results of the November poll were excellent and saw Labour achieve, for the first time, a majority of the vote, 55%.[63] One view of the municipal elections of 1926 is that they echoed 'the degree of strike activity that had taken place' in the different parts of the city. Thus, the Labour vote rose in wards like Hutchesontown, Parkhead and Kinning Park, 'which had witnessed large-scale clashes with the police', while Labour's vote remained the same or

[57] G. A. Phillipps, *The General Strike: The Politics of Industrial Conflict* (London 1976) p. 203.
[58] A. McKinlay & J.J. Smyth, 'The end of "the agitator workman": 1926–32', in McKinlay & Morris, *ILP on Clydeside*, p. 178.
[59] Glasgow ILP Federation, *Annual Report 1925–26*, p. 3.
[60] Glasgow ILP Federation, *Annual Report 1926–27*, p. 1
[61] Glasgow ILP Federation, *Annual Report 1926–27*, pp. 1, 4.
[62] Glasgow ILP Federation, *Annual Report 1926–27*, p. 2.
[63] *Glasgow Herald*, 3 Nov. 1926. Given that eleven wards were not contested by Labour this is almost certainly an over-exaggeration of Labour's support over the whole city.

slightly fell in 'the shipyard wards like Govan, Fairfield and Kingston'.[64] While there is certainly something to this pattern the most dramatic feature at the time was the success of Labour across the board.

There were twenty-six contested wards in 1926 and Labour won twenty-one of these. The five seats held by the Moderates, Maryhill, North Kelvin, Partick East, Partick West and Whiteinch, were all areas where Labour had traditionally failed to make an impact.[65] The eight gains made by Labour, however, were spread quite widely over the city and saw Labour strengthen its hold on marginal wards and make inroads into what were considered safe Moderate areas. Four of the seats gained, Cowcaddens, Kingston, Ruchill and Woodside were in wards where the representation since 1920 had been shared between Labour and the Moderates. The gains in Kinning Park, Sandyford, Townhead and Whitevale were more significant since these were areas where Labour had previously enjoyed no, or very little, success and were among the eight key wards identified by the ILP in 1921. These victories were certainly dramatic and, in the case of Kinning Park (a seat never before won by Labour) where John S. Clarke unseated the Lord Provost, verged on the spectacular.

With these gains it was possible to imagine a Labour administration. The ILP enthusiastically charted the electoral progress necessary to return a Labour Lord Provost in 1929. Seven wards were now regarded as critical and where the ILP branches should concentrate their efforts; Cowlairs, Cowcaddens, Kinning Park, Provan, Ruchill, Townhead and Whitevale. Four gains could be made in the 1927 polls and five the year after that, enough to give Labour a majority.[66] Such optimism, however, proved unfounded. In the 1927 local election Labour lost five seats to the Moderates whose majority on the Council rose to an effectively insurmountable twenty-five.[67] The tenuous nature of Labour's advance in 1926 can be seen in that the eight wards where Labour made gains, only one, Cowcaddens, registered a Labour victory in 1927. Likewise, Cowcaddens was the only ward of the seven identified by the ILP as critical for further advance which Labour won that year.

The immediate cause of Labour's poor performance in 1927 was identified as the 'birth control issue'.[68] This was a controversy over whether or not Glasgow's libraries should stock copies of *Birth Control News*. The issue went to a Council vote in October, shortly before the November poll, and saw the proposal heavily defeated with all the Moderates voting against but a

[64] P. Carter, 'The West of Scotland', in J. Skelley (ed.), *1926: The General Strike* (London, 1976), p. 138.

[65] The one exception was Maryhill where Labour had won two seats in 1920 but had lost every election thereafter.

[66] Glasgow ILP Federation, *Annual Report 1926–27*, p. 5. The report was published in March by which time Labour's representation had inched up to 51.

[67] *Glasgow Herald*, 2 Nov. 1927.

[68] Glasgow ILP Federation, *Annual Report 1927–28*, p. 5.

sizeable minority of Labour councillors voting in favour.[69] The *Glasgow Observer* called for Catholics to vote against those councillors who had supported the proposal, though the fall-out from the affair was far from clear-cut; four of the five councillors who lost their seats were themselves Catholics.[70] Two of the seats lost by Labour were among its strongest heartlands, Govan and Parkhead, though both were lost due to splits allowing a Moderate victory on a minority vote.[71] Somewhat complacently but, nevertheless accurately, the Glasgow ILP predicted that those seats 'will, of course, come back to Labour.'[72] If the breakthrough of 1926 proved to be a false dawn, so the downturn of 1927 was not as bad as it perhaps first appeared. The war of attrition continued with little change in the overall position of either party; after the polls in November 1930 Labour stood at forty-three councillors, still twenty-five seats behind the Moderates.[73]

The ILP's Dilemma: Socialism or Representation?

By 1924 and the formation of the first (albeit minority) Labour Government, the pattern of electoral politics seemed well set; essentially a two-horse race between Labour and the Conservatives. On the left positions had hardened and simplified after the flux of the war and immediate post-war years. The death of John Maclean in late 1923 effectively ended any hope of an independent Scottish socialist strategy. The formation of the Communist Party of Great Britain, small as it was, nonetheless provided a permanent left-wing alternative to Labour. But these were minority forces. Maclean and the CP were able to bother Labour but never seriously threaten its position. Within Glasgow the ILP remained the dominant political force, yet as real political power loomed tantalisingly before it, so doubts emerged over the whole project of labour representation. Doubts, ultimately, which would tear the ILP apart.

The experience of the first Labour Government convinced Maxton and Wheatley that Labour should not take office as a minority again or, if it did, should introduce a radical legislative programme that would force the Conservatives and Liberals to unite in opposition. This approach was anathema to the majority perspective of the Labour Party, which has tended to be identified solely with MacDonald, of taking office in order to prove Labour's 'fitness to govern'. The Labour Party, with Snowden as Chancellor and shadow Chancellor, was wedded to rigid financial orthodoxy against which the ILP, and Wheatley in particular, argued for the underconsumptionist economics of J. A. Hobson.[74] The ILP was therefore pursuing a quite

[69] McLean, 'Legend', pp. 223–4. See chapter Five for further discussion of this issue.
[70] T. Gallagher, *Glasgow: The Uneasy Peace* (Manchester, 1987), p. 192
[71] *Glasgow Herald*, 2 Nov. 1927.
[72] Glasgow ILP Federation, *Annual Report 1927–28*, p. 5.
[73] *Glasgow Herald*, 5 Nov. 1930.
[74] D. Howell, *A Lost Left:Three Studies in Socialism and Nationalism* (Manchester 1986), p. 255; I.S. Wood, *John Wheatley* (Manchester, 1990), p. 159.

separate political project to that of the Labour Party, especially when Maxton replaced Clifford Allen as Chairman in 1926.

The sharp differences between the two can be gauged from the rival party programmes; the Labour Party's *Labour and the Nation*, and the ILP's *Socialism in Our Time.* While the former included some definite measures of reform, it was rooted in orthodoxy and relegated socialism to some long-distant future. The latter, in contrast, sought to challenge mass unemployment and poverty by increasing working class expenditure through such means as a 'living wage' to be determined for each industry and family allowances to be provided through the state. In addition, the banks and 'key resources' such as the mines and railways were to be brought under public ownership, and the Government was to extend its control of currency, credit and investment.[75] As an economic policy, *Socialism in Our Time* had the advantage of recognising the long term decline of the staple export trades and seeking an alternative in promoting production for the home market, a strategy that relied upon increased working class purchasing power. However, the most important aspect of the new policy was the political consequences implicit within it.

For the first time the ILP had a 'distinctive policy', distinct that is from the Labour Party and, at much the same time, the ILP began to develop a quite different political strategy.[76] In reaction to the perceived timidity of the first Labour Government, the ILP began to question the Fabian inspired belief in the 'inevitability of gradualness' and sought a more direct and confrontational approach.[77] In the mid-1920s the ILP was at its height in terms of membership, finances and numbers of elected representatives. Much of this was due to the activity of Clifford Allen as Chairman who galvanised the party's internal organisation and attracted considerable middle class support and money.[78] Although Maxton and Wheatley were suspicious of what they perceived as Allen's middle class perspective, and Maxton would replace him as Chairman, it was, nevertheless, under Allen's leadership that the ILP swung left just as the Labour Party moved to the right. Allen, as well as Wheatley, articulated a view of Labour's political strategy that emphasised the necessity of a Labour Government adopting a radical programme and deliberately courting defeat, a defeat which would be the prelude to a more certain victory.[79]

---

[75] J. Paton, *Left Turn: The Autobiography of John Paton* (London, 1936), pp. 234–5. The policy was developed during 1925 by a study group within the ILP chaired by Hobson himself. *Socialism in Our Time* was the title given to the group's interim report, endorsed by the ILP Conference, while *The Living Wage* was the title of the eventual document. Howell, *Lost Left*, pp. 266–7.

[76] R.E. Dowse, *Left in the Centre: the Independent Labour Party 1893–1940* (London, 1966) p. 120–1.

[77] W.W. Knox, ' "Ours is not an ordinary Parliamentary movement": 1922–26' in *ILP on Clydeside*, pp. 164–5.

[78] Paton, *Left Turn*, pp 153–4.

This remained a strategy based upon political reform but it sought to commit a future Labour Government to, in Wheatley's words, 'a constructive but rapid transition'.[80] It was, needless to say, execrated by the Labour leadership. The ILP hoped the idea behind *The Living Wage* would appeal to the trade unions but it met instead with near unanimous hostility. The unions saw it as a direct challenge to the whole idea of collective bargaining and thus to their very *raison d'être*, while the notion of family allowances struck at the heart of the notion of the male breadwinner earning a family wage.[81] The ILP did make a real effort to popularise its message with an extensive series of industrial conferences but, while these were well attended, they failed in their object of getting the trade unions to embrace the policy.[82] The response of the Labour Party was equally negative. *Socialism in Our Time* was dismissed by MacDonald (almost certainly without having read it) as a series of 'flashy futilities' and it was effectively buried at the Labour Party Conference in 1926.[83]

The propaganda impact of the *Socialism in Our Time* policy was undoubtedly blunted by the General Strike and subsequent lockout as the ILP branches and membership threw all their efforts into supporting the miners in their long and bitter struggle.[84] While the ILP played no directive role in the General Strike – indeed union officials were hostile to ILP involvement – the experience only served to further sharpen the left wing's critique of the Labour leadership, both parliamentary and trade union.[85] John Wheatley's sense of disgust can be gauged from his comments shortly after the collapse of the General Strike:

> From the first moment of the struggle and indeed before it, prominent Labour leaders were whining and grovelling. Some, instead of going out to proclaim the justice of the workers' cause, spent their time damping the ardour of the courageous by wringing their hands and talking about a tragedy. The real tragedy was that in its hour of trial the labour movement was deserted by those in whom it had placed its greatest trust.[86]

For Wheatley, however, the perceived betrayal incubated a growing doubt about the viability of the Labour Party as a vehicle for socialism.

It was Wheatley who was the moving force behind the Cook-Maxton

[79] Paton , *Left Turn*, p 224; Dowse, *Left in the Centre*, p. 133
[80] Quoted in D. Howell, *Lost Left*, p. 264.
[81] Howell, *Lost Left*, p. 273.
[82] Dowse, *Left in the Centre*, p. 132.
[83] *Socialist Review* March 1926, quoted in Howell, *Lost Left*, p. 273. The Conference decision was to set up a joint Labour Party – TUC commission to examine the policy. This made its recommendations in 1930. MacDonald's ignorance or dishonesty can be glimpsed in his injunction to the ILP that it would be better served studying the ideas of Hobson. Dowse, *Left in the Centre*, p. 134.
[84] McKinlay & Smyth, 'Agitator Workman', pp. 178–9
[85] P.J. Dollan in *Socialist Review* June 1926, see Dowse, *Left in the Centre*, p. 128.

Manifesto of 1928 which further divided opinion within the ILP and antag-
onised relations with the Labour Party. This Manifesto and the political
campaign to be built around it was devised at a meeting in a House of
Commons committee room attended by the Clydeside MPs Maxton, Wheatley, Kirkwood, Buchanan and Stephen, A.J. Cook, President of the Miners'
Federation of Great Britain (MFGB), and Willie Gallacher of the Communist
Party, who claimed to have written the Manifesto.[87] It was Cook's inspirational
leadership of the miners during 1926, and the ILP's unstinting solidarity, that
brought him close to the ILP left wing. Cook and Maxton were perhaps the
two most charismatic and powerful orators the socialist movement possessed
and the idea behind the campaign was that they would address a series of
large scale meetings where the audience would be urged to purchase cards
pledging their support for the aims expressed in the Manifesto.

The vague programme of the Manifesto and the secrecy behind the
Campaign – the ILP was not involved or even informed about what was
intended – provoked a storm of criticism. *Forward* scathingly compared the
pledges to those made by 'reformed drunkards . . . at the Band of Hope.'[88]
Dismissed by contemporaries as a 'complete failure amounting indeed to
fiasco', it is clear that nothing substantive came out of the Manifesto.[89] Yet
the purposes behind it were of importance. Generally, the left wing of the
ILP wished to check the continuing rightward drift of the whole Labour
movement and to counter the apathy which they saw as its origin. Cook's
opposition within the TUC to the class collaboration exemplified in the
Mond-Turner talks made him the perfect trade union ally. There is considerable evidence that Wheatley was contemplating a new organisational
initiative; Maxton, however, at this stage, was clearly opposed to any split in
Labour's ranks and it was his perspective which prevailed.

The 'Cook-Maxton' episode brought a number of matters to a head. The
ILP was even further distanced from the trade unions, as Cook became
increasingly marginalised within the TUC. The Labour Party was not
deflected from its course, as it went on to adopt *Labour and the Nation* as
the official party programme in 1928. Finally, tensions within the ILP rose,
especially between the Maxton-Wheatley group, who dominated the national leadership, and the Scottish Division of the ILP led by Patrick Dollan.

This was the critical paradox which faced Maxton, Wheatley and the other
Glasgow MPs who shared their left wing perspective; while they controlled
the ILP at a national level they were outflanked by the right wing in their
own home territory. As John Paton put it, 'the prophets were without
honour in their own country.'[90] The critical figure in denying Maxton

---

[86] *Glasgow Evening Standard*, 22 May 1926, quoted in Wood, *John Wheatley*, pp. 171–2.
[87] Wood, *John Wheatley*, p. 176, who points out that the CPGB Central Committee
'criticised it as weak and sentimental'.
[88] *Forward*, 14 Jul. 1928, quoted in McKinlay & Smyth, 'Agitator Workman' p. 187.
See this article generally for a discussion of the Cook-Maxton manifesto.
[89] Paton, *Left Turn*, p. 294.

and his allies this support was Dollan who, alone of all the major Clydeside ILPers of the pre-1914 generation, did not enter Parliament but remained a constant figure in Glasgow's municipal politics. Dollan was elected chairman of the Glasgow Federation in 1917, a post he held until 1926 when he became Chairman of the Scottish Divisional Council. This, in turn, gave him a position on the NAC, wherein he waged a constant battle against the trend of the Maxton-Wheatley majority. Dollan's differences with his erstwhile allies had been apparent for some time, but the Cook-Maxton issue saw the lines being drawn unequivocally: 'Maxton and Dollan agreed politically on nothing after the issue of the Manifesto.'[91]

Dollan is often presented as if he were a 'Tammany Hall' US type politician, the man who pulled the strings behind the scenes in Glasgow and stitched up deals in smoke filled rooms.[92] There is undoubtedly a lot of truth in this picture but it does Dollan, and the Glasgow ILP, less than justice. Dollan was a talented journalist and politician whose decision to remain in local politics – he represented Govan on Glasgow Town Council from 1913 to 1947 – rather than seek a future at Westminster, appears to have been a deliberate one.[93] Prior to and during the war Dollan was a close colleague of John Wheatley's and was employed by the latter on his religious newspapers before going on to become assistant editor of *Forward* and Scottish editor of the *Daily Herald*. Dollan had been active as a young man in the Lanarkshire miners' union and with Wheatley helped build the links between the ILP and the Clyde Workers' Committee. During the Forty Hours Strike of January 1919 Dollan edited the daily *Strike Bulletin*, a role he repeated later in the year for the railwaymen during their dispute.[94] Links such as these, as well as the moral authority he gained during the war through his prosecution as a conscientious objector, were the source both of Dollan's popularity among the rank and file of the ILP and of the support he was able to mobilise within the Labour Party.[95]

Dollan's different perspective was evident in two issues even prior to the major conflict over the Cook-Maxton Manifesto; his support for Ramsay MacDonald's leadership and his opposition to Communist affiliation to the Labour Party. Dollan was not completely uncritical of MacDonald and even regarded his taking office in 1924 as 'the biggest mistake' he ever made.[96] However, as Maxton and Wheatley sharpened their critique of MacDonald's

---

[90] Paton, *Left Turn*, p. 335.

[91] Dowse, *Left in the Centre*, p. 145.

[92] McLean, *Legend*, p. 192, refers to Dollan's 'long reign as city boss' and that he 'ran the machine'.

[93] 'Patrick Joseph Dollan' entry in W.W. Knox (ed.), *Scottish Labour Leaders 1918– 1939: a biographical dictionary*, (Edinburgh, 1984), p. 94.

[94] Knox, *Labour Leaders*, pp. 93–5.

[95] 'He worked hard to stitch up an alliance with fellow moderates from the trade unions and the Co-operative Society', Gallagher, *Uneasy Peace*, p. 201.

[96] Quoted in Brown, 'Labour and Political Change', p. 303. This, of course,

leadership into a more outright opposition, so Dollan identified himself more closely with his national leader. Immediately after the 1924 general election Maxton proposed George Lansbury as leader of the Parliamentary Labour Party in preference to MacDonald. This received only a handful of votes but it was done to register opposition to the Labour's disappointing record in office, and not on the secondary matter of MacDonald's handling of the Zinoviev letter.[97] Dollan, on the other hand, defended the Government and MacDonald's record and at the Scottish Labour Party Conference in 1925 challenged the critics to either put up or shut up. Significantly, Maxton was the only delegate prepared to confront this view of uncritical support for the parliamentary leadership.[98]

In the same year Dollan defeated Maxton again, this time on the question of the affiliation of the Communist Party to Labour. Although with only a relatively small membership and no elected representatives the Communist Party or, rather, the *question* of the Communist Party, played a major role in Glasgow's labour politics. The Glasgow Trades and Labour Council, re-organised 1918 as the central Labour Party for Glasgow, soon had a considerable Communist membership among its delegates. However, as the Labour Party began to tighten up its procedures which effectively banned Communist affiliation and the adoption of Communists as Labour candidates, this led to intense conflict within the Trades Council.[99] The issue was debated by Maxton and Dollan at the Scottish ILP Conference in 1925, where the delegates voted by 127 votes to eighty-six against Maxton's appeal for allowing affiliation. Even though prominent MPs and allies of Dollan, such as Tom Johnston and Emmanuel Shinwell, were prepared to accept Communist Party involvement, Dollan remained totally opposed, castigating the CP as 'left wing disrupters'. However, his position appears to

---

was written much later and may be a case of Dollan being wise after the event.

[97] W.W. Knox, *James Maxton* (Manchester, 1987), p. 54. The 'Zinoviev letter' was published in the British press on 25 October 1924, four days before the general election which saw the Conservatives returned to office after Labour's nine month Ministry. Grigori Zinoviev was the head of the Communist or Third International (Comintern) and the letter instructed the British Communist Party to agitate in favour of the ratification of the Treaties between Britain and the Soviet Union which had been one of the major planks of MacDonald's foreign policy. The letter, which went on to detail the necessity of military preparations and ultimately 'armed insurrection', was a forgery which found its way from the Foreign Office to Fleet Street and the Conservative Party at the height of the election campaign and without MacDonald's express instructions. See G. Bennett, *'A most extraordinary and mysterious business': the Zinoviev Letter of 1924* (Foreign and Commonwealth Office, History Notes No. 14, London, 1999).

[98] I.S. Wood, 'Hope Deferred: Labour in Scotland in the 1920s', in I. Donnachie, C. Harvie & I.S. Wood (eds.), *Forward! Labour Politics in Scotland 1888–1988* (Edinburgh, 1989), p. 40.

[99] P.H. Liddell, 'The Role of the Trades Council in the Political and Industrial Life of Glasgow 1858–1976', (unpublished M.Sc. thesis, University of Strathclyde,

have been closer to the views of the ordinary ILP member. When the Trades and Labour Council held a referendum of its affiliated bodies on the question the result was overwhelmingly against affiliation, with ILP branches even more opposed than other affiliated bodies.[100] The outcome of these two debates in 1925 – on MacDonald's leadership and relations with the Communist Party – 'showed quite clearly that it was Dollan, and not Maxton or Wheatley, who was the dominant figure in the west of Scotland ILP.'[101]

The different attitudes towards the CP indicated quite different approaches to political strategy and mobilisation. The Glasgow ILP's electoral successes since 1918 had reinforced a narrow conception of labour representation, one that emphasised the return of candidates more or less as an end in itself. Of course, independent labour representation was the *raison d'être* of the ILP but previously it had been pursued along with a commitment to articulating protest and campaigning with different pressure groups. This was most famously and successfully done over housing, although during the war a whole series of other issues were pursued in a similar way, and this provided the basis both of the ILP's 'popular appeal' and 'pivotal role' within Glasgow.[102] After the defeat of industrial militancy in the early 1920s the ILP was left to concentrate on electioneering but without parallel involvement in grassroots protest movements. Such involvement was possible – in both the National Minority Movement (NMM) within the Unions and the National Unemployed Workers' Movement (NUWM) – but this would have meant co-operating with the Communist Party. While Maxton and Wheatley were prepared to build such temporary alliances, Dollan was not; neither the SDC nor the Glasgow Federation of the ILP gave support to any joint activity with the CP. Those individual branches which were willing to do so ran the risk of punitive measures. For instance three ILP branches were expelled from the Federation in 1927 over the issue of their support for Communist nominees as local Labour candidates.[103]

Dollan's perspective on labour representation sat alongside a similarly gradualist approach to that of MacDonald. When relations between the ILP and the Labour Party deteriorated rapidly with the return of a second Labour Government, Dollan argued that the (minority) Government could not be expected to introduce radical measures for which it had not gained prior approval from the electorate. But this was in effect what the ILP did expect of a Labour Government and had done so since 1925 at least.[104] Maxton and Wheatley had, in a sense, grown beyond a simple faith in labour

1977). p. 33 and generally for detail on the recurring issue of Communist influence within the Council.

[100] The referendum result was 60,227 to 18,780 for the Labour Party's resolution banning all CP affiliation. Twenty-four ILP branches voted in favour of the resolution and only seven opposed it. Knox, 'Not An Ordinary Movement', pp. 166–7.

[101] Knox, 'Not An Ordinary Movement', p. 167.

[102] McKinlay & Smyth, 'Agitator Workman', p. 180.

[103] McKinlay & Smyth, 'Agitator Workman', pp.193–4.

representation. The experience of the 1924 Labour Government taught them that giving a lead was absolutely necessary if any progress towards socialism was to be made. For Dollan, continuing to operate in municipal politics, the overriding purpose remained that of securing a Labour administration; an ambition which was frustratingly close to realisation and which would be jeopardised by any association with the Communists.

Such a position was made easier by the predominant position which the ILP enjoyed within the Labour Party in Scotland. In 1927, the first year individual membership of the Labour Party was collected, Scottish membership stood at just over 11,000 compared to 300,000 for the United Kingdom as a whole. There was little evidence of Labour Party activity in rural constituencies where the ILP took on most of the responsibilities, and in the industrial areas the Divisional Labour Parties remained largely shell organisations, controlled by either the ILP or the unions. At the 1929 general election sixty-seven out of sixty-eight Labour candidates were members of the ILP and thirty of these were direct nominees.[105] Where Dollan differed quite fundamentally from the likes of MacDonald and Snowden was in his commitment to maintaining the ILP as a distinct political entity.[106] At the national level he was not convinced that the ILP should surrender its separate status either by disbanding itself completely or by subsuming itself within the Labour Party. Moreover, Dollan jealously guarded the Glasgow ILP's local strength against any attempted encroachments by the Labour Party.[107]

When, in 1928, the ILP decided that it would finance only those MPs prepared to support *Socialism in Our Time*, a breach with the Labour Party became more likely, if not inevitable. The rationale behind this move was the perceived necessity of the ILP having its own distinctive identity and the means to pursue its own policies. While Labour remained in opposition, conflict between the two parties was manageable, but once Labour was returned to office in 1929 relations quickly deteriorated. Of the almost 300 Labour MPs elected in 1929 some two thirds were members of the ILP, although only thirty-seven of these were direct nominees.[108] However, the vast majority of these nominal ILPers were loyal to MacDonald and Labour rather than to Maxton and the ILP and there was an attempt made to have decisions reached at ILP group meetings in Parliament made binding on all, thus neutralising criticism of the Government. In order to avoid being swamped by this group Maxton had, in effect, to ignore it and declared he would honour the pledges made to his constituents.[109] While Dollan

[104] Dowse, *Left in the Centre*, p. 159.
[105] Brown, 'Labour and Political Change', pp. 365, 370, 375.
[106] Dowse, *Left in the Centre*, p. 148.
[107] McKinlay & Smyth, 'Agitator Workman', pp. 181–2.
[108] Paton, *Left Turn*, p. 317; Dowse, *Left in the Centre*, p. 152. Seventeen of the thirty-seven MPs were returned for Scotland where, in contrast, the Divisional Labour Parties returned only seven candidates.

criticised this cavalier treatment of the majority of MPs, and the Scottish ILP backed him against Maxton, the truth of the matter was that, 'Since the majority were out of sympathy with almost everything the party stood for, to have accepted their verdict was virtually impossible.'[110]

Very quickly the ILP parliamentary group dwindled to about eighteen MPs and this became the core of what was by now 'a permanent opposition within the Labour Party.'[111] The most notable stand which the ILP made against the Government was over unemployment, the issue on which Labour had campaigned at the General Election. The Maxton group raised a series of amendments to the National Insurance Bill which, although they became known as the 'ILP Minimum Demands' were actually based on Labour's own proposals to the Blanesborough Committee on Unemployment Insurance. The ILP particularly objected to the 'Not genuinely seeking work' clause in the Bill, and to the intended provision for the unemployed, e.g. the Government's Bill gave 32s. per week for a family of two adults and three children, whereas at the Blanesborough Committee Labour had proposed 45s.[112] Again and again, the ILP would base its amendments on Labour's own declared policy. As the *Socialist Review* put it: 'The present duty of the ILP itself can be stated in few words. It is to give general support to the Government so long, and only so long as, it does not defy the Labour Party Conference on a major issue.'[113]

The Labour Party's response was to tighten up the Standing Orders placed upon its MPs in parliament. These had been codified in 1928 and permitted MPs to abstain on a matter of conscience but expressly forbade voting against a decision of the PLP. In addition all prospective Labour candidates were to give an undertaking to abide by the Standing Orders.[114] Ultimately this would be the issue which would force the ILP to decide whether or not to stay in the Labour Party. For Labour the presence of a permanent, disruptive opposition existing within its own ranks was intolerable, and the Maxton group of MPs had proved to be the most telling of all the Government's critics.[115] Yet, for the ILP compliance with Standing Orders was equally impossible. It would have meant the negation of the political strategy developed since 1925 and the effective neutering of the ILP as a political entity. The 'great betrayal' of 1931 did not resolve the issue since the ILP saw the actions of MacDonald and Snowden as the logical outcome of Labour's gradualist perspective, a philosophy and strategy shared by the whole leadership and not just a guilty few.[116]

[109] Paton, *Left Turn*, p. 319.

[110] Dowse, *Left in the Centre*, p. 159.

[111] Paton *Left Turn*, p. 323.

[112] Paton, *Left Turn*, p. 318; Dowse, *Left in the Centre*, p. 155.

[113] *The Socialist Review*, April-June 1931, p. 169.

[114] The conscience clause was seen by Paton as 'a sop to the extreme pacifists'. Paton, *Left Turn*, p. 324.

[115] Knox, *Maxton*, pp. 84–6.

The ILP generally, and the left wing in particular, were dealt a body blow by the death of John Wheatley in May 1930. Wheatley had become the main protagonist of the ILP's economic strategy and of its political tactics. His writing and debating skills made him a powerful opponent who commanded respect, if not affection, from the Labour leadership.[117] Wheatley did not enjoy the same easy popularity as Maxton but their complementary gifts made them a formidable team. It must remain an open question whether or not Wheatley would have supported disaffiliation but, while there can be no final answer to such a question, it seems unlikely that the man who had been the most damning critic of the Labour leadership and of the decision to accept minority office again, would have shirked from the final break.[118]

The ensuing by-election in Glasgow created more friction between the ILP and Labour as John McGovern was selected by the Shettleston ILP to fight the seat. The nomination of McGovern and his election became shrouded in controversy as a series of charges were made against him by local right-wing forces in the Labour Party. These included claims that he had used delegates with forged credentials to secure his nomination, that he had opportunistically rejoined the Catholic Church for election purposes, and even that he had worked during the General Strike. Although he gave assurances that he would obey Standing Orders, McGovern went on to join with Maxton and the other rebel MPs in the Commons.[119] Later in the year there was another by-election in East Renfrewshire where another ILPer was selected to contest the seat for Labour. The candidate refused to give the loyalty pledge on Standing Orders and, two weeks into the campaign, the Labour Party announced it was withholding its endorsement and support. Not surprisingly, in what was a secure Tory seat, the ILP trailed some seven thousand votes behind the Marquess of Douglas and Clydesdale. 'This was really a declaration of war by the Labour Party, and was so regarded by the ILP.'[120]

Even so the leadership of the ILP had still not decided for disaffiliation. As late as November 1931 Maxton spoke out against disaffiliation at a Conference in Glasgow.[121] However, the Labour Party had refused to endorse

---

[116] Knox, *Maxton*, pp. 95–6.
[117] Oswald Mosley famously compared Wheatley to Lenin. For this and other contemporary views of Wheatley see, Howell, *Lost Left*, p. 29
[118] Knox, *Maxton*, pp. 100–1. Wood reviews the debate on either side and appears to suggest that had he lived Wheatley would have sought an accommodation with the Labour Party, Wood, *Wheatley*, pp. 198–9.
[119] 'John McGovern', in Knox, *Labour Leaders*, p. 177. McGovern himself claimed that *Forward* had 'twisted' an interview with him and he had not given any such assurances, J. McGovern, *Neither Fear Nor Favour* (London, 1960), p. 69.
[120] Paton, *Left Turn*, p. 339. See also *The Socialist Review*, Dec. 1930, pp. 57–8, which made a direct connection between Labour's action at East Renfrew and the Government's 'surrender to the capitalist parties over the Education Bill' to ask whether 'the breaking point' had been reached.

the ILP's sitting MPs at the General Election a few weeks earlier and continued to refuse to reach any accommodation over Standing Orders. These actions, and a critical decline in ILP membership, convinced Maxton that immediate disaffiliation was the only solution. The election had seen the ILP parliamentary group reduced to four, of whom three – Maxton, McGovern and Buchanan – stood for Glasgow constituencies while Kirkwood stood in nearby Dumbarton. In this 'unmitigated disaster' the ILP shared the fate of the Labour Party which managed to return fifty-two candidates in total and only seven in Scotland.[122]

At the Divisional conferences of the ILP held in January 1932 disaffiliation was the big question. At the Scottish conference Maxton argued passionately in favour of breaking with the Labour Party but the majority supported Dollan, though while voting for continued affiliation the delegates also wanted Standing Orders to be amended. This was the position taken by most of the Divisions and was reaffirmed at the ILP's national conference in March. However, there was no realistic prospect of any accommodation being reached with the Labour Party over Standing Orders and a specially convened conference was called for July to decide the matter once and for all. In June the National Committee voted to recommend disaffiliation – with only Dollan opposed – and the following month delegates to the Special conference confirmed this by 241 to 142 votes.[123] This decision was not taken lightly; there was little expectation that the ILP would replace the Labour Party. For John Paton, the General Secretary of the party who had previously opposed disaffiliation, it was a Hobson's choice; either a long, slow death within the Labour Party (being inside had not stemmed the haemorrhage of members), or a quick death by disaffiliation which at least offered the possibility, 'that we might so command the circumstances as to emerge triumphantly a stronger Party than ever before.'[124] Paton did oppose the 'clean break' strategy and wanted the disaffiliation to be on the national level only. His hope was that this would force the initiative onto the Labour Party to act against members in their localities, and that faced with disciplinary measures more members would choose to remain with the ILP. However, the clean break prevailed and very soon old comrades were facing each other across the electoral barricades.

---

[121] Dowse, *Left in the Centre*, p. 177.

[122] I. Donnachie, 'Scottish Labour in the Depression', in Donnachie, Harvie & Wood, *Forward!*, p.54.; The 'total' Labour figures include six MPs who had not been endorsed by the Party. These include the four ILPers which meant that in Scotland the ILP had more MPs than the Labour Party, though Kirkwood soon moved to Labour. F.W.S. Craig, *British Electoral Facts 1832–1987* (Aldershot, 1989), pp. 30–1.

[123] Dowse, *Left in the Centre*, pp. 178,183; McKinlay & Smyth, 'Agitator Workman', pp. 197–8.

Conclusion

The fall-out of from the disaffiliation of the ILP will be detailed in chapter six, but here we shall conclude on the divergence between Labour's performance at the Municipal and Parliamentary polls. Labour's continuing success in the latter threw into sharp relief its position in the former, where it appeared stuck as a permanent, if substantial, minority. In the general election of 1929, the first held under the equal franchise for men and women, Labour were returned to power at Westminster as the largest single party; while in Scotland Labour gained an overall majority of seats and in Glasgow won ten of the City's fifteen divisions. On a strictly proportionate basis Labour was over-represented in Glasgow; with 52% of the vote it got two thirds of the seats. Moreover, as in 1922 and 1923 Labour benefited from a split right-wing vote; the Liberals contested four seats in 1929 and their intervention gave Labour victory in Partick.[125] Even with these qualifications, however, the contrast with the municipal situation is very clear.

One explanation for this discrepancy may be the more restricted franchise which operated at the municipal level. As discussed earlier (see Introduction) the municipal franchise differed in certain important respects from the parliamentary franchise. Essentially the Representation of the People Act established residence as the qualification for a parliamentary vote but retained occupation as the qualification for the municipal vote.[126] This created an anomaly for women in that a single woman could qualify for the local vote at the age of twenty-one while a married woman had to wait till she was thirty. Of more significance, however, was the difficulty that young single men had getting the municipal vote. While the two franchises were much the same for women, in the case of men only one million of the four million men given the parliamentary vote under the 1918 reform, also qualified for the municipal vote.[127] Whether and to what extent this had an adverse impact on Labour's performance in local elections is difficult to establish. One view is that there was no class bias operating, 'As contemporaries agreed, it was single people, of all classes, who failed to qualify for the municipal franchise.'[128]

However, irrespective of the judgement of posterity it is clear that Labour felt it was losing potential voters. The Scottish Council of the Labour Party took issue with the 1918 legislation on exactly this point, i.e. the treatment of lodgers, and claimed that the situation was worse than it had been previously. Labour also pointed out the absurdity of single and married women being treated differently and was to call, repeatedly, for a simplified Register

[124] Paton, *Left Turn*, p. 388.
[125] Craig, *Election Results 1918–1949*, p. 594.
[126] M. Pugh, *Electoral Reform in War and Peace, 1906–1918* (London, 1978), p. 112.
[127] D. Tanner, *Political Change and the Labour Party 1900–1918* (Cambridge, 1990), p. 389.
[128] Tanner, *Political Change*, p. 389.

based on adult suffrage for national and local elections.[129] William Regan, the Glasgow ILP Organiser and a Town councillor, spelt out the electoral impact much more clearly:

> The Parliamentary register is infinitely more favourable to Labour than the Municipal register. Thousands of young men (and they are usually Labour supporters) are entitled to the Parliamentary vote on reaching 21, but are disfranchised at the local poll through the absence of a property qualification. Again, in the middle-class parts of every Ward there are large houses comprising young ladies who qualify for the Municipal vote through their property, but who being under 30 years have no Parliamentary vote. These well-to-do young ladies are usually anti-Labour.[130]

There is fairly strong evidence from the electoral registers to substantiate these claims. Although the discrepancy varied, there was always a shortfall in the municipal register compared to the parliamentary. For the city as a whole this was some tens of thousands of voters but, since some parts of the municipal burgh lay outside the contours of the parliamentary burgh, it is impossible to establish the precise difference. However, it is clear that there were marked discrepancies amongst the various parts of the City. In the middle class parts of the City there was no major disparity between the two electorates; in fact, more people seemed to have the municipal than the parliamentary vote. Thus, in 1922 in the two southern suburban Divisions of Pollok and Cathcart there was a higher number of municipal than parliamentary electors.[131] This could be explained simply by the fact that in both the municipal wards covered a larger area than the parliamentary divisions. But, in Hillhead, where the Parliamentary boundary was exactly that of the Municipal Wards of Kelvinside and Partick East, the same pattern can be seen; there were some 772 more municipal electors than parliamentary. In contrast, the working class areas of the city had considerably fewer people with the municipal than the parliamentary vote. In Shettleston (comprising the wards Shettleston & Tollcross and Parkhead) and Gorbals (comprising Hutchesontown and Gorbals wards) the municipal electorate was only about 85% of the parliamentary.[132] In addition, all the middle class wards had a majority female electorate.

The article by Regan quoted above was written after the local elections of 1920 and its author was at pains to draw out the implications for the next general election. By combining the wards into their respective divisions,

---

[129] Scottish Advisory Council of the Labour Party, *Report of Fourth Annual Conference 1918*, p. 4. See also *Report 1919*, pp. 11, 45–6, and *Report 1921*, p. 37.

[130] *Forward* 13 Nov. 1920; Brown, 'Labour and Political Change', p. 142.

[131] The number of 'additional' municipal electors were 2435 in Pollok and 1014 in Cathcart. Figures are taken from the *Glasgow Post Office Directory 1922–23*.

[132] In other localities, such as mining areas, there was an even greater disparity between the national and local electorates, due to young miners continuing to live with parents or as lodgers. S. MacIntyre, *Little Moscows* (London, 1980), p. 180.

Regan was able to show that five Divisions now had Labour majorities: Shettleston, Bridgeton, Springburn, Gorbals and Govan. In addition he pinpointed four more, St. Rollox, Maryhill, Tradeston and Camlachie, where municipal minorities ought to be converted into parliamentary majorities. This was because of the more generous parliamentary franchise, and the expectation that Labour would gain votes that had gone to independent and unofficial Labour candidates at the local polls. We have already established that Labour's ten gains at the 1922 general election were foreshadowed by its performance at the local poll shortly beforehand.[133] However, these figures show only six seats with clear Labour majorities; the five given by Regan plus St. Rollox. In fact Regan's analysis proved very prescient as the nine Divisions he identified were all won by Labour in 1922. The additional gain of Cathcart was due to the unforeseen divisions between National Liberals and Unionists and was never repeated.

Immediately after the General Election the ILP conducted examinations into the successful campaigns in the various Divisions. Maryhill, which was narrowly won in a three-cornered contest, was given particular attention. On the basis of municipal contests Labour expected a vote of over 10,000 but, in addition, there were 3,640 category 'D' voters in the Division, 'young men who have only the Parliamentary vote.' Labour were 'confident of capturing the young men's vote' and they directed special effort towards the 'D' voters. Recognising that some municipal electors did not have the Parliamentary vote, nevertheless, 'we felt that the young men voters would more than compensate us for that loss.' Labour's calculations were uncannily accurate: they polled 13,058 votes and John Muir took the seat from the Conservatives by a majority of 2,107.[134] Labour's success in Maryhill during the 1920s, they won the seat in 1922 and 1923, lost it in 1924 but regained it in 1929, contrasts with their municipal performance. Three wards, Maryhill, North Kelvin and Ruchill, comprised the Division and none were safe Labour seats; North Kelvin never returned a Labour councillor, Maryhill was solidly Moderate after 1920 with a single Labour victory in 1929, and only Ruchill gave Labour any sort of success, with three victories between 1921 and 1930. Tradeston and Camlachie showed very similar patterns; the Parliamentary Divisions were solidly Labour in the four general elections of the 1920s but this success was not replicated at the municipal level

The franchise, therefore, remained an issue after 1918 and not only for the restrictions placed on young women qualifying for the parliamentary vote. There appears to have been an equal determination not to allow young men unfettered access to the local franchise.[135] Labour certainly felt that

---

[133] McLean, *Legend*, pp. 162–3. See page 17 above.

[134] *Forward*, 2 Dec. 1922.

[135] Robert Munro the Liberal Secretary for Scotland in 1918 refused an amendment from William Adamson, Labour MP from Fife to make registration by lodgers free from financial qualification. 'Munro rejected this as tantamount to adult suffrage for lodgers . . .'. Pugh, *Electoral Reform*, pp. 122–3.

this had a detrimental effect upon their support as they were more likely to be the major recipient of such votes which, given the radicalising effect of the war years and after on young workers, seems a likely proposition.[136] It is interesting to note than even when the discrepancy in the treatment of young women was ironed out of the parliamentary franchise in 1928 there was no comparable reform of the local government franchise. It is possible, therefore, that had there been full adult suffrage at every level of government Labour would have enjoyed greater success in municipal elections, that a number of the more marginal wards might have shifted to Labour and the Moderate majority been under greater pressure.

However, under the system which was in operation, the Moderate coalition proved to be remarkably successful. Apart from the odd scare, as in 1926, the broad anti-Socialist alliance proved to be disciplined and resilient. Labour's emergence as a major political force was apparent at the municipal elections of 1919 and 1920, and its dominance of Glasgow appeared assured with the dramatic triumphs in the General Election of 1922. However, Labour found it impossible to translate this success into the formation of a socialist Town Council. Looking back at the end of a decade of trying to wrest control of the Council from the Moderates, the Glasgow ILP concluded that, in terms of increasing Labour representation, 'No progress had been made since 1920.'[137]

[136] On young workers attracted to the ILP during the war see McKinlay, 'Doubtful Wisdom', pp. 127, 139.

[137] Glasgow ILP Federation, Management Committee, minutes, 23 May 1930. This was a meeting called to discuss increasing Labour representation with the ILP Town councillors. Perhaps revealingly, of the 33 councillors invited only eight bothered to attend.

CHAPTER FOUR

The Irish and Labour

The relationship between the Irish and Labour demands specific attention simply because of the massive significance accorded to the political role played by the Catholic-Irish community in Scotland. The orthodox analysis of the Irish is essentially a negative one: prior to the first World War it was the Irish who held Labour back because their primary commitment to winning Home Rule for Ireland ensured that they voted Liberal rather than Labour. Furthermore, once the constitutional status of Ireland had been settled by 1922 the Irish did come over to Labour but, though their electoral support was crucial, they brought with them the corrupting influence of their 'machine' politics. This is the view of the Irish which has become a mainstay of historical explanation.[1] The perspective taken here is quite different and it is intended to show that the Irish were simply never sufficiently numerous to play such a determining role – it often appears to be forgotten that they were a minority – and that their relationship with Labour was both more complicated, and more positive, than the usual chronology allows for.[2]

The traditional view of the Irish and Labour before the War is offered by J.G. Kellas:

> One important factor which weakened the Labour movement in Scotland was the hostility of the Roman Catholics. As long as Home Rule depended on the Liberals, the Catholics voted for them and the Labour party was deprived of much of its potential working class vote.[3]

From regarding the Irish as a contributory factor to attaching to them the whole blame for the weakness of Labour is but a short step. Elsewhere, Kellas

---

[1] It is to be found in the following, J.G. Kellas, *Modern Scotland: The nation since 1870* (2nd. Edition, London, 1980); T.C. Smout, *A Century of the Scottish People* (London, 1986); C. Harvie, *No Gods and Precious Few Heroes* (Edinburgh, 1993); I. McLean, *The Legend of Red Clydeside* (Edinburgh, 1983); M. Fry, *Patronage and Principle: A Political history of Modern Scotland* (Aberdeen, 1987); M. Keating, *The City That Refused To Die* (Aberdeen, 1988); I. Levitt, *Poverty and Welfare in Scotland 1890–1948* (Edinburgh, 1988).

[2] The most thoroughgoing critique of the 'orthodoxy' is J.F. McCaffrey, 'Irish Issues in the Nineteenth and Twentieth Century: Radicalism in a Scottish context?', in T.M. Devine (ed.), *Irish Immigrants and Scottish Society in the Nineteenth and Twentieth Centuries* (Edinburgh, 1991). See also T. Gallagher, *Glasgow: The Uneasy Peace* (Manchester, 1987); I.S. Wood, 'John Wheatley, The Irish and the Labour Movement in Scotland', *The Innes Review*, xxxi (1980).

[3] Kellas, *Modern Scotland*, p. 140.

has been even more forthright, 'It was the attitude of the Irish working class which prevented the emergence of a strong Labour movement in Scotland, until Irish Home Rule was solved.'[4] The work of William Walker adds weight to this view by emphasising the Church-oriented basis of Irish nationalist politics hostile to both secular ideologies, especially if they smacked of socialism, and any weakening of the Home Rule vote.[5]

This essentially negative picture has been modified by other historians who have commented upon the positive, active role played by individual Irishmen and Irish organisations alongside of, and within the Labour movement. Wood in particular questions Walker on, 'Whether Irish na-tionalism in Scotland was always inimical to any immigrant rapport on class issues with Scottish trade unionists and radical movements.'[6] Similarly, McCaffrey sees the Irish vote in Scotland as, 'a conditional vote, organised and given to whatever power in the State would accede to Catholic wishes as expressed in this conjunction of religion and nationality'.[7] Furthermore, by attempting to quantify the Irish electorate, McCaffrey calls into question the supposed significance of the 'Irish vote', especially before the 1918 Reform Act, as well as indicating cracks in its supposed monolithic nature. Thus, on occasion the Irish vote, or parts of it, went to Labour, while a general level of enfranchisement of 50% of Irish male householders must have seriously limited the impact of that vote, even if it was united.[8]

The Catholic-Irish Community

Irish migration to Scotland began in the late eighteenth century as increasing numbers of migrant workers decided to stay on permanently. The developing economy with its constant need for labour was a strong pull of attraction and even before the famine the number of Irish born in Glasgow was 44,000 or 16% of the total population.[9] Thereafter, the Irish continued to arrive (though for many Scotland was simply a temporary stage in a longer journey);

---

[4] J.G. Kellas, 'The Mid-Lanark By-election (1888) and the Scottish Labour Party (1888–1894)' *Parliamentary Affairs,* xviii (1965) p. 323.

[5] W.M. Walker, 'Irish Immigrants in Scotland: their Priests, Politics and Parochial Life', *Historical Journal,* xv (1972), pp. 649–67. Walker deals only with the Irish in Dundee, not in Scotland as a whole, and he says almost nothing about the Irish National League.

[6] I.S. Wood, 'Irish Immigrants and Scottish Radicalism', in . MacDougall (ed.), *Essays in Scottish Labour History,* I (Edinburgh, 1978) p. 68. See also Wood, 'Wheatley, The Irish and Labour', p. 73 where he is more definite on this point.

[7] J. McCaffrey, 'Politics and the Irish community Since 1878' in D. MacRoberts (ed.), *Modern Scottish Catholicism* (Glasgow, 1979), p. 146.

[8] J. McCaffrey, 'The Irish Vote in Glasgow in the Later Nineteenth Century: a preliminary survey', *Innes Review,* xxi (1970), pp. 30–6.

[9] W. Knox, 'The Political and Workplace culture of the Scottish Working Class, 1832–1914', in W.H. Fraser & R.J. Morris (eds.), *People and Society in Scotland, Vol. 2 1832–1914,* (Edinburgh, 1990), p. 141.

in 1851 the number of Irish-born in Scotland was 207,000 and in 1901 this figure remained more or less unchanged at 205,000.[10] The tiny indigenous Catholic population was simply swamped by these new arrivals and ultimately in Scotland the terms 'Irish' and 'Catholic' became synonymous.[11] Yet not all the Irish were Catholic: with the majority of Irish migrants to Scotland coming from the nine counties of Ulster and including industrial workers as well as peasants, a large proportion of the incomers were Protestants. Estimated at 25% of the Irish born in Glasgow in the 1860s, it is impossible to give an accurate breakdown thereafter but the numbers remained substantial.[12] Although not all of these were skilled artisans, many were industrial workers from Belfast and this, as well as their Protestantism, made it easier for them to assimilate with the host community.[13]

It was the Ulster Protestants who brought the Orange order to Scotland and it was often felt that the violent clashes between Orangemen and Catholics in industrial Scotland was a continuation of Irish sectarianism. Many Scottish Protestants did not look kindly on this other Irish import, yet the Order flourished and provided Scottish Conservatism with much needed working class support.[14] While the attention recently given to the Protestant Irish provides a welcome addition and corrective to much of the existing historical record, it remains the case that the bulk of immigrants were Catholic and it was these people and their descendants whom most contemporaries were referring to when they spoke, disparagingly or otherwise, of the 'Irish'.

The Catholic population of Scotland declined throughout the eighteenth century and has been estimated at only 30,000 souls by 1800. Thereafter, fuelled by Irish incomers it rose substantially; by 1851 it has been estimated at 145,900 and by 1901 at 446,000 or 10% of the Scottish population. Most of this number were concentrated in the south-west central area, especially Glasgow and Lanarkshire. In 1851, 66,300 Catholics accounted for 12.5% of the population of the county of Lanark and in 1901 there were 186,100 Catholics in the City of Glasgow, 17.6% of the total population.[15] This was an

---

[10] B. Collins, 'The Origins of Irish Immigration to Scotland in Nineteenth and Twentieth Centuries', in Devine, *Irish Immigrants and Scottish Society*, p. 1.

[11] The Scottish Catholic clergy resisted this Irish colonisation for some time but ultimately the number of priests needed by the rapidly growing community could only be provided from Ireland or the Scots born descendants of Irish migrants. Gallagher, *Uneasy Peace*, pp. 11–12, 42–7.

[12] Gallagher, *Uneasy Peace*, p. 27; Collins, 'Origins of Irish Immigration', pp. 14–15.

[13] G. Walker, 'The Protestant Irish in Scotland' in Devine *Irish Immigrants and Scottish Society*, pp. 44–66.

[14] E. McFarland, *Protestants First: Orangeism in 19th. Century Scotland* (Edinburgh, 1990), pp. 160–89; see also A.B. Campbell, *The Lanarkshire Miners: A Social history of their Trade Unions 1775–1874* (Edinburgh, 1979), and Walker, 'Protestant Irish'.

[15] Estimated population figures from J. Darragh, 'The Catholic Population of Scotland, 1878–1977', in *Modern Scottish Catholicism*, pp. 211–47; see also Gallagher, *Uneasy Peace*, p. 9.

overwhelmingly working class community, indeed, of the poorer working class as most found work in the unskilled sector of the jobs market.[16] Prejudice, discrimination and the independent, but seriously underfunded, Catholic education system were reasons why young Catholics failed to move up the jobs ladder in Scotland. Their lack of social mobility has been unfavourably compared not only to the experience of Irish migrant communities in the USA, but also in chronically sectarian Liverpool.[17]

Statistical data on occupation by religion is not available, but the Census of 1911 does provide valuable information on the occupations of persons of Irish birth resident in Scotland. The principal occupations of Irish born males in Glasgow are tabulated below.

The eleven principal occupations listed in Table One are those in which more that 500 Irish-born males were employed and together they represent 42.4% of the Irish-born male workforce compared to 22.8% of the total male workforce. No fewer than four are explicitly described as labouring jobs and these alone account for just under 20% of the Irish-born male workforce, compared to just 6.4% of the total male workforce. In all of these occupations with only two exceptions the Irish are over-represented in terms of their overall proportion of the occupied male population. The essentially unskilled, or at best semi-skilled manual nature of the Irish worker is well attested.

Some added light on social structure of the Irish community is provided by Table Two. As we might expect the Irish are very much under-represented in the Professions – Law, Medicine, Education.[18] The numbers employed as Builders, Masons, and Bricklayers contrasts sharply with the figure in Table One for the labourers in these trades; in the former the Irish are under-represented while in the latter they are massively over-represented. Barmen and Publicans are included here due to the significance attached to the 'drink trade' within the political life of the community and, conforming to the myth about Catholics and publicans, the Irish are over-represented in these two groups. However, the importance of the drink trade possibly arises from the fact that it was one of the few commercial opportunities open to them.

There are two ways in which this information is limited. One is that it tells us nothing about the majority of the Irish community, i.e. those who were actually born in Scotland and, secondly, there is no way of distinguishing between Protestant and Catholic. Although historians of the Protestant-Irish have warned about assuming all Protestants from Ulster were skilled workers, it is still reasonable to assume that significantly more Protestant Irish

---

[16] J.E. Handley, *The Irish in Modern Scotland* (Cork, 1947), pp. 122–63.

[17] Gallagher, *Uneasy Peace*, pp. 60–1.

[18] There had been little change over the previous decades as in 1880 there were only six Catholics studying in Glasgow University, five in medicine and one in law. Gallagher, *Uneasy Peace*, p. 61.

Table 1: Principal Occupations of Irish-Born Males in Glasgow, 1911.

Total Irish-born male workforce = 26,062
Total Male Workforce = 253,210
Irish-born as proportion of total workforce = 10.3%

OCCUPATIONS	(A)	(B)	(C)
General labourers	1959	7293	26.9%
Dock/Quay labourers	1561	3973	39.3%
Ironfounders	1497	9155	16.4%
Iron, steel, tube manufacture	1040	5246	19.8%
Builders', masons' Bricklayers' labourers	995	2112	47.1%
Vanmen, Lorrymen, Carriers, Carters	866	11017	7.9%
Gas Works Service	832	2557	32.5%
Undefined workers in Engine and machine making	646	7970	8.1%
Omnibus and tram service	583	2883	20.2%
Boot, &c. – Makers, Dealers	550	2871	19.2%
Labourers in Engineering Works	525	2775	18.9%
TOTAL	11054	57852	19.1%

Note:
Column A = No. of Irish born employed in each occupation
Column B = No. of all employed in each occupation
Column C = Irish-born as proportion of all employed in each occupation

Table 2: Other (Selected) Occupations of Irish-Born Males in Glasgow, 1911.

OCCUPATIONS	(A)	B)	(C)
Barmen	215	1172	18.3%
Inn, Hotel Keepers: Publicans, Beersellers, Wine and Spirit Merchants, Agents	296	1954	15.2%
Builders, Bricklayers, & Masons	231	2826	8.2%
Advocates, Solicitors	1	473	0.2%
Physicians, Surgeons, Registered Practitioners	9	520	1.7%
Schoolmasters, Teachers, Professors, Lecturers	35	1036	3.4%

would be found in the skilled trades than their Catholic counterparts.[19] The census figures, therefore, would seem to underestimate the unskilled nature of the Catholic-Irish workforce. Furthermore, most historical and literary accounts agree that there was little change between generations, 'until the 1950s and 1960s at the very earliest.'[20]

[19] Walker, *Protestant Irish*, pp. 58–9; McFarland, *Protestants First*, p. 10.
[20] Gallagher, *Uneasy Peace*, p. 59.

The Nationalist Vote, 1885–1895

By the end of the nineteenth century, when Labour began its effort to establish an electoral presence in Glasgow, the Irish were an established part of the political life of the City. The collapse of 'fenianism' in the late 1860s left the way open for the constitutional home rule movement. Isaac Butt, the founder of the Home Government League in Dublin in 1870, was invited to Glasgow the following year to spread the agitation to the mainland. Out of his meeting emerged the Home Government Branch (HGB) which, through all the vicissitudes of the nationalist movement in the following decades, was to remain 'the most influential sector in Great Britain of the movement.'[21] The emergence of Parnell and the formation of the Irish National League of Great Britain (INL) in the 1880s saw greater efforts to mobilise the Irish electorate. Parliamentary elections were all important but there was also concern at local government level, especially as regards School Boards, to secure Irish or Catholic representation.[22] A Catholic Union was set up by Archbishop Eyre in Glasgow which worked closely with the INL branches in getting Irish voters onto the electoral register.[23] Therefore, there existed not only an Irish community, but also an Irish vote. Given the overwhelmingly working class nature of this community it is hardly surprising that Labour would seek to make direct appeal to it.

The year 1885 saw the Irish political forces in Glasgow develop a greater cohesiveness. This was the year of the first general election since Parnell had assumed the leadership of the Irish Party and it was to be fought under his new, aggressive tactics which, in this instance, meant the unusual step of recommending that the Irish community in Britain should vote for Conservative candidates as Parnell felt that the best hope of Home Rule came from this direction. The *Glasgow Observer* was also established in the same year, giving the Irish community in the city their first regular journal since the demise of the *Free Press* in 1868.[24] Moreover, unlike its predecessor, the *Observer* did not clash with the hierarchy but was in broad agreement with the Church over political matters; the closeness of the relationship indicated by sales of the *Observer* at the back of the Chapel.[25]

The one point of friction was the differing emphasis put on Home Rule and Catholic education, with the *Observer* insisting on the primacy of the former over all other considerations. The results of the School Board elections in 1885 were analysed by the *Observer*, 'to demonstrate the self-

[21] Handley, *Irish in Modern Scotland* , p. 270.

[22] Wood, 'Irish Immigrants', pp. 70–1.

[23] McCaffrey, 'Politics and the Irish Community', p. 146.

[24] Handley, *Irish in Modern Scotland*, pp. 278–9.

[25] A practice that continues today. O.D. Edwards, 'The Catholic Press in Scotland since the Restoration of the Hierarchy', in MacRoberts, *Modern Scottish Catholicism*.

confidence that Catholics could feel through effective electoral organisation.'[26] While the cumulative vote used for School Board elections allowed direct Irish-Catholic representation, such success could not be repeated at either the Parliamentary or even Municipal level. Nevertheless, it could encourage an awareness of electoral strength and further efforts at organisation, as well as raising unrealistic hopes of securing Irish-Catholic MPs and town councillors. The rapid development of the INL meant that it, 'could claim from 1885 to be the fastest growing political organisation in Scotland'; at its strongest it had over a hundred branches and while Glasgow had relatively few, the City was home to the largest branches and the most prominent activists such as John Ferguson.[27]

Parnell's instruction to vote Tory in 1885 cut across established Irish voting behaviour and the interests of the Irish working class in Britain. The disciplined response within Irish ranks emphasises the dominance of the national question to the Irish community. Nevertheless, there were some problems in realising total support for the leadership's call. The most prominent figure in this respect was John Ferguson who had openly questioned Parnell's policy.

In and around Glasgow there were a number of candidates run by the left-wing, pro-land nationalisation organisation the Scottish Land Restoration League (SLRL), which did have sympathisers amongst the Irish community. Ferguson supported the candidature of James Shaw Maxwell in Blackfriars & Hutchesontown, who also received the endorsement of Michael Davitt.[28] Of the five SLRL challenges, only this one and Bridgeton were serious, the other three candidates being run as reprisals against the Liberals for not allowing two straight fights against the Tories.[29] Shaw Maxwell's support for the Irish Land League had made him 'particularly popular with many of the Glasgow Irish' and this may have had something to do with his relatively high poll.[30] While Ferguson was censured by the Executive for his role at the election, a majority of his own branch, the HGB, gave him a vote of confidence, and his stature in the movement seems to have encouraged the Executive to leave matters alone.[31] There is no suggestion of a split away from the Executive but it does seem likely that a number of Irish were prepared to follow Ferguson's example and in Blackfriars the local INL was

[26] McCaffrey, 'Politics and the Irish Community', p. 147.

[27] Wood, 'Irish Immigrants', p. 71.

[28] Wood, 'Irish Immigrants', p. 72.

[29] *Labour Leader*,1 Dec. 1905. Article by J. Bruce Glasier, 'Socialism Twenty Years Ago'. See also J.J. Smyth, 'Labour and Socialism in Glasgow: the Electoral Challenge Prior to Democracy' (unpublished Ph.D.thesis, University of Edinburgh, 1987), pp. 13–17, 75–6.

[30] Wood, 'Irish Immigrants', p. 72. While the three spoiling candidates averaged a derisory one per cent, the two bona fide candidates in Hutchesontown and Townhead managed 14.4% and 12.1% of the poll respectively. F.W.S. Craig, *British Parliamentary Election Results 1885–1918* (London, 1974), pp. 503–4.

[31] Handley, *Irish in Modern Scotland*, p. 276.

divided on the matter with many supporting Shaw Maxwell.[32] As we shall see, this sort of division within a supposedly monolithic vote was to be a recurring phenomenon.

The general election of 1886 saw no radical or labour candidates (the term 'labour' was sometimes applied to the SLRL candidates), but Keir Hardie's challenge at the Mid Lanark by-election in 1888 saw Ferguson step out of line once again. While so much has been written about Mid Lanark as a milestone in the formation of the Labour Party it only has this significance in retrospect; at the time it was simply part of a series of 'one off' initiatives which cumulatively led to the beginnings of independent labour represen-tation.[33] A great deal has also been made of the role of the Irish vote which, it has been argued, by being withheld from Hardie, was the prime cause of his defeat.[34] Yet, given estimates of the total Irish electorate in the con-stituency of only some 900 (10% of the total), even had Hardie won all of these votes he would still have come last.[35] In fact it seems likely that Hardie did receive some Irish support. Handley, who tends to downplay the Labour and Socialist influence on the Irish community, comments that Hardie's stand, 'caused a split in the Irish vote', and that 'A third of the delegates at a conference of Hardie's supporters were Irishmen.'[36]

Even so Hardie's performance was not as good as Shaw Maxwell's had been: 8% of the poll compared to over 14%. Hardie's low poll, after much optimism, may have been due to an increasing awareness that he was not going to win and therefore a vote for him would be 'wasted'. Even John Ferguson was secretly urging withdrawal while still helping to organise the campaign. Ferguson reckoned Hardie would be lucky to get 300 votes and hoped to broker a deal whereby 'labour' would declare for the Liberal in return for Liberal support for Hardie the next time round.[37] Ferguson's own preference was for labour to work through the Liberal Associations, though he approved of continued agitation and became one of the Honorary Presidents of the Scottish Labour Party formed later in 1888.[38]

The 1892 general election saw, for the first time, a definite Labour challenge at the polls. In Scotland seven 'Labour' candidates stood: three from the Scottish Labour Party (SLP) with two in Glasgow seats, and four from the Scottish United Trades Council Labour party (SUTCLP) with one

---

[32] McCaffrey, 'Politics and the Irish Community', p. 148.

[33] For Mid Lanark and the Scottish Labour Party see Smyth, 'Labour and Socialism', pp. 57–70.

[34] Kellas, 'Mid-Lanark By-election', pp. 322–3.

[35] H. Pelling, *The Social Geography of British Elections 1885–1910* (London, 1967), p. 408; McCaffrey, 'Politics and the Irish Community', p. 150.

[36] Handley, *Irish in Modern Scotland*, p. 277.

[37] ILP Archive, Francis Johnston Correspondence, 1888/43, John Ferguson to R.B. Cunninghame-Graham, 11 April 1888. In the end no such deal was struck and Hardie managed over 600 votes.

[38] ILP Archive, Francis Johnston Correspondence, 1888/43, John Ferguson to Keir Hardie, 17 May 1888. See Chapter One p. 4.

in Glasgow. All stood against Liberals and all lost heavily, though in Camlachie and Tradeston, the Labour intervention may have been responsible for the Liberals losing the seats to Liberal Unionists.[39] However, for the Irish this was an election where maximum effort and unity had to be thrown behind the Gladstonian Liberals who had, apparently, committed themselves to Home Rule. The *Observer* was in no mood to encourage any sympathies for Labour candidates. It recognised Labour's right to assert its own independence but questioned the bona fides of the Labour candidates: Cunninghame Graham (Camlachie) was 'a Scottish landlord', Bennet Burleigh (Tradeston) was a 'Unionist journalist' and even Keir Hardie was dismissed as a carpet bagger. Warming to its theme, the *Observer* concluded that 'Irish workers will note the game of these men is obviously to put Home Rule to one side, and also to put the land question out of sight.'[40] The fact that Bennet Burleigh had come within 159 votes of winning Camlachie for the Liberal Unionists in 1886 gave this view a degree of credence.

The immediate provocation for this attack was a statement by Cunninghame Graham that he was quite pleased about Michael Davitt's defeat at the Waterford by-election by John Redmond, leader of the Parnellites, which group the *Observer* violently opposed. However, the fundamental difference remained that of rival attitudes to the Liberal Party, upon which all hopes of Home Rule seemed to lie. Yet, not all Irish opinion in Glasgow was so hostile to Labour: John Ferguson, in particular, tried to find middle ground where both Liberal and Labour support could be accommodated.

Ferguson's argument was that Home Rule and the cause of labour were inextricably intertwined. The early movement, led by Butt, had looked to the Irish aristocracy to achieve Home Rule but this had led nowhere, whereas the new movement, led by Parnell, had been stimulated by 'economic and democratic forces'. Not only were the Irish masses galvanised by the new approach of Home Rule and land reform but so were the British working men; the 'labour' candidates of 1885 were supportive and Highland crofter agitation had been based on the Irish example. According to Ferguson, 'I know of no labour leader who is not upon the Irish side.'[41] Ferguson wanted the Liberals to leave the 'two or three dozen of Labour candidates' unopposed and also wanted to avoid 'another Irish blunder' like Mid-Lanark when Parnell opposed Hardie in order to please Gladstone.

[39] In both these seats the combined Liberal and Labour vote would have defeated the successful Liberal Unionists. Tradeston was already held by the Liberal Unionists but Camlachie was a Liberal seat. Craig, *Election Results 1885–1918*, pp. 505, 509.

[40] *Glasgow Observer*, 9 Jan. 1892.

[41] Ferguson's position was stated at some length in a letter to the press entitled, 'The Revolt of Labour and the Triumph of Home Rule'. It was published in full in the *Glasgow Observer*, 9 Jan. 1892.

This was little different to the attitude of Hardie who, like Ferguson, compared the Labour party to the tactics and history of the Irish Party.[42] The SLP conference in January 1892 contemplated twelve candidates in Scotland (plus one in Carlisle). But the 'independent' nature of these men was not clear since Hardie claimed Cunninghame Graham to be the officially adopted Liberal candidate for Camlachie and Bennet Burleigh was 'likely' to be adopted by the Liberal Association in Tradeston.[43] In the event both had to fight against official Liberal opponents and this was the dilemma which could not be avoided for ever: what did the proponents of Labour representation do when the Liberals made it clear they were not going to accept labour candidates? Unless Labour abandoned its ambitions a clash was inevitable.

Ferguson's strategy relied on avoiding such a clash indefinitely or until Home Rule had been achieved. This proved impossible. Relations became further strained when Hardie claimed that Liberal Conference decisions on land nationalisation and the eight hours' day were nothing but 'a device to catch the Labour vote.'[44] Since Ferguson had been partly responsible for achieving these votes he was compelled to publicly contradict Hardie. It was something he was loath to do since he did not wish to further muddy the waters but, despite being as diplomatic as possible, this public disagreement further sharpened the differences between Labour and the Irish. Ferguson went on to say, 'I look to the Liberal party as the real instrument to obtain reform, and to Mr. Gladstone as the noblest British statesmen in our annals.'[45] There could be little doubt where Ferguson would stand when the crunch came. After the election he was expelled from his position of Honorary Vice-President of the SLP for having appeared on Liberal platforms in seats contested by Labour.

How many Irish votes the SLP candidates got is an open question and Cunninghame Graham certainly did not expect much in early 1892 when he blamed their opposition to him as due to 'the attacks of reactionary priestcraft.'[46] However, the dispute with Ferguson cannot be reduced to that and is, rather, evidence of the complexity of politics within the Glasgow Irish community. McCaffrey points out that in the 1890s, 'there is evidence of a growing interest within the Catholic community in social questions', with regular public discussions on *Rerum Novarum*. This is also related to fears about Irishmen voting for 'no-hope' Labour candidates. After the 1892 election the *Observer* fulminated against 'traitors' who had supported Labour

[42] For Hardie see *Scottish Leader*, 4 Jan. 1892 and for Ferguson's explicit comparison see the same 6 Jan. 1892.
[43] *Scottish Leader*, 4 Jan.1892.
[44] *Scottish Leader*, 4 Jan. 1892.
[45] *Scottish Leader*, 6 Jan. 1892
[46] ILP Archive, Francis Johnston Correspondence, 1892/2, R.B. Cunninghame Graham to Keir Hardie, 9 January 1892.

in Camlachie and Tradeston; the virulence in itself indicating that significant numbers had done just that.[47]

Despite the failure of the Liberal Government to secure the Home
Rule Bill, the general election of 1895 again saw the INL throw its weight
behind the Liberals. A complicating factor was the education issue and
the view taken by many in the hierarchy that Catholics should support
Tories since they at least wanted to have religion taught in schools.[48] The
Observer strenuously opposed this attitude which threatened to push
Home Rule into the background and argued that any injunction to vote
Conservative would be directly opposed by the Irish Party. The issue was
clear cut, the 'first duty' of the INL was to 'get Home Rule for Ireland'.
Moreover, there would be great difficulty in getting any Irish support for
Tories since the Irish vote was a radical and social reform vote.[49] On the
other hand, the *Observer* was just as hostile to the ILP candidates as it was
to the Tories; indeed, it insisted on regarding them as opposite sides of
the same coin.

Any vote for Labour, in the eyes of the *Observer,* was not only a wasted vote
but a direct vote for the Tories since Labour's policy was not based on
actually winning seats but on keeping the Liberal out. The example of
Camlachie in 1892 was kept in mind when, 'Cunninghame Graham, posing
as a Labour candidate, succeeded in doing the work of the wrecker and
handing over the seat to the Tories.'[50] On this occasion, apparently, there
was no dispute between the *Observer* and the INL in Glasgow with one of the
Bridgeton branches refusing the ILP candidate permission to even address
the membership. John Ferguson was fully behind the Liberals, more so than
in 1892. He no longer spoke of Labour replacing the Liberals and even
contradicted his view of three years before that Labour was simply doing
what the Irish Party had done. There was a clear hardening in his attitude
towards the ILP candidates: 'they now have to be opposed because they will
not agree to form the combination for the advance and support of the
Liberal party upon its great programme.'[51]

The ILP stood five candidates in 1895, a challenge not repeated on the
same scale until 1918, but its performance was poor; an average of just under
7.5% of the poll with Robert Smillie doing best with just under 11% in
Camlachie. The result was also bad for the Liberals, who were left with just

---

[47] McCaffrey, 'Politics and the Irish Community', pp. 148–9. *Rerum Novarum* was the
famous Encyclical by Pope Leo XIII in 1891 which proscribed Socialism but
embraced social reform. Catholic socialists such as John Wheatley argued that
British socialism being reformist rather than revolutionary was in harmony with
the injunctions of the encyclical. See D. Howell, *A Lost Left* (Manchester, 1986)
pp. 230–1.
[48] *Glasgow Observer,* 13 Jul. 1895.
[49] *Glasgow Observer,* 13 Jul. 1895.
[50] *Glasgow Observer,* 13 Jul. 1895.
[51] *Glasgow Observer,* 13 Jul. 1895.

two of the City's seven seats, though it is not clear that the ILP intervention was responsible. Most of the Unionist majorities were very small, but only in one seat, St. Rollox, would the combined Liberal–ILP vote have been enough to win and this was the seat where the Labour vote was proportionately the lowest. The *Observer* did not immediately blame 'traitors' for these disastrous results; there was a common agreement that it had been mostly due to the absence of working class voters due to the 'Fair' holidays.[52] However, Smillie's relatively high poll may have been due, as in 1892, to a level of Irish support from within the HGB. It was a few months later, in the run up to the municipal election, that the *Observer* laid the blame for the Liberal defeat in Camlachie at the door of the HGB: 'It is notorious that the Home Government Branch did all it could safely do against Baillie Chisholm in Camlachie, and only by a sort of death-bed repentance came into line at the eleventh hour . . .'[53]

The re-opening of this old wound was the prelude to a new and much more significant division within Irish opinion over the role of the Irish vote at municipal elections and, in particular, its relationship to Labour candidates.

The Municipal Alliance and Irish Disagreements

Although the general election of 1895 appeared to have worsened relations between the Irish and Labour, this was only true of the *Observer*. By contrast the INL drew closer to the ILP and the Trades Council. As already discussed, the ILP in Glasgow followed the lead of John Ferguson in municipal politics and the INL played a significant role in the formation of and early years of the Workers' Election Committee (WEC), a development which further split Irish opinion.[54]

The crucial divide lay between the HGB and the *Observer*.[55] In 1894 the *Observer* came under the sole ownership and control of Charles Diamond who was a keen advocate of temperance and the local veto; although he could agree with men such as John Ferguson that the Irish vote was largely a working class and social reform vote, he was determined that nothing should stand in the way of Home Rule – neither the ILP nor the Cardinal of Westminster. The HGB was the oldest and largest nationalist organisation in Scotland as well as the wealthiest and, hence, the most independent of all the INL branches. It also had a number of publicans amongst its membership and office bearers. The branch, or at least elements within it, had given succour to Labour candidates in 1885, 1892 and 1895, much to the chagrin of the *Observer*. However, it was the open support given by the HGB to ILP

[52] *Glasgow Observer*, 20 Jul. 1895. The *Observer*, John Ferguson and the parish priest in St. Rollox all agreed on this point.
[53] *Glasgow Observer*, 26 Oct. 1895.
[54] See Chapter One pp. 41–6.
[55] Handley, *Irish in Modern Scotland*, pp. 284–6.

candidates for the Town Council that really brought the simmering dispute out into the open.

During the general election campaign in 1895 Hugh Murphy, President of the HGB, had sailed close to the wind in following the instructions of the Executive. He had spoken of the duty of unity in the Irish camp but, unlike Ferguson, he made no direct criticism of the Labour candidates. The *Observer* regarded the ILP candidates as open enemies and later fulminated at the HGB's 'coquetting' with Smillie in Camlachie.[56] Only a few months after the general election Murphy was working assiduously for the ILP candidates at the municipal polls and it was he who proposed George Mitchell of the ILP at the Committee meeting of the Second Ward. Speaking in support of Mitchell as a distinctively Labour candidate Murphy argued:

> during the past ten years they had seen candidates calling themselves temperance candidates, and candidates calling themselves publicans' candidates, but they found that all in the Town Council, Liberal, Tory, Publican and Temperance united to put down the working man (cheers). These men only used the workman as a ladder to get into power and then kicked them away.[57]

For the *Observer* this was 'dabbling in political heresy' and it urged its readers, 'Do Not Support the ILP'. It was particularly critical of Hugh Murphy who, it argued, should go and join the ILP outright like, 'the other Home Government men who have gone before him into the camp whither most of them tend.'[58] In the eyes of Diamond the ILP was effectively anti-Home Rule due to its opposition to the Liberals at parliamentary elections and Mitchell, 'the brains carrier' of the ILP in Glasgow, had been particularly active in the Camlachie contests of 1892 and 1895 which the Liberals had lost. Any success for the ILP would simply add to their prestige in the City and so weaken the cause of Home Rule. This argument was directed at those pro-Labour Irish who took the view that parliamentary and municipal politics were distinct and they could take a clear class line in the latter. For the *Observer*, such 'water-tight compartment fighting is really impossible'.[59]

The strongest point that figures like Murphy had in their favour was that ILP councillors would be supporters of John Ferguson's municipal programme. The *Observer* accepted this, as it did that the programme was a 'good thing'. While it wanted supporters of the municipal programme returned to the Council, it did not if they were opponents of Home Rule: 'then we stick by the greater and let the lesser go'. Ferguson's programme would just have to wait until sufficient Home Rulers could be found to support it.[60] However, Ferguson did not have to wait long and the sub-

---

[56] *Glasgow Observer*, 13 Jul., 26 Oct. 1895.
[57] *Glasgow Observer*, 26 Oct. 1895.
[58] *Glasgow Observer*, 26 Oct.1895.
[59] *Glasgow Observer*, 9 Nov. 1895.
[60] *Glasgow Observer*, 26 Oct. 1895.

sequent municipal elections saw his position boosted by the return of a sizeable group of Labour councillors.[61] The creation of the WEC and the electoral success of the Stalwarts in this period is significant in showing the proclivity of the Irish community to support Labour, but also in indicating the limitations of that Irish vote.

The INL began to make its own plans in preparation for the re-division of wards and the imminent local general election in 1896. It attempted to establish a Central Municipal Election Council to promote Irish representation by bargaining the Irish vote in wards where it was numerous, but not 'overwhelming', for support in wards where Irish candidates were certain to lose.[62] However, this begged the question of exactly where the Irish were strong enough to return their own candidates. The one branch which opposed the idea of a Central Council was the Sir Charles Russell, one of whose delegates stated that he had, 'canvassed [Blackfriars] over and over again and he did not think that the Irish held overwhelming power in that district at least.'[63] Blackfriars was commonly regarded as an area with a sizeable Irish vote yet here was a local Nationalist denying its significance. This assessment was echoed by other INL branches who wanted concerted Irish action but realised it could never be fully independent. This, and an existing sympathy with Labour, explains why there was no sign of the Irish Central Municipal Council at the poll in 1896, but the INL were actively involved in the WEC.

In the 1896 election the *Observer* spoke of twelve wards, 'where the Irish electors had a special interest',[64] but this could refer to a candidate who had expressed sympathy with the Irish, as in Maryhill or, where the name of the Irish candidate was announced from the pulpit of the local chapel, as in Anderston. John Ferguson was the only Irishman strong enough to stand on his own and his situation was somewhat distinct. Apart from anything else Ferguson was not a Catholic. Of these twelve wards, the only 'Irish' successes were in the east end wards of Dalmarnock, Calton and Mile End where the candidates were actually WEC nominees, only one of whom, John Cronin, was an Irish-Catholic and even he was an ILPer. The fourth east end ward, Whitevale, saw Hugh Murphy, nominated by the WEC and INL, fail by only 131 votes, while Joseph McGroary, a similar Labour-Nationalist candidate, failed by over 1,000 votes in Cowcaddens. Elsewhere the 'Irish' candidates were easily beaten.[65]

The WEC successes in 1896 muted the *Observer's* criticisms but its opposition to links with the ILP and to the HGB continued throughout the 1890s. Its main target remained Hugh Murphy but it even turned on John Ferguson, accusing him of being a Parnellite and a supporter of the

[61] See Chapter One, pp. 41–6.
[62] *Glasgow Observer*, 26 Oct. 1895.
[63] *Glasgow Observer*, 26 Oct. 1895.
[64] *Glasgow Observer*, 7 Nov. 1896.
[65] *Glasgow Herald*, 4 Nov. 1896.

Tories.[66] What is clear from the results in 1896 was that Irish candidates were not strong enough to stand on their own; to have any chance of success they had to be allied to some other group, to seek a wider legitimation by identifying with other interests. This meant Labour.

New Perspectives on Labour

It became increasingly clear that the Liberals were dragging their feet over the Irish question with the development of an 'Imperialist' wing under Lord Rosebery. This was brought into clearer focus in 1900 both in terms of Liberal commitment to Home Rule at the general election and attitudes to the Boer War. Hugh Murphy proposed a policy of standing independent candidates against Liberal imperialists and even voting for 'the genuine [Tory] Jingo' against 'the Liberal Jingo'.[67] Since he believed a Conservative victory to be inevitable it would be easier for Irish voters to support 'independent' candidates, i.e. Labour. The *Observer* still clung to its faith in the Liberal Party and it counselled voting for anti-Boer Liberals, so long as they supported Home Rule.[68] However, there was to be no clash between the HGB and the *Observer* at the General Election.

The Liberal candidates in four of the city's constituencies re-affirmed their support for Home Rule and received Irish support. In Central there was no contest, with the sitting Tory being returned unopposed. In Blackfriars & Hutchesontown the sitting Liberal would not give the undertaking to support Home Rule and Irish opinion was united against him and in favour of Andrew Bonar Law, the future Tory leader.[69] There was only one Labour candidate, in Camlachie, which offered the rare spectacle of the HGB and the *Observer* united in support, since there was no Liberal in the field.[70] The HGB passed an unanimous vote in his favour and the *Observer* approved of him as 'just the kind of man the constituency ought to have.'[71] Diamond's paper had not changed its mind over Labour candidates handing seats to Unionists in three-cornered contests, but this did not arise in Camlachie on this occasion since, 'the Liberals and Labour people have come to a wise, mutual understanding on the matter.'[72]

The 1900 election is famous in Glasgow's history as the only occasion when Unionists won all the seats. The role of the Irish is difficult to establish

[66] Because he supported Labour municipal candidates against Liberals. Handley, *Irish in Modern Scotland*, p. 285.
[67] *Glasgow Observer*, 8 Sept. 1900.
[68] *Glasgow Observer*, 15, 29 Sept. 1900.
[69] Wood, 'Irish Immigrants', p. 81; Gallagher, *Uneasy Peace*, p. 68.
[70] The candidate was A.E. Fletcher who was the nominee of the Scottish Workers' Representation Committee but was also endorsed by the Liberals. I.G.C. Hutchison, *A Political History of Scotland 1832–1924* (Edinburgh, 1986), p. 182.
[71] *Glasgow Observer*, 15 Sept.1900.
[72] *Glasgow Observer*, 29 Sept.1900.

since the two constituencies where Irish influence was reckoned greatest were fought under very particular circumstances. In Blackfriars & Hutchesontown the Irish electors were advised to vote Tory to punish the recalcitrant Liberal. A Liberal majority of almost 400 was turned into a deficit of just under 1,000 but, given the scale of the pro-Unionist swing throughout the city, it is hardly likely that Irish action was critical. Likewise, in Camlachie, even with united Irish support, Labour was unable to wrest the seat from the Unionist.

The 1900 election and Irish backing for Fletcher in Camlachie marks a watershed in the practical arrangements between the Irish and Labour, at least as regards parliamentary elections in Glasgow. In 1906 not only the HGB but also the INL Executive and the *Observer* would support Labour candidates in Glasgow in three-way contests. However, this did not indicate a straightforward shift from Liberal to Labour allegiance, as in the municipal arena the attitudes of the HGB and the *Observer* were almost reversed.

Both British Working Men and Irishmen

Just as the *Observer* began to regard Labour as a potential ally, though it remained insistent on judging each candidate individually, so the HGB retreated from the Stalwart alliance. This three-way conflict largely revolved around the phenomenon of Scott Gibson, whom the HGB firmly supported, while the *Observer* was as scathing in its condemnation of him as was the ILP.[73] Furthermore, as the 'forces of the democracy' rapidly began to disintegrate and the ILP dominated the WEC, so the Irish felt their erstwhile allies were denying them fair representation. Out of this tangled web certain threads can be grasped. One being that the Irish identified themselves as 'Progressive' or 'Labour' voters (the labels being interchangeable) but, they expected a *quid pro quo* in that they had a separate identity within the larger democratic framework and should receive reciprocal rights:

> The Irish voters in the city are progressive voters; perfectly willing to vote on the progressive side, since their interests lie that way, if only the progressive party would have the courage and loyalty to agree to give comrades' rights to their Irish allies.[74]

The nadir in Irish-Labour municipal relations occurred in 1906 on the death of John Ferguson when the ILP insisted on regarding his Calton seat as 'labour' rather than 'Irish'.[75] Yet, in the parliamentary elections of that year the co-operation between the two had never been closer.

A crucial factor in Labour acquiring Irish support lay in having their

---

[73] See chapter one pp. 52–7 on the rise of Scott Gibson, his relationship with the HGB and his impact upon Labour.

[74] *Glasgow Observer*, 9 Nov. 1901. This was a major shift from the outright hostility of the 1890s.

[75] See chapter one p. 59.

candidates in the field first. In the case of Blackfriars & Hutchesontown George Barnes began his campaign in earnest as early as 1902, and Irish hostility to the Liberal in 1900 made the adoption of a Labour candidate solid on Home Rule that much easier. In Camlachie, the absence of a Liberal candidate in 1900 allowed Labour to justifiably claim priority in challenging the sitting Unionist. There was some local hostility to Barnes among the Irish, with a move from within the William O'Brien branch of the UIL for a repeat vote for Bonar Law. Though this has been described as a 'major split' it seems clear that the majority endorsed the Executive's directive and Barnes.[76]

While Barnes secured a historic first victory for Labour in Glasgow and pushed the Liberal into third place over 1,000 votes adrift, Labour came last in Camlachie where a Liberal Unionist topped the poll.[77] Irish support may have been difficult to organise given that Labour's candidate was Joseph Burgess. Yet the UIL made it clear that no matter their low opinion of Burgess in Glasgow's municipal affairs, they were solidly behind him at the general election; he was the choice of the UIL Executive, he was first in the field, and he was judged sincere over Home Rule.[78] For his part, Burgess, speaking at an ILP meeting, declared himself 'delighted' with UIL support with which he was certain of victory.[79] In the event he did not win, though he did get 2,568 votes and 30% of the poll. This represented a drop of 539 votes on the 1900 election which, considering there was now a Liberal in the field, was not a bad performance; nevertheless, it indicated how far Labour had still to go to achieve an electoral breakthrough, even when it had Irish support.

After the lack of friction over Irish support for Labour at the Elections of 1900 and 1906, controversy resumed in 1910. There was no difficulty over George Barnes in Blackfriars & Hutchesontown; he had proven himself a popular MP to Irish-Catholic opinion, solid on Home Rule and detached from the secular position on education. The Liberals had accepted their defeat in 1906 and did not contest the seat in January 1910 when Barnes was triumphantly returned with 62% of the poll.[80] However, in Camlachie there was another three-cornered contest; Labour still had ambitions for the constituency and put forward J. O'Connor Kessack, whom the HGB was eager to support. The decision of the UIL Executive to support the Liberal, Cross, provoked perhaps the deepest split in Irish ranks in Glasgow, as the officers of the HGB resigned en masse.

---

[76] Wood, 'Irish Immigrants', p. 83; see also Handley, *Irish in Modern Scotland*, p. 290.

[77] Craig, *Election Results 1885–1918*, pp. 503, 505. The combined Liberal-Labour vote was some 2000 more than the winning Unionist.

[78] *Star*, 6 Jan. 1906. For the clash between Burgess and Scott Gibson, and the UIL's eventual split with Gibson, see chapter one, pp. 13, 16.

[79] *Star*, 6 Jan. 1906.

[80] The result in the December election was more or less the same. In a straight fight with the Conservative Barnes was returned with 59.1% of the votes cast. Craig, *Election Results 1885–1918*, p. 503.

Though the *Observer* claimed that there was no split in the ranks in Camlachie and that the Executive mandate was 'enthusiastically adopted' by a 500 strong meeting of 'Nationalist electors', its own report of the passionate debate aroused within the HGB proved otherwise. At a tumultuous meeting one member of the branch declared:

> he had been at an Irish meeting in Camlachie where 95% of those present were agreed that they were no longer to be kept in the slums by Mr. Cross [Liberal candidate] or Mr. Mackinder [Liberal Unionist candidate].[81]

The significance of this remark is that it emphasises that class issues, rather than Home Rule, confronted Irish workers in Britain. At another Irish meeting in the College Division of Glasgow, it was declared that the Irish in that division, 'would have to consider their position as British working men as well as their position as Irishmen.'[82]

At the January election the Irish vote seems to have stayed with Labour in Camlachie; O'Kessack's poll of 2,443 was just 125 adrift of Burgess's 1906 total, a fall of only 1.1% in the share of the vote; the Unionist vote marginally increased and the Liberal vote fell slightly. However, in the December election there was a significant shift even thought the result remained the same; Labour lost 904 votes while the Liberals gained 660 to come within twenty-six votes of the Unionist. What is important, in terms of Irish influence, was the more or less unanimous backing of the Liberal.[83] The drop in O'Kessack's vote could be explained simply by anti-Unionist voters giving up on Labour after three unsuccessful efforts, but the gain in Liberal votes corresponds very closely to the estimate of 700 Irish electors in the constituency.[84]

At the municipal level Irish relations with Labour had recovered from the low point of 1906 but there was still considerable uncertainty and scope for disagreement. It had now become a standard refrain that the Catholic-Irish were 'working people' whose vote was a 'progressive' vote. But still, according to the *Observer*, it should receive recognition of its specific interests and some degree of recognition from their allies.[85] The relationship remained a complex and subtle one influenced by class, religion and ethnicity.

In the municipal polls of 1910 Labour enjoyed one of its best results for many years: two sitting members were returned unopposed, three candidates were returned out of five contests and the other two only narrowly

---

[81] *Glasgow Observer*, 22 Jan. 1910.

[82] *Glasgow Observer*, 22 Jan. 1910.

[83] *Glasgow Observer*, 10 Dec. 1910.

[84] *Scotsman*, 18 Jan, 1910, cited in S. Cooper, 'John Wheatley: A Study in Labour Biography' (unpublished Ph.D. thesis, University of Glasgow 1973), pp. 49–50; see also *Scotsman*, 18 Nov. 1909, cited in McCaffrey, 'Politics and the Irish Community', pp. 43–4.

[85] *Glasgow Observer*, 29 Oct. 1910.

defeated. The major issue was the question of the tramway surplus and whether it should be used to reduce the rates or used to reduce fares, which was the policy of the Trades Council. The election results were an overwhelming rejection by the working class wards of the Corporation's preferred strategy and the rates' subsidy policy was subsequently dropped.[86] On this issue the *Observer* took its stand on the same side as the Trades Council, except in two seats. In Townhead the Labour candidate, Hugh Lyon, was opposed because of his previous opposition to Irish-Catholic candidates and his opponent's views on the tramway surplus were endorsed. In Maryhill George Carson was opposed because the Trades Council, of which he was Secretary, had adopted the 'secular solution' to the education question, and this was regarded as a direct threat to Catholic schools. Although admitting that, in normal circumstances Carson was a man whom the Irish could readily support, on this occasion the *Observer* declared, 'He should be asked to drop the "Secular Solution" or drop the Catholic vote.'[87] In the event both Lyon and Carson won their seats – in wards where the Irish claimed influence – with very comfortable majorities; a fact which suggests that in municipal affairs either Labour could do without the Irish vote altogether or get that vote without 'official' sanction.

Things ran much more smoothly in 1911, mainly because two Nationalist figures were standing and were given clear support by 'the leaders of the Labour Party'.[88] However, although both lost, the arrangement was criticised by younger Labour figures such as Patrick Dollan and Tom Johnston who saw it as a 'deal' made by some sitting Labour Councillors with unfortunate links to the drinks trade, especially as both men were publicans.[89] However, this was only a prelude to a more significant development, the formation of the Glasgow Labour Party which restricted candidates to members of affiliated bodies. While both the HGB and the *Observer* had been prominent in calling for greater Labour organisation the shape it eventually took, with no place for the UIL, came as a shock. It was particularly galling that, at that time, there were no Catholic councillors. The *Observer* reacted furiously: whereas 'Jews and atheists' could be freely returned, it fulminated, 'The Catholics of Glasgow, the Irish Nationalists of Glasgow (the terms are entirely synonymous) have no representative professing their creed or policies in the Corporation of Glasgow'.[90]

Yet, this dispute, which seemed to have the potential to shatter Irish-Labour relations quickly fizzled out. At the 1912 polls the *Observer* specified

---

[86] *Glasgow Herald*, 2 Nov. 1910; Glasgow Trades Council, *Annual Report 1910–11*.
[87] *Glasgow Observer*, 29 Oct. 1910. The *Observer* was also intent on settling old scores with Shaw Maxwell who was standing in Cowcaddens but by this time he had no connection with Labour and his defeat is of little interest.
[88] *Glasgow Observer*, 4 Nov. 1911.
[89] *Forward*, 11 Nov. 1911.
[90] *Glasgow Observer*, 2 Nov. 1912.

which Labour candidates were to be supported and which were to be opposed and declared the result satisfactory. But it added, 'we have fought as much as we want to fight', and appealed for peace by requesting Labour to revise the offending rule.[91] The following year the antagonism was much more muted. Labour Party rules remained unchanged but this did not stop Labour offering considerable support to the Irish candidate, ex-Baillie O'Hare, in Cowcaddens. Although O'Hare was defeated the *Observer* regarded the overall results as excellent and satisfied itself that the exclusion of Nationalists would not last another year.[92]

Beyond the bluster there is a clear sense of the *Observer* deliberately pulling its punches, of not wishing to indulge in a war which it could not hope to win. *The Observer* was always keen to claim the determining significance of the Irish vote; for instance in 1912, of the five Labour candidates standing in the 'old' city wards, the only two who won were those given the *Observer's* mandate. Yet Irish opposition to Carson and Lyon in 1910 had been ineffectual, and did not prevent John Wheatley winning Shettleston in 1912, to become the only Catholic on the Corporation.[93]

There can be no doubt that an identifiable 'Irish' vote existed in Glasgow. However, establishing just how influential it was it is more difficult; on some occasions the Irish vote appears decisive, yet on other occasions of no consequence. It needs to be underlined again that the Irish were a minority. Only in Liverpool were there sufficient Irish congregated together to secure direct representation.[94] In sharp contrast, Irish Nationalists could never have secured a parliamentary seat in Glasgow, nor could they establish their own group on the Corporation. Furthermore, since the Irish were to be found among the poorer, more transient working population, their level of enfranchisement was very low.[95] Of course, it was not in the interests of Irish-Catholic spokesmen to draw attention to these weaknesses. Perhaps contemporaries were too gullible in believing the boasts of a large and disciplined electoral force.[96]

Moreover, as we have seen, this vote cannot be regarded as a constant undivided unit; the recurring conflict between the *Observer* and the HGB indicates clearly enough that the Irish community seldom spoke with one

---

[91] *Glasgow Observer*, 9 Nov. 1912.

[92] *Glasgow Observer*, 10 Nov. 1913.

[93] Chapter one, pp. 67–8.

[94] The Nationalists had been organised independently in Liverpool municipal politics since the 1870s and T.P. O'Connor held the constituency of Scotland as an Irish Nationalist from 1885 to 1929. P. J. Waller, *Democracy and Sectarianism: a Political and Social History of Liverpool, 1868–1939* (Liverpool, 1981), p. 89.

[95] 'Whilst it is possible that as many as one in six Irish men were entitled to vote, only one in ten ever did.' S. Fielding, *Class and Ethnicity: Irish Catholics in England, 1880–1939* (Birmingham, 1993), p. 81. See also Matthew, McKibbin & Kay, 'The franchise factor in the rise of the Labour party', *English Historical Review*, xci (1976), p. 750.

[96] Fielding, *Class and Ethnicity*, pp. 27–8. And some historians also.

voice. The poles of attraction for the Irish in Britain were Liberal and Labour, with the recognition that in the long-term the latter would prevail. This understanding, based on the class nature of the Catholic-Irish population, was reached first by John Ferguson and the HGB and eventually by the originally hostile *Observer*. The Irish remained careful never to completely subsume their identity within Labour and continued to press for some degree of separate recognition. At the municipal level this was at first possible through the WEC and the Stalwarts, though ultimately this democratic alliance fractured. The later success of John Wheatley showed that Irish-Catholic representation lay within the Labour movement as part of that movement, not as Irish nationalist allies to it.

In Parliamentary elections Home Rule still predominated. In the 1890s Labour as a political force hardly existed. Even as its cohesiveness and identity developed it remained, at a UK level, wedded to the Liberals. Labour figures may have railed at the Irish workers for failing to vote in his own class interests but this was a disposition shared by most British workers. Up to 1914 only the Liberals could deliver Home Rule and it was expecting a great deal of the Irish to jettison that alliance.[97] Yet, even here support for Labour was strong and divisions within Irish opinion ran deep. The bitter controversy surrounding the UIL Executive's command to vote Liberal in 1910 in Camlachie, the HGB's home constituency and where Labour had enjoyed considerable success in municipal elections, can only be explained if we accept that voting Labour had become an established practice for many Irish workers.[98]

Post-war: The End of Nationalist Politics

The impact of the war upon the Irish-Catholics in Scotland was both critical and contradictory. The events of the war and its aftermath further hastened the integration of their community yet, at the same time, threw up a new and more virulent opposition from within Scottish society. Ingrained hostility to their Catholicism increasingly adopted a more racial tone which was to find dramatic expression in the rise of a militant Protestant political movement in the 1930s.[99]

Just as the leaders of the Irish National Party embraced the war effort so too did the Catholic Irish in Scotland; encouraged by their political leaders, by the *Observer* and by their bishops, they took the King's shilling in

---

[97] Fielding, *Class and Ethnicity*, pp. 79–80 makes similar points for England.

[98] Similar debates within the UIL where the local branch supported the Labour candidate can be identified in North East Lanarkshire and Manchester South West. See Hutchison, *Political History*, p. 260 and Fielding, *Class and Ethnicity*, pp. 99–100.

[99] The electoral impact of this movement in discussed in Chapter Six. See Gallagher, *Uneasy Peace*, pp. 150–7; S. Bruce, *No Pope of Rome: Anti-Catholicism in Modern Scotland* (Edinburgh, 1985), pp. 54–65.

substantial numbers.[100] However, by the end of the war the UIL had shrunk to insignificance. The effect of the 1916 Easter Rising, and especially the execution of the leaders, and the Nationalist leaders' inability to get the Government to make the Home Rule Act a reality, saw the UIL being superseded by Sinn Fein.[101] Charles Diamond, initially hostile to the Dublin uprising, quickly changed tack and threw the weight of the *Observer* and his other titles behind the separatists. At the same time he was arguing for a clear division between Ireland and Britain – the Irish in Britain should wind up the UIL and join Labour.[102]

1922 is usually taken as the year in which the transfer of Irish loyalties to Labour in the West of Scotland was more or less completed. That this was the same year in which Labour made its major electoral breakthrough seems to clearly establish the closeness of the relationship. However, explaining why the transition occurred is a matter of some debate. According to T.C. Smout, the reason is to be found in Labour's acceptance of the 1918 Education (Scotland) Act which gave state provision to Catholic schools.[103] For McLean, with his emphasis upon 'machine politics', the Irish allegiance to Labour occurred only after the latter began to downplay its anti-drink stance following the prohibition referendum in 1920.[104] Other historians, however, deny this linkage and see a more complex development involving the political and military changes in Ireland (1921 saw the end of the war with Britain and the following year the Irish Civil War) and also stress the fact that the Irish-Catholic community was not immune to the war-time and post-war social and political developments within Scotland.[105]

The problem with locating this political shift so firmly after 1918 is that it fails to encompass the wider picture and the changes already evident both before and during the War. As we have seen the Irish in Glasgow actively supported Labour, both in parliamentary and municipal elections since Labour's first emergence as a political entity. The support was qualified and inconsistent but in this it was little different from other allies of Labour such as the Co-operators. Furthermore, even before the general election of 1918 had been called, the *Observer* had thrown its weight unreservedly behind Labour as, in the title of an editorial, 'Ireland's Only Hope'.[106] A subsequent issue referred to previous sympathy offered by local Labour representatives to the Irish-Catholic community and welcomed Labour's current programme:

---

[100] Gallagher, *Uneasy Peace*, p. 86.
[101] Fielding, *Class and Ethnicity*, p. 101.
[102] Diamond made this point as early as February 1915. Gallagher, *Uneasy Peace*, p. 87.
[103] T.C. Smout, *A Century of the Scottish People 1830–1950* (London, 1986), pp. 270, 274.
[104] McLean, *Legend*, pp. 180–3, 241. Prohibition was firmly supported by the Labour movement, STUC, ILP etc., but the popular vote was for 'No change'.
[105] Gallagher, *Uneasy Peace*, pp. 97–8; McCaffrey, 'Irish Issues', pp. 126–33.
[106] *Glasgow Observer*, 3 Aug. 1918.

What is in it to which an Irishman cannot subscribe? In each and every reform tabulated the Irish toiler is keenly interested, for is he not virtually – yes, actually – "the hewer of wood and the drawer of water"? As to Ireland, their platform is – "The right of self-determination for all peoples." Surely that is all sufficient for anyone . . .[107]

At the same time the Irish were becoming aware of the extent of the impact the Representation of the People Act upon the electoral strength of the working class in general and their own community in particular. Once again the *Observer* emphasised the class nature of the community. The Act was:

> certain to add to the voting power of the workers, and should prove of immense value to the Catholics of this country, who are in the majority of cases in the ranks of the toilers . . . for the first time the Voting Power of the Irish in Scotland can become proportionate to their number.[108]

The inadequate electoral registers in 1918 and the inability of so many soldiers to cast a vote, also affected the Catholic Irish adversely, as did the collapse of the UIL which meant that much electoral work had been neglected. The Irish vote does seem to have swung behind Wheatley in Shettleston who secured one of Labour's best results at the general election, though still defeated.[109] Just as the true strength of Labour would only be revealed after 1918, so too with the Irish. At the same time, in a new and uncertain situation and with expectations of a possible four-fold increase in the Irish vote, it would have been surprising had there not been some thoughts of running independent Irish candidates. This did occur in post-war municipal elections but not in any systematic manner. The formation of a distinct 'Irish Labour Party' in Glasgow in 1918 was savaged by the *Observer* and quickly disappeared.[110]

Of more significance was the emergence of ex-Nationalists as members of the ILP and as Labour candidates after 1918. It is here that allegations of publican influence and corruption seem to lie. At the municipal polls of 1921 the *Glasgow Herald* (whose hostility to Labour at this time often bordered on the hysterical) drew specific attention to the Irish Nationalist and Catholic background of a number of Labour candidates. Interestingly, the same information had been collated by the Glasgow Unionist Association for its own propaganda purposes.[111] However, to regard this as in some way suspect would be to view a straightforward political development

---

[107] *Glasgow Observer*, 31 Aug. 1918.
[108] *Glasgow Observer*, 3 Aug. 1918.
[109] Gallagher, *Uneasy Peace*, pp. 87–8.
[110] *Glasgow Observer*, 31 Aug, 1918; Gallagher, *Uneasy Peace*, p. 89; McLean, *Legend*, p. 199.
[111] *Glasgow Herald*, 28 Oct. 1921; NLS, Acc 10424/15, Scottish Conservative and Unionist Association, Archive.

through the lens of a conspiracy theorist. Most of the men involved had been members of the HGB which, as we have seen, had been the most consistently pro-Labour Irish organisation before 1914.[112] Given that record and the history of the past few years it was surely logical that they should join Labour outright. Moreover, it is far too easy to exaggerate the influence of what was a very small number of councillors who do not appear to have acted in collusion, were unable to dominate any ward, and were, of course, part of a minority party.[113]

The Catholic population of Scotland numbered over half a million by 1911 and increased further to 662,000 by 1931. At this later date the number in Glasgow reached almost 300,000 or 24% of the total population of the City.[114] If we accept that this translated into a similar proportion of the electorate, then we can make some estimate of the increase in the Irish-Catholic vote.[115] In late 1909 the *Scotsman* estimated the number of Irish voters in the seven Glasgow constituencies. Relating these figures to the electorate at the January 1910 election puts the Irish proportion between a low of 6% in Central to a high of 13% in Blackfriars & Hutchesontown, or 8.3% overall.[116] These figures illustrate just how limited the Irish vote was prior to 1914 and also indicate the increase in its size as a result of the reform of 1918. Yet the question of how influential it was remains.

For some commentators the Irish influence was critical. Thus, Labour owed its very 'position in local government' in Glasgow 'to the power of the Catholic machine to deliver large numbers of loyal voters'.[117] Now there can be little doubt about the marked propensity of Catholics to vote Labour, or the value of that support to the Labour Party over a long period.[118] Yet, given that these voters remained a minority, not too much should be read into this pattern. It could be argued that if the Irish influence was

[112] Even McLean recognises this point. McLean, *Legend*, p. 199.

[113] Gallagher, *Uneasy Peace*, p. 102

[114] Darragh, 'Catholic Population of Scotland', pp 228, 241.

[115] The Glasgow Unionists considered the Roman Catholic vote in the 1930s to be 25 per cent of the city's electorate. NLS, Acc 10424/9 'Sir Lewis Shedden's file relating to Glasgow municipal elections, 1896–1939.' While that was likely so for parliamentary elections the more restricted nature of the local franchise is likely to have made this less for the municipal electorate.

[116] See McCaffrey, 'Politics and the Irish Community', pp. 153–4, for *Scotsman* figures. Electorate figures from Craig, *Election Results 1885–1918*, pp. 503–9.

[117] M. Savage, 'Whatever happened to Red Clydeside?', in J. Anderson & A. Cochrane (eds.), *A State of Crisis*, (London, 1989), p. 232. Savage explains this loyalty as due not to drink or education but to Labour's 'vague commitment to Irish independence'.

[118] See McLean, *Legend*, also, I. Budge & D.W. Urwin, *Scottish Political Behaviour* (London, 1966), pp. 61–3, and M.G. Clarke & H.M. Drucker, *Our Changing Scotland: A Yearbook of Scottish Government 1976–77* (Edinburgh, 1976), p. 12 which refers to a poll taken in the Glasgow area just after the February 1974 General Election which found that amongst Catholics who had voted, 79.3% voted Labour.

limited overall it was predominant in specific wards. There were, on occasion, Irish Catholic candidates who were returned as 'Independents' or 'Independent Socialists' but these were few and far between and usually ended up being adopted by Labour.[119] Further, as shown above, the number of Labour councillors in the 1920s who were Irish Catholics was really quite limited.

While it was loyal to Labour overall, the Irish or Catholic vote did, however, remain 'conditional' and, as the Irish question receded, so education and birth control became the major issues upon which Catholic opinion would seek to influence elected representatives and elections.[120] Although denominational schooling cut across Labour's traditional belief in secular education, there was, in practice, little disagreement with Catholics over the issue. Indeed, it has been astutely remarked that both Labour and the Catholic Church were 'lucky in the timing of the 1918 settlement'.[121] For Labour it was easier to accept the newly-established system – which was not of its making – than to campaign for the establishment of a secular system. Furthermore, Labour was notoriously weak in elections to the Local Education Authorities (LEA) which were elected under proportional representation (single transferable vote) and were dominated by the Churches. Indeed, what little success Labour enjoyed in the Glasgow LEA was largely due to the transference of Catholic votes, a favour not necessarily reciprocated.[122] While a great deal of contemporary attention was focused on the threat by a supposed 'unholy alliance' between Catholics and Socialists to dominate the LEA, it is clear that this was never a possibility and that Catholics did co-operate with the Moderate-Protestant majority.[123] The education issue was still important and increasingly so in the 1930s as the cry of 'No Rome on the Rates' helped fuel the rise of Alexander Ratcliffe's Scottish Protestant League (SPL). However, it is interesting that the Glasgow Unionists actually defended the 1918 arrangement, at least privately, against the violent and dishonest propaganda of the SPL: 'there seems no fairer plan than that established by the Act of 1918 under which both Protestant and Catholic parents obtain for their children at school the kind of religious education which they respectively find acceptable.'[124]

The mobilisation and direction of the Catholic vote became more complicated due to the vagaries of Charles Diamond's own political loyalties. From being a Labour candidate himself Diamond began to express a distinct anti-Socialist message, turned back towards the Liberals and even dreamed of a Catholic Centre Party on the European model. The *Observer* once again insisted on judging each and every candidate on its merits but it

---

[119] Gallagher, *Uneasy Peace*, pp. 101–2.
[120] The same holds true for England. See Fielding, *Class and Ethnicity*, pp. 105–6.
[121] Gallagher, *Uneasy Peace*, p. 108.
[122] *Glasgow Herald*, 7 Apr. 1919; McCaffrey, 'Irish Issues', p. 129.
[123] *Glasgow Herald*, 23 Feb. 1922; McCaffrey, 'Irish Issues', pp. 128–31.
[124] NLS, Acc 104249/9, 'Report on Glasgow Municipal Elections 1933'.

is clear that it could not deflect the consistent pro-Labour tendency of most Irish electors.[125] It was one thing for the *Observer* to trumpet the electoral power of the Catholic vote but, just as before 1914, analysis of election results throws doubt on such claims and presents a more complicated picture.

The birth control issue is regarded as one in which Catholics had a special interest. As we saw in the previous chapter it became a live political matter in Glasgow in 1927 over the attempt to get the Corporation to allow the city libraries to take a copy of the journal *Birth Control News*.[126] According to the *Observer*, 'the mere mention of birth control is enough to set the Catholic electorate on its hind legs' and Catholics were urged to vote against those in favour accepting the journal.[127] As such, the birth control issue ought to reveal the influence and discipline of the Catholic vote.

Since only Labour Councillors had voted in favour of accepting *Birth Control News*, any mobilisation of the Catholic vote would be directed against Labour. In its analysis of the election *Forward* concluded that the issue had adversely affected Labour's performance, yet commented that, 'It is very difficult to express definite views on the effect of the Birth Control controversy in the election.'[128] The overall loss of five seats made this one of the worst November polls for Labour, though in two cases the damage was self-inflicted and not directly connected to birth control: in Parkhead the sitting member, who retained the backing of the District Labour Party and the Trades Council, had been expelled by the ILP who stood a candidate of their own; in Govan the sitting member was a lapsed ILPer who had failed to secure nomination but still stood against a candidate chosen jointly by the ILP and the Trades Council. In both instances the split vote allowed Moderates to succeed. While Govan and Parkhead were safe Labour seats the three wards where Labour lost in straight fights – Kingston, Provan and Ruchill – were marginal constituencies in the 1920s with representation fluctuating between Labour and Moderate; defeats here were not especially surprising.

Moreover, if, in the words of the *Observer*, the Catholic vote was to be directed against 'Birth Control propagandists', its accuracy was that of a blunderbuss rather than a sniper's rifle. Of those who voted in favour of accepting *Birth Control News*, a number were actually opposed to birth control but took a democratic line that journals should not be banned from public access. *Forward* pointed out that of the five defeated Labour candidates four 'were pronounced anti-Birth Controllers' and Catholic.[129]

---

[125] Diamond's idiosyncratic political views and criticisms of Labour are detailed in Gallagher, *Uneasy Peace*, pp. 186–96.

[126] Chapter three pp. 109–10.

[127] *Glasgow Observer*, 5 Nov. 1927, quoted in Gallagher, *Uneasy Peace*, p. 192. Directions were also given by priests encouraging a vote for the Moderates. *Forward*, 12 Nov. 1927.

[128] *Forward*, 5 Nov. 1927.

[129] It also argued that the *Observer* had 'twisted' the issue into a vote for accepting the journal being the same thing as advocating birth control. *Forward*, 5, 12 Nov. 1927.

The one clearly pro-birth control candidate was James Gould in Ruchill who was defeated by 128 votes in a ward the Moderates had won in four out of the previous six years. However, in Springburn, a safe Labour seat, the mobilisation of the Catholic vote against the Rev. Richard Lee may have reduced his majority but was not enough to unseat him.[130] Furthermore, it would appear that the anti-Labour injunction was not universally popular with Catholics, with some degree of protest being registered in Springburn and Woodside.[131] The *Observer*, however, did not let the matter rest but returned to the issue in the general election of 1929.

At this election Diamond declared in favour of the Liberals while recognising that most Catholics, being 'wage-earning people', were still disposed to vote Labour. The *Observer's* response, therefore, was to give a seat-by-seat guide as to whom Catholics should vote for in Scotland; most of the favoured candidates were Labour, but included some Liberals and even Unionists. Particular hostility was directed towards five Labour candidates who, as Glasgow councillors, had voted in favour of *Birth Control News* two years previously, and the advice was crystal clear, '*None of the five should get any Catholic vote at this election.*'[132] The five candidates and their constituencies were: John S. Clarke (Maryhill), Dr. R. Forgan (West Renfrew), William Leonard (Greenock), James Welsh (Paisley) and J. Winning (Kelvingrove). A sixth offender was Jennie Lee (North Lanarkshire) whose attempt to deny that birth control was a political issue was judged as 'mere eyewash to avoid answering the question'.

Of course, 1929 was a good year for Labour throughout the UK with the return of the second Labour Government and in Scotland Labour recorded its best ever performance with thirty-six MPs. Of the six constituencies listed above only two were not won by Labour; Kelvingrove was a solid Unionist seat which Labour never won; and Greenock was safely held by Sir Godfrey Collins for the Liberals until his death in 1936 when Labour at last secured the constituency at the subsequent by-election. The other four seats could not be regarded as 'safe' Labour seats and, indeed, three of them – Maryhill, West Renfrew and North Lanark – had been Unionist at the last poll. Jennie Lee had taken her Lanarkshire seat at a by-election in March 1929, against the *Observer's* opposition, and thus these three can all be regarded as Labour gains. Paisley had been Asquith's seat until 1924 when Labour secured it for the first time. Welsh was a new candidate in 1929 and the *Observer* confidently predicted his defeat because of the Catholic support which would

---

[130] Rev. Lee had voted for accepting the journal but was opposed to birth control. *Forward*, 12 Nov. 1927.

[131] See 'Open Letter to Father McCann', by Dr. S.H. Bennett in *Forward*, 12 Nov. 1927. Dr. Bennett was the Labour candidate in Woodside and was opposed to birth control. This, however, did not stop Father McCann, parish priest of St. Columbus encouraging his parishioners to vote Moderate.

[132] *Glasgow Observer*, 25 May 1929. Emphasis in original. Cuttings from this issue were found in the SCUA archive, see NLS, Acc 10424/8(v) The Roman Catholic Vote 1929–36.

be withdrawn from him. In the event Welsh polled 56% of the vote, giving him a clear victory over both Liberal and Conservative opponents.[133]

If we accept that a Catholic vote had played some role in the municipal election of 1927, it is impossible to see any influence at the general election in 1929. Just as before 1914, Irish support for Liberals was helpful when the general tide was running in their favour but was not sufficient to halt a general Unionist advance, so the same can be said about the Catholic vote and Labour from 1918.[134] The actual historical record suggests that the Catholic electorate was neither so unified nor so powerful as it is often depicted. A recent study of the Orange Order comes to a very similar conclusion. There was an 'Orange vote' which was meant to be uniformly pro-Unionist yet, if it explains the political complexion of certain wards and constituencies, it signally fails to do so for others.[135]

Conclusion

While it is mistaken to depict the Catholics as an immigrant community, since the majority had been born in Scotland from the later nineteenth century, nonetheless they were widely regarded as outsiders.[136] Just as the Irish Catholic community were about to commit themselves to Scottish civil society, so worsening economic conditions made them in the eyes of some the obvious scapegoat for all Scotland's ills; Willie Gallacher pointed out that while the fascists in Germany were anti-Jewish those in Scotland were anti-Irish.[137] However, anti-Irishness was not confined to confirmed fascists but was much more widespread. Its roots lay deep in Scotland's Presbyterian past, a history that had done much to shape Scottish self-identity and to which Catholicism was perceived as a direct threat. This, of course, had always been the case but after the Great War a much sharper, more virulent, racial aspect emerged; Irishness as much as Catholicism now threatened to 'swamp' Scotland and denude her native stock, and the Church of Scotland was chief among those raising the alarm.[138]

---

[133] Electoral information taken from F.W.S. Craig, *British Parliamentary Election Results 1918–1949* (Chichester, 1983).

[134] McCaffrey, 'Politics and the Irish Community', p. 147.

[135] G. Walker, 'The Orange Order in Scotland Between the Wars', *International Review of Social History*, xxxvii (1992), pp. 177–206.

[136] B. Aspinwall, 'The Catholic Irish and Wealth in Glasgow' *in* Devine, *Irish Immigrants and Scottish Society*, p. 100.

[137] *Forward*, 4 Nov. 1933.

[138] See the inflammatory report by the Church and Nation Committee of the General Assembly in 1923, subsequently published as a pamphlet, *The Menace of the Irish Race to Our Scottish Nationality*. S.J. Brown, ' "Outside the Covenant": The Scottish Presbyterian Churches and Irish Immigration, 1922–1938', *Innes Review*, xcii (1991), pp. 19–45; see also the same author's 'The Social Vision of Scottish Presbyterianism and the Union of 1929', *Records of the Scottish Church History Society*, xxiv (1992), pp. 91–3. This period and issue is discussed in depth by Gallagher, *Uneasy Peace*, chapter four. See also Bruce, *No Pope of Rome*, p. 46.

The War itself and its aftermath in Ireland was one reason for this hostility. Irish sacrifices in the trenches were overshadowed and forgotten by the impact of the Easter Rising and the War of Independence and all Catholics were associated with the 'treachery' of Sinn Fein in the Empire's hour of need. The massive casualty lists from the Western Front, in which the sons of the clergy were prominent, encouraged bitter recriminations.[139] There was an active Sinn Fein presence in Glasgow and in the international upheavals of the post-war world the connection was even made between Irish republicanism and Bolshevism.[140] Over and above this, however, was the changed economic climate, the crisis facing the heavy industries and mass unemployment. As Gallagher has argued it is the lack of confidence within Scotland after the war that explains the hostility directed towards the Irish.[141]

The lack of Irish migration to Scotland in the inter-war years did not stop calls for such migration to be checked, or for the repatriation of those whom it was claimed were receiving poor relief. In 1929 even the *Glasgow Herald* was forced to admit, after detailed investigation, that any migration was a mere 'trickle' and official Government responses showed there was no problem over poor relief.[142] Nonetheless, political capital continued to be made out of these issues, and not just by Alexander Ratcliffe. Speaking in the Glasgow Conservative Club just before the general election of 1931, Sir Robert Horne, MP for Hillhead and an ex-Chancellor of the Exchequer, expressed his views on the 'Irish invasion'. Conflating 'Catholic' with 'Irish', Horne declared that the latter accounted for 25% of the population of Glasgow and it was they who caused most of the City's problems. They were:

> responsible for the class of representation they got, and most of the trouble which arrived in their midst and which had a very serious effect on their trade and industry. There were very few people who wanted to come to the Clydeside to establish industries unless they could demonstrate that they were not being over-ridden by the Irish revolutionaries in their midst.[143]

---

[139] See 'Sectarianism in Scotland', a film by George Rosie, part of the Secret Scotland series broadcast by Scottish Television, 26 June 1997.

[140] For Sinn Fein presence and activity in Glasgow and Scotland see Gallagher, *Uneasy Peace*, pp. 90–7.

[141] Gallagher, *Uneasy Peace*, pp. 135–7.

[142] *Glasgow Herald*, 25 Mar. 1929, quoted in Gallagher, *Uneasy Peace*, p. 167. See also Handley, *Irish in Modern Scotland*, pp. 3–9, 11. In 1928 the Government had already produced figures contradicting those of the Church of Scotland; both immigration from the Irish Free State and numbers of Irish-born claiming poor relief had not risen but had actually fallen. Brown, 'Outside the Covenant', pp. 32–3.

[143] *Glasgow Observer*, 24 Oct. 1931. The Church of Scotland also blamed Catholics for the large number of Labour MPs and the industrial militancy on Clydeside. Brown, 'Outside the Covenant', pp. 27–8 and, Brown 'Social Vision of Scottish Presbyterianism', pp. 92–3.

Although the Unionists claimed they were non-sectarian, anti-Irish senti-ment was undoubtedly a common reflex within the Party. How far the constant drip of such prejudices fed the rise of militant Protestantism is a moot point, but the success of the SPL in the 1930s certainly encouraged a more explicit anti-Irish message from Unionist politicians. With the Liberal Party reduced to a handful of seats in Scotland, and the National Party of Scotland standing on a manifesto commitment to restrict Irish immigration, it is no great mystery as to why Irish-Catholics in Scotland should have been so solidly pro-Labour.[144] Specific circumstances tended to make Labour the obvious choice for Catholic workers but this was mainly because of their general position within society.[145] Their support for Labour was primarily because they were working class and, increasingly, part of the labour movement; it was not the result of deals stitched up in pubs by 'machine' politicians.[146]

[144] On Nationalist anti-immigration policy see *Glasgow Observer,* 25 May 1929. While Scottish Nationalist opinion did contain those like Christopher Grieve who had strong pro-Irish sentiments, the majority opinion was hostile to both the Irish and Irish immigration into Scotland. See R. Finlay, *Independent and Free: Scottish Politics and the Origins of the Scottish National Party 1918–1945* (Edinburgh, 1994), pp. 65, 94, 193.

[145] Even McLean who sets great store by the Irish vote recognises 'the overwhelming importance of class as a determinant of the Labour vote and can only conclude that, 'religion is not negligible.' McLean, *Legend,* p. 227.

[146] '. . . Catholic support for Labour did not spring out of direct efforts of bodies such as the Catholic Union or Labour political organisers to marshal their votes but rather as part of a more general convergence to Labour which was such a marked characteristic of the political and social evolution of the times.' McCaf-frey, 'Irish Issues', p. 132.

CHAPTER FIVE

Labour's Women

Looking back from the early 1960s Jean Mann, ILPer, Labour councillor and ultimately Labour MP (she was elected for Coatbridge in 1945), wrote in her memoirs that a Housewives' Union, though mooted in 1918, was never formed because '. . . the vital needs of men and women were akin – housing, health, pensions, full employment, family allowances, and a living wage. So long as there were men to fight for these, women were content to let them, and joined in the fight.'[1] This easy association of male and female needs appears naive and sustainable only if demands such as equal pay and birth control are left out of the reckoning. Yet, the point is, nonetheless, a valid one; Mann's list of issues were critical to the working class, both men and women, in the post-war period. These issues were also identified with the ILP which, in its agitation and appeal for mass support for Labour, directed particular efforts towards women. This was, however, very much an appeal to *housewives* and emerged out of the war-time struggles over housing. Before 1914 Labour's attitude to women was much more ambivalent.

The pattern of most women's lives, in which their adult years were concentrated on the domestic roles of wife and mother was, in itself, a major barrier to their participation in trade union and political affairs. Unlike most men, working class women could not expect (nor necessarily wish) to spend their life in full time paid employment. Nor were the occupations open to them as young workers particularly amenable to organisation. Therefore it was much less likely that they would join a trade union or, if they did, sustain membership over a lengthy period and so gain the experience of membership, acting as delegates, branch officers, etc. which was so critical to the career of activists within the movement. For instance, by 1910 Glasgow Trades Council had only seven women delegates out of total of 288 members.[2] It is hardly surprising that only a few women rose to prominence: in an exhaustive biographical study of labour leaders in inter-war Scotland there are seven women compared to fifty-six men and only two women became Labour MPs over the same period.[3]

---

[1] J. Mann, *Woman in Parliament* (London, 1962), p. 232.

[2] Glasgow Trades Council, *Annual Report 1910–11.* Five of the women represented the National Federation of Women Workers and two represented the Weavers (Women).

[3] W.W. Knox, *Scottish Labour Leaders 1918–1939: A Biographical Dictionary* (Edinburgh, 1984); C. Burness, 'The Long Slow March: Scottish Women MPs, 1918–45', in, E. Breitenbach & E. Gordon (eds.), *Out of Bounds: Women in Scottish Society 1800–1945* (Edinburgh, 1992), p. 166.

Numbers alone can only tell us part of the story and fail to convey the complexities and indeed drama of women's political involvement; after all within our period women *did* achieve the vote. As regards the suffrage, and so much else within the labour and socialist movement, women had to struggle with and against men at one and the same time. Moreover, there was no single woman's view; whether it be the vote, employment, family allowances, there was constant debate among women rather than just a dialogue between women and men. While most male socialists and trade unionists tended to emphasise women's domestic role and commitment, the fact is that many women also sought to protect and improve the lives of women at home. If women's emancipation was to be real it had to start where working class women actually were. Such an attitude and perspective was not, 'the expression of a male-dominated ' "false consciousness" . . . At its base was the conviction that the home should and could provide the base for the liberation of women rather than their insuperable bondage.'[4]

Women, Employment and Marriage

Underpinning women's limited participation in the labour movement was their very different experience of paid employment compared to men. Whereas most men were identified by the census as 'occupied', less than half of women were so regarded; for instance in both 1911 and 1931 only 39% were formally 'occupied'. Moreover, If we take the age range between twenty-five to forty-four as representing the time in their lives when most people were likely to have a family of their own we can see that the difference is even more marked. In 1911 in Glasgow 31% of women aged between twenty-five and forty four were designated as occupied compared to 99% of men in the same age group.[5] Yet, these general figures tell only part of the story of what were two almost totally different labour markets. As has been remarked for the period 1891 to 1914:

> Glasgow's female labour market differed in three crucial respects from its male counterpart. It offered relatively few openings for school leavers to acquire a skilled training; its occupational range was much more restricted; and only a minority of women was listed as gainfully employed in successive Censuses.[6]

[4] P. Thane, 'The Women of the British Labour Party and Feminism, 1906–1945', in H.L. Smith (ed.), *British Feminism in the Twentieth Century* (London, 1990), p. 129
[5] *Census of Scotland*, City of Glasgow 1911 and 1931. Unfortunately the post WW1 Censuses reports do not provide the same age and gender specific information.
[6] J.H. Treble, 'The Characteristics of the Female Unskilled Labour Market and the Formation of the Female Casual labour market in Glasgow, 1891–1914'. *Scottish Economic and Social History*, vi (1986), p. 33

A fourth element, or the combined effect of the other three, could be added; that of wages. Women's actual and expected earnings were significantly lower than male earnings. Relegated primarily to unskilled jobs where the supply of labour tended to exceed the demand, it is hardly surprising that, 'women workers were massively over-represented among the ranks of the low paid . . .'[7]

Behind the poor wages paid to women was not just the fact of the jobs they happened to be in but the predominant attitudes of why women worked and what they should be paid: the notion of 'pin money', that a woman's wage was merely a supplement to the wages of her husband. It was this that led to 'competition' between single and married women, which helped keep female earnings down. As Professor Smart of the Glasgow Municipal Commission remarked:

> the single woman has to suffer from the fact that she is single: that is to say, while the wages of wives and daughters are supplementary to the wages of the head of the house, and therefore increase his ability to pay rent, the wages of single women are determined by the competition of these supplementary women, and therefore remain low. [8]

While it is impossible to distinguish figures for single women who were dependent solely upon their own earnings and single women who lived with their parents and were contributing to a larger, household income, we do at least know the number of wives who were returned as employed. In Glasgow in 1911 there were 7047 married women listed as occupied, some 5.5% of the total number of married women, and only 6.5% of the total number of occupied females aged fifteen and over.[9] As Treble has pointed out, 'This distinctive pattern [of female employment] owed everything to the impact of matrimony upon the female labour market.'[10] And this 'impact' had been an increasing influence since the middle of the nineteenth century: in 1851 the proportion of married women working had been three times as great, at 17%.[11]

This pattern reinforced ingrained social attitudes towards women's employment generally, that since women were unlikely to work for long before marriage took them out of the workforce more or less permanently there

[7] Treble, 'Female Unskilled Labour Market', p. 34.
[8] Glasgow Municipal Commission on the Housing of the Poor, *Minutes of Evidence* (Glasgow 1903), p. 532.
[9] *Census of Scotland*, City of Glasgow 1911. While it is widely recognised that the census has a marked tendency to under record women's employment, particularly that of married women, it remains a necessary source and can still identify broad patterns. On the limitations of the census see E. Gordon, 'Women's Spheres', in W.H. Fraser & R.J. Morris (eds.), *People & Society in Scotland, Vol. 2 1830–1914*, (Edinburgh, 1990), pp. 208–9.
[10] Treble, 'Female Unskilled Labour Market', p. 35.
[11] E. Gordon 'Women's Employment in Scotland', (unpublished paper, Glasgow University, 1979).

was little point in educating or training them beyond a rudimentary level.[12] In spite of the fact that many women did not marry it is, nonetheless, from this perspective that we have to approach the subject of working class women and political involvement. The overwhelming significance of marriage and the expectation that, upon getting married, a woman should stop working for a wage was central to perceptions of women and work in this period.[13] Particularly among skilled workers it became a crucial element to their notion of 'respectability', an indication of their earning capacity and status, that their wives should not 'work'. This domestic ideology went further than simply the male egotism of artisans, however, as even Margaret Irwin objected to any young married woman going out to work, 'if her husband is earning good wages'.[14]

The ILP and the 'Woman Question'

Though there was a wide acceptance among socialists that there was a 'woman question', the issue was, conveniently, left over until the attainment of actual socialism when all inequality would be transcended. There was little debate on the specific content of what might constitute female emancipation.[15] Early socialist indifference to women's suffrage can partly be explained by the property basis of the demand. Further factors included a general hostility towards electoral politics, and a concentration upon social issues, which were regarded by many as being distinct from constitutional or mere 'political' matters. Furthermore, there was also an antipathy or sheer indifference to political issues affecting women. This attitude was well expressed by H.M. Hyndman, leader of the Social Democratic Federation (SDF):

> I have never been able, while fully admitting the justice of giving suffrage to all women, if they claim it, to get up much enthusiasm for female suffrage by itself . . . I cannot believe in Suffrage, limited practically to well-to-do women as being worth serious effort . . .[16]

[12] Treble, 'Female Unskilled Labour Market' p. 36; H. Corr, 'An Exploration into Scottish Education' in *People & Society*, p. 302; J. McDermid, 'Catholic working class girls' education in Lowland Scotland, 1872–1900', *Innes Review*, xlviii (1996), pp. 68–80.

[13] In 1911 fully one third of women in the twenty-five to forty-four age range were single, i.e. neither married nor widowed. *Census of Scotland*, City of Glasgow 1911.

[14] Glasgow Municipal Commission, p. 534. Irwin was a long standing campaigner for women's trade unions and was the first Secretary to the Scottish Trades Union Congress.

[15] In William Morris's socialist utopian romance *News From Nowhere*, women's role remained primarily domestic or 'semi-domestic'. See P. Anderson, *Arguments within English Marxism* (London, 1980), p. 166.

[16] H.M. Hyndman, *Further Reminiscences* (London, 1912), p. 287, quoted in M. Ramelson, *The Petticoat Rebellion: A Century of Struggle for Women's Rights* (London, 1972), p. 81.

The concentration of the SLP and ILP upon attempting to gain representation at the local as well as national level and gain specific reforms had more of a bearing on women's concerns, and was also more amenable to the question of the suffrage. Much of the ILP's responsiveness was due to Keir Hardie. Of all the socialist leaders, Hardie had the most advanced perception of women as a distinct 'constituency'. Although much of Hardie's championing of the Women's Social and Political Union (WSPU) may have been due to his long-standing friendship with the Pankhurst family, his concern with female emancipation had much deeper origins. However, despite his assertion that 'The sex problem is at bottom the labour problem', Hardie offered no particular socialist perspective on the subject; his arguments were based on 'democratic' grounds alone.[17]

For Hardie, women were potential electoral assets to labour, a view which went against the perceived wisdom of women as innately conservative. As early as 1894 he suggested to the SLP in Glasgow that it should choose a woman as a candidate in the School Board elections.[18] Such a perspective, based on notions of women's inherently nurturing and caring natures, could be seen in its own way as being quite restrictive in its view of the potential for women's political involvement. Prior to 1914 in Glasgow it was in the School Board and Parish Council elections that Labour occasionally promoted women, the more important Town Council elections remaining the preserve of male candidates.[19] Yet, there were also feminists who argued that to be female was to be different and that women's active involvement in politics would necessarily change it for the better.[20] This position echoed that of Hardie, who remained one of the most constant supporters of women's suffrage. Furthermore, it had the benefit of encouraging women's active participation within labour politics.

Part of the SLP's contribution to encouraging women's involvement lay in it having a separate Women's Branch or 'Scottish Women's Party' as it was styled prior to the Scottish party joining with the national ILP. While we know little about the Women's Party, it did survive until 1898 and its membership peaked in 1896 – the year labour made its first major assault on Glasgow municipal politics – when it boasted fifty paying members.[21] The

[17] K. O. Morgan, *Keir Hardie: Radical and Socialist* (London, 1975), pp. 162–3; see also C. Benn, *Keir Hardie* (London, 1992), p. 200.

[18] *Labour Leader*, 31 Mar., 7 Apr. 1894.

[19] Agnes Pettigrew Hardie was returned to the Glasgow School Board as a Labour member in 1909. Knox, *Scottish Labour Leaders*, p. 136. Before the War no female municipal candidates were selected by Labour in Glasgow.

[20] See S. Holton, *Feminism and Democracy: women's suffrage and reform politics in Britain 1800–1918* (Cambridge, 1986), in particular chapter one, "Feminising Democracy": the ethos of the women's suffrage movement'.

[21] *Archive of the Independent Labour Party*, Directory of Branches 30 November 1896 (Harvester Press microform) On the Women's Labour Party see J. Smyth, 'Labour and Socialism in Glasgow 1880–1914: The Electoral Challenge prior to Democracy (unpublished Ph.D. thesis, University of Edinburgh, 1987), pp. 217–8.

perennial problems of branch finances was even more pronounced and Kate Taylor, the Secretary, made an appeal to 'monied people in the country' in order to aid the Glasgow women establish a 'club', not only for local need, but also to 'serve as one of the centres of the forward "women's movement" now so rapidly developing'.[22]

The Scottish Women's Party or Branch was itself both an expression of and contributor to this women's movement. One of its contributions was to raise the matter of votes for women within the labour movement. At the fifth annual conference of the SLP, the Women's Labour Party introduced a motion, 'That this conference urges the Government to take steps at once to extend the Parliamentary Franchise to women.'[23] As it stood this resolution was, basically, the standard women's suffrage demand for the vote on the same terms as men. However, the movers accepted an amendment, moved by a delegate of the SDF, which turned the issue into an adult suffrage motion, i.e. that all men and women should have the vote. A decade later and the suffrage debate within the labour and socialist movement would revolve around this exact point – women's suffrage versus adult suffrage.

Although the debate at the conference was perfunctory, a number of points made by men are worth mentioning. One was the argument that the resolution be extended to cover all women, married and single. This was because the municipal franchise, 'had only been given to single women, with the result that their votes had simply been handed over to their spiritual advisers.'[24] This reflected the widespread belief that the existing women's vote in local matters was determined by the Churches, a point we shall return to below. The movers of the original resolution had no objection to extending its coverage to married women. An attempt was then made, by a delegate of the Glasgow Shoemakers, that the resolution be dropped altogether since, 'the proper sphere of women was the home; but if they went further in the direction in which they had been going, the time would soon come when men would remain at home to discharge the maternal duties, and the women could go out to do all the work.'[25] Although this contribution to the debate raised a laugh among the delegates, of more significance is the fact that it was unable to find a seconder and fell.

The following year the Women's Labour Party took the fight into the National ILP. At the Annual conference held in Newcastle the Glasgow women successfully amended a somewhat vague resolution by the National Administrative Council (NAC), 'in favour of every proposal for extending electoral rights and democratising the system of government', so that it

[22] *Labour Leader*, 14 Apr. 1894. However Taylor managed it, the money was raised as the women's party moved into Brunswick Street shortly after.

[23] *Labour Leader*, 5 Jan. 1894. The seconder of the motion was Mrs. Neilson, formerly of the Socialist League and attending the SLP conference as a delegate from the Ruskin Society.

[24] *Labour Leader*, 5 Apr. 1894.

[25] *Labour Leader*, 5 Apr. 1894.

included specific reference to 'men and women' after 'electoral rights'. The actual formulation was suggested by Hardie, as he put it, 'in order to avoid opening up a wide question', presumably a coded reference to women's suffrage. However, Mrs Pearce, the Women's Labour Party delegate, declared that 'this would satisfy her.'[26] The Scottish Trade Union Congress debated the issue in 1898 when Margaret Irwin favoured votes for women on the same terms as men, but she was opposed by Robert Smillie, and Congress agreed on the compromise of 'universal adult suffrage'.[27] Adult suffrage would remain the universal socialist and labour position until 1903 when the ILP decided to promote a female suffrage bill.[28]

The ILP did not have a separate women's section, as the Liberal and Conservative Parties had, and this equal membership of the sexes probably encouraged a greater female participation.[29] Amongst socialist organisations the ILP also had a better record. This may have been partly to do with the fact that it was the largest socialist party and the pro-feminist attitudes of prominent male leaders such as Hardie and George Lansbury undoubtedly helped. More fundamentally, however, was the actual practice and outlook of the ILP which distinguished it from the SDF and the Socialist Labour Party. The SocLP, so significant in the development of the shop stewards' movement on Clydeside, placed its emphasis on industrial and workplace struggles which, only too easily, ignored the predicament facing women in the home. Although the SDF and the British Socialist Party (BSP), as it became, was more politically oriented it, nevertheless, shared in the myopic attitude to women.[30]

The ILP, on the other hand, was neither industrially based nor was it dominated by an economic-reductionist approach to theory – in fact it was not burdened by theory at all. This, and its concentration on electoral politics, allowed the ILP to base its propaganda on much more than exploitation at the workplace.[31] This did not make the ILP immune from anti-feminism or guarantee equality in practice; but there were significant numbers of female activists within the party, at both the local and national level. Annie and Ada Maxton, sisters of James Maxton and active members of the ILP in their own right, recalled that there tended to be a bigger

[26] ILP, *Report of Third Annual Conference* (1895) p. 10. Mrs Pearce was almost certainly married to C.W. Bream Pearce, a wealthy businessmen who was a financial supporter of Hardie. Benn, *Keir Hardie*, pp. 107, 118.

[27] S. Lewenhack, 'Women in the Leadership of the STUC 1897–1970', *Scottish Labour History Journal*, vii (1973), pp. 7–8.

[28] J. Liddington & J. Norris, *One Hand Tied Behind Us: The Rise of the Women's Suffrage Movement* (London, 1978), pp. 179–80.

[29] Liddington & Norris, *One Hand Tied Behind Us*, p. 45.

[30] For a detailed discussion of the SDF and its women members see, K. Hunt, *Equivocal Feminists: The Social Democratic Federation and the woman question 1884– 1911* (Cambridge, 1996).

[31] 'Taking about Herstory', interview with Sheila Rowbotham, *Radical Scotland*, xxii, (August/September 1986).

proportion of women speakers at ILP meetings that those of other socialist parties.[32]

In the same year, 1903, that the ILP voted in support of women's suffrage Mrs Pankhurst was elected onto the NAC and the Pankhurst-dominated WSPU was formed. These events were indicative of the growing strength of the women's suffrage movement and an increasing involvement of working class women; in particular, the emergence of what has been termed a 'radical suffragist' campaign based among the women textile workers of Lancashire and Cheshire can be identified.[33] The WSPU, in a very real sense, grew out of the ILP and shared much the same background as the working class radical suffragists. But the WSPU soon chose to concentrate solely upon the vote and influencing middle and upper class women, a growing social exclusiveness marked by its shift from Manchester to London in 1906.[34] However, the new credo of the national leadership did not, necessarily, operate elsewhere and in Glasgow the links between the WSPU and the ILP were to remain close.

Women's Suffrage in Glasgow

From the mid-1900s the women's suffrage campaign moved to a new height of activity. Much of this was due to the formation of the WSPU and its creation of a new 'militant' movement alongside the older, 'constitutional' movement. In Glasgow the WSPU was clearly a left-wing body; indeed, the constitution-alist Glasgow and West of Scotland Society for Women's Suffrage (GWSSWS), itself established in 1902, assumed the new body to be an ILP organisation.[35] As the Glasgow WSPU was set up in late 1906 it was helped by another new arrival on the scene, the socialist weekly *Forward* which began publishing in October of that year. Under the sympathetic editorship of Tom Johnston, the pages of *Forward* were always open to the suffragettes and, like Keir Hardie, he was a consistent advocate of the cause. The very first issue of the paper carried a large advert for a meeting to be addressed by the Pankhursts in the City Halls and in the second issue Johnston himself wrote a lengthy piece describing the women's movement as, 'another Chartist revival', and argued for the connection between women's rights and socialism:

> We can never have socialism without complete democracy, and every privilege broken, every barrier burst, every sex and social hallucination swept aside makes clearer the road and clearer the eyesight for the struggles which are before the people of this and all other countries.[36]

[32] Interview by author with Annie and Ada Maxton, 3 September 1979.
[33] The phrase 'radical suffragist' is used by Liddington & Norris, *One Hand Tied Behind Us*, to distinguish the textile workers both from the NUWSS (which they had close ties to nonetheless) and the WSPU.
[34] Ramelson, *Petticoat Rebellion*, pp. 131–4.
[35] E. King, 'The Scottish Women's Suffrage Movement', in *Out of Bounds*, p. 135.
[36] *Forward* 13, 20 October 1906. Johnston also published a pamphlet, *The Case for Women's Suffrage and Objections Answered* (Glasgow, 1907).

Although the Pankhursts and the heroism of the suffragettes have tended to overshadow the less dramatic contributions of other suffrage campaigners, we now have a picture of a more complex and varied movement. Alongside the WSPU there was the Women's Freedom League (WFL), the United Suffragists, Sylvia Pankhurst's own East London Federation and, of course, the continuing efforts of the non-militant societies affiliated to the NUWSS.[37] Even the distinction between militant and constitutionalist was not absolute, as there was often over-lapping membership between societies and many women recognised a symbiotic relationship between the two wings. It was only in 1912 that the WSPU's increasing use of violence made co-operation impossible.[38] Furthermore, the history of the movement in Scotland differed in important ways from that of England. For instance, while the WSPU's escalating militancy in the immediate pre-war years has been seen as a mark of desperation that cost the organisation members, in Scotland, the lack of progress in Parliament encouraged women into the WSPU at this time and there is no evidence of any defections resulting from the increasingly militant acts.[39]

In Glasgow the links between Labour and the women's movement were complicated. The socialist influence within the WSPU and the WFL meant that relations between the militants and the ILP remained close. When the Pankhursts turned on Labour and even Keir Hardie, *Forward* still carried a regular feature, 'Our Suffrage Columns', which was a voice for the Glasgow WSPU. When *The Suffragette* was banned by the Government, *Forward* (and the SocLP) offered to print it in Glasgow, and in 1913 Johnston organised stewards from among sympathetic dock workers for one of Mrs Pankhurst's biggest meetings.[40] It was not only socialists who supported the women's cause, though it was perhaps socialists who were closest to the militants; Glasgow Town Council was a long-standing supporter of votes for women and the Glasgow Presbytery was one of only two in the Church of Scotland to pass a supportive resolution.[41] This indicates the support which existed, particularly among Liberals, and which was to cause the constitutionalists some difficulties as the NUWSS swung firmly behind the Labour Party in 1912. While the Edinburgh society was willing and in many cases, keen to support Labour candidates in by elections such as South Lanark and Mid-

---

[37] There now exists an extensive historiography of the suffrage movement. Of particular interest to Scotland is the work of Holton, *Feminism and Democracy*; King, 'Scottish Women's Suffrage'; and L. Leneman, *A Guid Cause: The Women's Suffrage Movement in Scotland* (Aberdeen, 1991).

[38] Holton, *Feminism and Democracy*, p. 31.

[39] Leneman, *A Guid Cause*, pp. 109, 140.

[40] Helen Crawfurd, 'unpublished autobiography', n.d. p. 108, Marx Memorial Library, London, copy in Glasgow Caledonian University Library; R. Challinor, *The Origins of British Bolshevism* (London, 1977), p. 153.

[41] Leneman, *A Guid Cause*, pp. 148, 164, 168, 170.

Lothian, the Glasgow Society, overwhelmingly Liberal, was determinedly opposed.[42]

The great fear of suffrage campaigners was that a further reform might be passed which would either extend the suffrage among men or even give manhood suffrage, but which would exclude women and would put their cause back by years. Thus the formulation of the WSPU demand for 'votes for women as are or may be granted to men'. The logic of directing their campaign against the Liberals was a recognition that anything less than a full Government supported Bill had little or no chance of getting through Parliament and the later attack on the Labour Party was because it was effectively supporting the administration.[43] The ILP's formulation of words was very close to that of the women's campaign but it was unable to get the Labour Party to budge from straightforward adult suffrage, even when Keir Hardie threatened to resign over the issue in 1907.[44]

A genuine campaign for universal suffrage could have squared the circle and allowed all socialists and suffragists to co-operate fully and openly. But, in spite of the existence of an adult suffrage society, there is no suggestion that such a campaign was ever likely. In Hardie's opinion the adult suffrage society was merely a spoiling device by those opposed to votes for women, 'it holds no meetings, issues no literature . . . it is never heard of, save when it emerges to oppose the Women's Enfranchisement Bill. Its policy is that of dog in the manger.'[45] Yet, at the same time Hardie did not regard universal suffrage as being in the realms of practical politics.[46] For most women in the Labour movement, therefore, there was a clear choice to be made over women's suffrage or adult suffrage.

For many women this was a difficult choice as they found their loyalties split in attempts to reconcile their socialism with their feminism.[47] The standard argument by adult suffragists was that to enfranchise women under the same terms as men would mean reinforcing the forces of reaction and property as the vast majority of women who would fulfil the property requirement would be middle or upper class. Women suffragists replied by attempting to show that, on the contrary, most women enfranchised

---

[42] Holton, *Feminism and Democracy*, pp. 107–8, 'relations between the Glasgow Society and the Scottish ILP were particularly poor'.

[43] The WSPU adopted an anti-Labour policy in late 1912. Liddington & Norris, *One Hand Tied Behind Us*, p. 250.

[44] Liddington & Norris, *One Hand Tied Behind Us*, p. 234. The ILP constitution stated that it was, 'in favour of adult suffrage with full political rights and privileges for women, and the immediate extension of the franchise to women on the same terms as men.' *Forward*, 16 Feb. 1907.

[45] Quoted in Liddington & Norris, *One Hand Tied Behind Us*, p. 232.

[46] Holton , *Feminism and Democracy*, p. 58.

[47] See Liddington & Norris *One Hand Tied Behind Us*, pp. 161–4 on the difficulty of this choice.

would be working class.[48] Ironically, the argument that votes for women would disadvantage Labour and could help postpone manhood suffrage was used by Conservative women.[49] In Glasgow, opposition to the pro-women's suffrage position of Hardie and Johnston could come from ILP women. Agnes Pettigrew expressed the adult suffrage case in the pages of *Forward*, arguing that as that as matters stood 'votes for women' was a middle class measure which would only work to the advantage of the Conservative Party and weaken Labour.[50]

At the same time as the militant suffrage movement was developing Labour tried to build its own women's section. This was the Women's Labour League (WLL) which had three branches in Glasgow by the end of 1914.[51] Its function was essentially a supportive one of working for the party's candidates at elections (its President was Margaret, wife of Ramsay MacDonald) and it tended to echo Party policy on most issues, including the suffrage.[52] At its 1914 conference, held in conjunction with the Party conference, the WLL attacked the militant tactics of the WSPU as divisive and the result of a 'sex war' attitude. The Executive, while expressing itself, 'as keen as anybody for women's suffrage', accepted that there were other, more immediate issues that should have prior claim on the Labour Party's attention, such as the Dublin lock-out and the South African General Strike.[53] The general view of such 'labour women' was that the struggle for women's emancipation was part and parcel of the wider struggle for socialism and for the emancipation of the working class, which was to be effected through the Labour party and the trade unions. Thus their strategy was to work from within the Labour movement to fight for improvements in the wages and living conditions of the working class. However, put in simplistic terms the WLL line could read, 'The role of women in revolutionising society is to join the Women's Labour League.'[54]

To the members of the WSPU this position not only failed to counteract anti-feminism within working class organisations, but was also a betrayal of women's interests. Janie Allan, who edited *Forward's*, 'Our Suffrage Col-

---

[48] Even a Labour Party survey showed that the majority of women who would have qualified to be working class. See P. Hollis, *Ladies Elect: Women in English Local Government 1865–1914* (Oxford 1987), p. 32.

[49] Leneman, *A Guid Cause*, p. 33.

[50] *Forward*, 16 Feb. 1907. There could be no doubting Pettigrew's labour and socialist credentials. A member of the ILP she was Secretary of the Shop Assistants' Union and was elected to the Glasgow School Board in 1909. In the same year she married George Hardie, brother of Keir Hardie, who became Labour MP for Springburn in 1922. On his death in 1937 Agnes won the seat at the subsequent by-election. See Knox, *Scottish Labour Leaders*, pp. 136–7, biography of Agnes Pettigrew Hardie.

[51] *Forward*, 16 Jan. 1916.

[52] Liddington & Norris, *One Hand Tied Behind Us*, pp. 235–6.

[53] *Forward*, 31 Jan. 1914.

[54] *Forward*, 31 Jan. 1914.

umns', attacked this willingness to relegate the vote and women's issues
generally from primary consideration: 'So long as women are willing to
accept the last place, so long will they find there is no other place for
them'.[55] What makes this dispute particularly interesting is that Allan had
some years previously been vice-president of the WLL.[56] The narrow focus
of Christabel Pankhurst was not shared by the Glasgow women who were
aware of the limitations of the vote but argued that it was the necessary first
step in the continuous battle for equality. This perspective was expressed in
'Our Suffrage Columns' more or less on the eve of the First World War:

> But the vote, after all, is only a weapon not a stronghold, a symbol not a
> magic key. The possession of the weapon is necessary for the greater
> conflicts; and the symbol of equality and responsibility is necessary to
> the self-respect of women.[57]

Such was the massive symbolic value attached to the vote that, perhaps, it
was the single most telling factor behind a woman's decision to participate
actively in the movement. Helen Crawfurd of the Glasgow WSPU recalled
that, 'the members who became most prominent in the WSPU were middle
class women, to whom the best-paid professions were closed because of their
sex.' In her view the majority of activists were

> serious thoughtful women who were far from satisfied, not only with
> their position, but with the unjust social laws, over which they had no
> control. It was gall and wormwood to these intelligent women to see the
> most ignorant and undeveloped men allowed to participate in elections
> as voters while they were debarred.[58]

The most thorough history of women's suffrage in Scotland supports
Crawfurd's recollections of the social composition of the movement. Militant or constitutional – all three organisations, WSPU, WFL and GWSSWS,
were overwhelmingly middle class.[59] Generally speaking it can be said that
while the militants attracted a considerable number of socialists to their
ranks they did not attract a working class membership. The constitutionalists
in Glasgow, conversely, were hostile to socialism, but did have some working
class input through the affiliation of the Co-operative Women's Guilds,
though whether they welcomed this is another matter.[60]

Socialist women like Janie Allan, sister of James Allan, owner of the Allan

---

[55] *Forward,* 7 Feb. 1914.
[56] King, 'Scottish Women's Suffrage', p. 138.
[57] *Forward,* 1 Aug. 1914.
[58] Crawfurd, 'autobiography', pp. 87, 113.
[59] 'Nearly all the women about whom anything is known were of independent
means.' Leneman, *A Guid Cause,* p. 129.
[60] The GWSSWS 'took fright when the Co-operative Women's Guild branches
started to apply en masse for membership.' King, 'Scottish Women's Suffrage',
p. 136.

Shipping Line and also a socialist, played prominent roles in the militant campaign and, in Allan's case was a major financial supporter of the WSPU.[61] If Allan had been a suffragette before becoming a socialist, Helen Crawfurd's political trajectory was the other way round, and she joined the ILP on the outbreak of the war. Though brought up in a Tory family Crawfurd was to play a significant role in the rent strike and the peace campaign and by the end of the war she was the most prominent woman in the Scottish ILP before leaving for the Communist Party.[62] Another significant socialist was Teresa Billington-Greig who, although from Manchester, was living in Glasgow at this period and was instrumental in establishing the WSPU in Scotland before breaking with the Pankhursts in 1907 and setting up the WFL.[63]

Alongside women such as these, representative of the movement's membership, were a smaller group of working class activists such as Jennie MacCallum, a factory worker and Annie Rhoda Craig, wife of a stevedore and ILPer, who attacked Winston Churchill's car in Glasgow in 1912.[64] While very little is known about these women there is a fair amount of biographical detail on one woman, Jessie Stephen. Born in London in 1890, her family moved to Scotland, eventually settling in Glasgow. Her father, a socialist, was a tailor who was frequently unemployed and Jessie followed him into the ILP when sixteen, also joining the WSPU about the same time. Despite having won a scholarship, she had to leave school to work as a domestic servant. Jessie's contributions to the cause included acid attacks on post boxes, her neat domestic's uniform arousing no suspicion of her incendiary intent. Active in organising a trade union she moved to London to work for the Domestic Workers of Great Britain, returned to Glasgow during the war, then to London again to work for Sylvia Pankhurst and the Workers' Suffrage Federation.[65]

In her role as an activist Jessie Stephen would appear to have been more of an exception rather than a typical member.[66] Indeed there was a

[61] King, 'Scottish Women's Suffrage', p. 138.

[62] Crawfurd, 'autobiography'. See also biography of Crawfurd by H. Corr in Knox, *Scottish Labour Leaders*, pp. 81–6

[63] Leneman, *A Guid Cause*, pp. 42–3; King, 'Scottish Women's Suffrage', pp. 135, 140.

[64] Leneman, *A Guid Cause*, pp. 109, 129.

[65] For biographical information on Jessie Stephen see interview with her in *Spare Rib*, xxxii (1975). I am also very grateful to Audrey Canning for additional information on Stephen from her forthcoming entry in the *New Dictionary of National Biography* (Oxford, forthcoming).

[66] Leneman makes the point that we simply do not know how many working class suffragettes remain in obscurity and, quotes from an interview with Stephen conducted by Brian Harrison where she says there was, 'a tremendous number of working class women'. Leneman, *A Guid Cause*, pp. 93–4. However, this contradicts her view in *Spare Rib* (1975) where she refers to general sympathy with the cause, not active involvement.

reluctance by the WSPU to involve working class women in militant actions because, if caught, the punishment they received in the courts and in prison was particularly severe. To an extent the middle class status of the archetypal suffragette gave them a degree of protection; they were more confident and articulate in dealing with officials and female prison warders tended to defer to such prisoners. For working class women the whole legal process could be much more traumatic; one woman, arrested in Glasgow in 1912 for breaking windows, could not make herself understood in court and her resolve broke: 'I jist broke ane . . . I'm sayin' a'm kind o' vexed noo that I did it, but I'll pay for the damage if ye like.'[67]

Despite being convinced that the suffragettes enjoyed considerable support among working class women (and men), Jessie Stephen was aware, because of her own background, that the growing tendency towards violent outrages by the WSPU had an alienating effect on working class women.[68] This was partly why Teresa Billington-Greig left both the WFL and the militant movement generally as early as 1911. Regarding the movement as too extreme and too narrowly focused, she wrote:

> Votes for women we must have, and many other things for women, but votes for women over-hurried and at any price may cost us too dear. A slower, bigger and more outspoken movement alone would have had any chance to appeal to the women who are industrially enslaved.[69]

Yet, this view did not differ from that of women like Jessie Stephen who saw the vote as 'only a means to an end'. Recalling the 'aspirations of the ordinary member of the WSPU', she said, 'These were about jobs, about wages, about the present matrimonial laws. . . . Some of these women had deep convictions about the economic structure of society, and there was the question of housing, and the question of making life easier for women in the home, and maternity benefits. . . .'[70]

In the main, therefore, it would appear that working class women were supportive of the demand for the vote but found the democratic workings of the constitutional societies, such as organising petitions and holding meetings to be the most acceptable methods. Yet, this does not mean that they were anti-militant or diametrically opposed to direct action. As we shall see below, the rent strike during the war, which made housing and the home a mass political issue, saw respectable housewives of the women's guilds prepared to take on the forces of the state.

---

[67] *Glasgow Herald*, 11 Mar. 1912, quoted in King, 'Scottish Women's Suffrage', p. 137. Recognition of this class difference does not lessen the heroism of the women who were sent to prison and especially those who suffered the tortures of forced feeding.

[68] *Spare Rib*, (1975).

[69] T. Billington-Greig, *The Militant Suffrage Movement* (London, 1911), quoted in Liddington & Norris, *One Hand Tied Behind Us*, p. 251.

[70] *Spare Rib*, (1975).

Labour and the 'Old Women': Politics pre-1914

It was often pointed out by pro-women suffrage campaigners that the exclusion of women from the parliamentary vote was made a greater anomaly since they already had the vote in municipal affairs. For instance, Tom Johnston argued that, 'no evil effects have followed' from women voting in local elections.[71] Yet, at the same time it was accepted by socialists like Johnston that the existing female electorate was a reactionary, anti-labour force which could, at least on occasion, play a critical role.

Essentially women householders, but not married women, were able to qualify for the municipal franchise.[72] In Glasgow in 1901 there were some 23,223, women voters, or just over 17% of the total municipal electorate.[73] Within the twenty-five wards at that time there was a variation from under 10% to over 30%, with no fixed gradation by social class; the 'slum' area of Cowcaddens had more women voters, both numerically and proportionately than middle class Dennistoun – 1258 female electors (20%) to 887 (15%). Those wards with the lowest proportion of women voters were the 'artisan' wards of Springburn and Cowlairs (both 9%) and the 'business' wards of Blythswood and Exchange (10% and 7% respectively). However, those wards with the highest proportions of female electors were the most clearly middle class, residential areas such as Kelvinside and Park (28% and 30% respectively).

As we saw in chapter one labour was doing badly in the municipal polls in the early to mid-1900s and in its attempts to explain its lack of success focused on the female voter. Thus, William Stewart, the defeated Labour candidate for Dalmarnock at the 1904 poll:

> In reality we did win on the men's vote. There are twelve hundred women voters, mostly controlled by the churches, and the most of them voted against labour, the result being that Mr. Harvie joins his friend Mr Willock as the representative of the old women – of both sexes.[74]

Stewart actually listed other reasons why Labour did not win: previous Labour nominees had lost the confidence of the constituency; Tories and Liberals combined; religion was used to denigrate Labour, as was temperance; the unpopular sitting candidate was replaced by a new man; a third candidate was introduced, 'to confuse the issue'. And yet, despite all this, the

[71] Johnston, *Case for Women's Suffrage*, p. 10.
[72] The legislation was introduced in England first and then Scotland. At first all female householders were included but a legal decision in 1872 removed married women. B.K. Lucas, *The English Local Government Franchise: A Short History* (London, 1952), pp. 166–7; Hollis, *Ladies Elect*, pp. 31–33.
[73] *Glasgow Post Office Directory 1901–1902.* This year is used because it was the last year in which the Directory made a clear distinction within the electorate by sex. 17% was also the proportion accounted for by women in England & Wales, Hollis, *Ladies Elect*, p. 31.
[74] *Labour Leader*, 11 Nov. 1904.

defeat was, ultimately laid at the door of the 'old women' or the 'bible women'. The following year, after a second defeat, Stewart's explanation remained unchanged, 'So we were beaten comrades by the old women of both sexes.'[75]

Before dismissing Stewart's explanations as the self-serving excuses of a failed candidate it is worth establishing what substance they contain. Those women who managed to get on the electoral register would likely have been 'old' in that they had to be householders and would tend, when not unmarried, to have been widowed. The influence of the Churches upon women was testified by many, as was religion's general hostility to socialism. Helen Crawfurd, who was brought up in the Gorbals in the 1880s in a strongly religious and Tory household, recalled that, as a child, 'If I heard the word [socialism] I fled as from the devil'.[76] Married in 1898 to a Presbyterian Minister, her growing awareness of inequality and questioning of women's subordinate role received the stern admonition from her husband, 'Woman, that is blasphemy'.[77] At a more general level, Crawfurd could see that, while working class men were organising and educating themselves, this was a very one-sided development. 'The women in Scotland, however, were still bound hand and foot to the Church in its various forms, to evangelical religion and even spiritualism.' Critical of male socialists in this period for not doing enough to involve women she also felt that she was better able to appeal to women because she herself had been 'extremely religious.'[78]

Numerically, the women voters of Dalmarnock could have swayed the result: there were around 1200 female electors and Labour lost by 358 votes in 1904 and 750 votes in 1905.[79] However, women only accounted for about 15% of the total municipal poll in Dalmarnock and when Stewart lost for a third time in 1906 – this time coming bottom of the poll and over 2,000 votes adrift of Scott Gibson – he did not mention the 'old women'.[80] Yet, in the elections of 1908 the women voters were again identified as the 'deciding factor' in Labour's defeat. Once again Labour saw itself up against an 'unholy alliance' of publicans and temperance parties, Liberals and Tories and the Churches and its success in attracting women to the polls in Hutchesontown was put down to, 'the spreading of the stereotyped lies and the slanders regarding the private character and religious views of the Socialist Candidate.'[81] Socialists had to defend themselves constantly against

[75] *Labour Leader*, 17 Nov. 1905.
[76] Crawfurd, 'autobiography', p. 13
[77] Crawfurd, 'autobiography', p. 45.
[78] Crawfurd, 'autobiography', pp 48–9.
[79] *Glasgow Herald*, 2 Nov. 1904, 8 Nov. 1905. Female electorate extracted from *Glasgow Post Office Directory*.
[80] *Labour Leader*, 16 Nov. 1906.
[81] *Forward*, 7 Nov. 1908. Similar excuses were made in other wards such as Townhead and Anderston where defeat 'was due to the Bible women and the charity soup kitchens.' *Glasgow Herald*, 4 Nov. 1908.

the charge that they were advocates of enforced 'free love' and it is more than likely that such an identification, plus the label of atheist, would have harmed them in the eyes of many religious women.

The true picture behind Labour's local fortunes at this time was that the electoral alliance behind the Workers' Election Committee (WEC) had collapsed and the ILP was, as yet, unable to re-organise a successful campaign. While there was almost a mark of desperation in Labour's explanations for its poor performances at this time, the language used reveals something about personal attitudes towards women held by male socialists. Even Tom Johnston was not immune to such conceits. After the municipal election of 1906, at which Labour fared particularly badly, Johnston attacked the 'Temperance Party' for its hypocritical opposition to Labour and characterised them as, 'old women wearing trousers to pose as men.'[82] The derogatory sense attached to the repeatedly used phrase, 'old women', is quite clear as is the implicit assumption about woman's inferiority to man. Few socialists would publicly have defended such a proposition and most would have argued the basic equality between men and women but, to varying extents, these attitudes did exist and can be glimpsed in throwaway remarks about wearing trousers. Nonetheless, Johnston was, at the same time, a committed supporter of women's suffrage and women's rights generally. His choice of words do not reveal him as a secret misogynist, but the pejorative tones do indicate a tension between official political views and more personal, possibly unconscious, antipathies towards women.[83]

This could have a debilitating effect on the wider political and organisational involvement of women. It has been pointed out that in regard to women inhabiting leading positions, the STUC has a much better record, historically, than the all-British TUC; indeed the first Secretary of the Scottish congress was a woman, Margaret Irwin.[84] However, in accepting the position Irwin insisted it be an interim appointment only and she had already refused nomination as Chairman. In both instances her reason was the same, she 'feared that at this early stage of the Congress work, it might be somewhat prejudicial to its interest were the post to be filled by a woman.'[85] However, concentration on leadership obscures the reality of most working class women's lives which were dominated by marriage and family.

[82] *Forward*, 17 Nov. 1906.

[83] Ernest Belfort Bax of the SDF was the most openly and crudely misogynist of British socialists. See Hunt, *Equivocal Feminists*, pp. 57–63 on Bax. Trotsky, writing about his period in Vienna in 1907, described how the leading Austro-marxists 'revealed' their true selves, 'in informal talks . . . much more frankly than in their articles and speeches', including 'their vileness towards women.' Trotsky, *My Life* (London, 1979), pp. 214–5.

[84] S. Lewenhak, 'Women in the Leadership of the STUC 1897–1970', pp. 3–23.

[85] Quoted in Lewenhack, 'Women in the Leadership', p. 6; also A. Tuckett, *The Scottish Trades Union Congress: The First Eighty Years, 1897–1977* (Edinburgh, 1986), p. 39.

With this in mind, the organisation which takes on greater significance is the Scottish Co-operative Women's Guild (SCWG). Run by and for housewives, the Guild simply dwarfed all other women's organisations within the labour movement: established in 1892 with twenty-two branches and a membership of 1,500, by 1913 it had grown to 157 branches and 12,420 members.[86] Although established with very modest aims, it was the Guild which provided most women with their initial experience of organisation; nearly all the Labour women activists of this period appear to have been Guild members, and its own history is an accurate gauge of the position of women within the broader movement in Scotland.

While the Co-operative Women's Guild in England had been formed in 1883, in Scotland there were only unofficial women's groups run through Co-operative Educational Committees. Influenced by the English example and with the encouragement of a few sympathetic men, a group of women from the Kinning Park Co-operative society took the lead in setting up their own Guild and then the Scottish-wide body; in an echo of the wartime rent strike the initial assembly was a kitchen meeting.[87] The founding document of the SCWG stated that: 'Its object is to assist in the propaganda of Co-operation, and to draw a closer bond of union between the wives, mothers and daughters of Co-operators, by mutual aid and social intercourse.'[88]

Much of the Guild's effort was directed towards raising funds for Co-operative causes and most of their 'social intercourse' revolved around cookery and dressmaking lessons and discussions. As such the Guild reinforced women's domestic role and was seen in this light by male Co-operators, an attitude expressed in the maxim, 'The Guild should be to the movement what the wife and mother is to the home.'[89] Despite such a limited perspective, the Guild was crucial in two inter-related areas: in breaking down the institutional barriers to women's active involvement in the broader labour movement, and in developing the abilities of individual women. Kinning Park seems to have been about the most progressive Co-operative society and certainly it was the pioneer of the Guilds, yet it was not until 1916 that it elected its first woman director.[90]

The influence of the Guild may have been slow and gradual in making itself felt but it was real nevertheless. It was through the work of the Guild that women began to take up positions within the Co-operative societies and the Guild itself became recognised by the labour movement as a significant entity with the right to delegate representation on local Labour Representation

[86] A. Buchan, *History of the Scottish Co-operative Women's Guild* (Glasgow, 1913), pp. 50, 112.

[87] Buchan, *Co-operative Women's Guild*, see chapters one and two.

[88] Buchan, *Co-operative Women's Guild*, p. 50.

[89] James Deans in his Preface to Buchan, *Co-operative Women's Guild*.

[90] P.J. Dollan, *History of the Kinning Park Co-operative Society Ltd.* (Glasgow, 1923), p. 94.

Committees.[91] Alongside such activity the Guild also debated and adopted positions on the important political issues of the day. The SCWG was an early advocate of women's suffrage, petitioning the government on the subject in 1893 and in 1905 it rejected the Labour party's position of adult suffrage.[92] The Guild chose to affiliate to the constitutionalist wing of the suffrage movement rather than the 'militant party', though it is impossible to say whether individual women were active in the WSPU or WFL.[93]

There can be little doubt that the Guild was of major significance in the self-development of many working-class women, particularly housewives, whose isolation within the home should not be under-estimated. The space provided by the weekly Guild meeting, free of any male domination, was crucial in allowing the members to 'be their natural selves, and freely express their ideas and opinions.'[94] Within such an atmosphere women could more easily learn the mechanics of organisation and gain the confidence to chair meetings and speak in front of an audience. What was learned within the Guild could then be applied elsewhere. This was done to most dramatic effect in the rent strike which was described by one early labour historian as, 'an agitation instigated and conducted by Kinning Park members' in South Govan.[95]

Housing: Labour Discovers the Housewife

In the immediate pre-war period and in the early years of the war a new, more positive attitude towards women and women voters began to be expressed by Labour in Glasgow. Partly this reflected the national resolution of the vexed relationship between Labour and the women's suffrage issue. At its annual conference in January 1912 the Labour Party decided on a formulation which, while still in favour of adult suffrage, declared that the Party in Parliament would refuse to support any suffrage bill that did not include women. This decision made no impact on the WSPU but for the NUWSS, especially with the defeat of the Conciliation Bill in March, it paved the way for a closer understanding with Labour and the National Union decided to support Labour candidates with activists and finance in subsequent by-elections.[96] While the NUWSS helped Labour in the Scottish by-

---

[91] The Maxton sisters regarded the Guild as, 'quite a power to be reckoned with.' Interview with Annie and Ada Maxton 3 September 1979.
[92] Gordon, *Women and the Labour Movement in Scotland 1850–1914* (Oxford, 1991), p. 269.
[93] Buchan, *Co-operative Women's Guild*, p. 68; Gordon, *Women and the Labour Movement*, p. 268; 'King, Scottish Women's Suffrage', p. 136.
[94] Buchan, *Co-operative Women's Guild*, p. 10.
[95] Dollan, *Kinning Park*, pp. 86, 93. South Govan was where the rent strike originated and was covered by the Kinning Park Co-operative Society. Amongst the Kinning Park Guild members who took leading roles in the strike were Helen Barbour and Agnes Dollan, wife of Patrick.
[96] Holton, *Feminism and Democracy*, pp. 73–5; Liddington & Norris, *One Hand Tied Behind Us*, p. 247.

elections at Leith, Mid-Lothian and South Lanark this new departure was not universally popular among suffragists; the steadfast Liberals of the Glasgow Society were strongly opposed.[97]

But, alongside this development Labour's own local perspective had also begun to change, albeit gradually. After yet another poor showing at the municipal elections in 1909, *Forward* did not castigate the 'old women' but, on the contrary, argued that socialism was struggling because it had 'neglected the women.'[98] As detailed in chapter one, it was from this point on that Labour's electoral fortunes began to recover, resulting, within a few years, in a sizeable Labour presence on the City Council.[99] This new-found success was built on the politicisation of the housing issue and the galvanising of public support through new, popular organisations such as the Glasgow Women's Housing Association (GWHA). With housing established as the priority issue in municipal politics, Labour's attitude towards the female electorate became much more positive. In early 1915 *Forward* was urging that the President of the GWHA, Mrs Laird, be adopted as a municipal candidate as part of a strategy which linked Labour's housing policy and a direct appeal to women voters: 'Housing is, above all, a woman's question. Women have already enough votes and influence to turn the balance in favour of the Labour Party – which is the only housing party – in two-thirds of the wards in Glasgow.'[100]

If the housing situation in Glasgow in 1914 was bad, the war only served to make matters worse. Andrew McBride, founder of the Labour Party Housing Committee (LPHC) in Glasgow in 1913, described a situation of near 'famine' as no new houses were being built and so much of the existing stock was 'admitted to be unfit for human habitation'.[101] The rapid expansion of Clydeside's heavy industries to meet the needs of the military attracted more workers into the area, thereby exacerbating the problem. Moreover, many people had to travel long distances to and from work, opportunities, through higher wages, to move to a better house were thwarted, and newly-married couples were faced with a complete shortage of housing. All of this raised tensions and fed into the burgeoning industrial unrest.[102] With a sharp increase in the cost of living, tenants became very sensitive to the perceived opportunism of landlords in pushing up rents.

Evictions of tenants for arrears, particularly those involving dependants of men under arms, hardened attitudes even more and provided flash points

[97] Holton, *Feminism and Democracy*, pp. 107–8: Leneman, *A Guid Cause*, p. 197.
[98] Quoted in Gordon, *Women and the Labour Movement*, p. 274.
[99] See chapter one, pp. 65–9.
[100] *Forward*, 16 Jan. 1915.
[101] Quoted in J. Melling, *Rent Strikes: People's Struggle for Housing in West Scotland 1890–1916* (Edinburgh, 1983), p. 40.
[102] PP 1917, *Report of the Royal Commission on the Housing of the Industrial Population of Scotland Rural and Urban*, Cd. 8731 Ch. XXXIV 'Bad Housing as a Factor in Industrial Unrest'. See chapter two, pp.81–2.

for the expression of outrage and hostility. For example, in Shettleston in June 1915 a crowd gathered at the eviction of a soldier's family and John Wheatley had to dissuade them from attacking the landlord's home. The report in *Forward* read, 'The women particularly were greatly and indignantly excited. Wheatley said that this was pre-eminently a strike for a poor woman and that poor women should undertake it. At the end of the meeting, some 500 women went to the ILP rooms and handed in their names as pickets.'[103] This incident illustrates the combination of spontaneous direct action and more or less immediate organisation which was such a marked feature of the rent strike and the basis of its success.[104]

It was actually in Govan, among the more respectable working class tenants, where the strike originated in the spring of 1915 and which remained the major bulwark of the struggle. The movement continued throughout the summer, flaring up in one area after another, but by the autumn it had become a more cohesive and threatening campaign and was successful in convincing the Government to pass a Rent Restriction Act before the year was out. What forced the Government's hand was the threat of the housing unrest spilling over into the factories and shipyards and affecting the production of war material. However, this should not detract from the significance of the rent strike itself and the actions of the women behind it. For those working class housewives the home was their point of production and the struggle waged over housing had, for them, much more direct personal resonance than either industrial struggles or campaigns for formal political rights. This is not to argue that such concerns did not affect women or to regard them as in opposition to domestic concerns, but it is simply to emphasise why housing galvanised these women into direct action.

The rent strike was, at heart, a housewives' campaign. Defence of the home was the prime responsibility of the wife and mother, particularly so in wartime with so many men absent, and the nature of tenement life meant that any defence of an individual flat was almost bound to become a collective act involving the whole close. Indeed, the strike could only be carried out on a collective basis. Much of the organisation of the strike effectively took place at home. Close committees were formed by women and kitchen meetings held to discuss their immediate situation and organise their defence. Homes were made secure by maintaining mass pickets against intended evictions and, when necessary, forcibly driving away factors and sheriff officers. This willingness to physically confront and even assault male figures of authority gave the rent strike much of its impact. Alongside such

---

[103] *Forward*, 19 Jun. 1915.

[104] 'Local mobilisation and direct personal contact laid the foundations for collective action in a way that a general appeal by Labour organisations could not have done.' Melling, *Rent Strikes*, p. 64. Melling's account of the rent strike is by far the most thorough and there is no need to repeat its detailed coverage here.

actions, however, there had to be a more general level of organisation and this was provided by the GWHA.[105]

The organisation of the GWHA was significant both in terms of its methods of activity and its leadership. Its most active members included prominent Labour women such as Agnes Dollan and Helen Crawfurd, the ex-suffragette, but also local figures such as Mrs Mary Barbour, Mary Laird and Mrs Ferguson. They, like the women on strike, were working class-housewives and their methods of organisation were geared to their own situation. Alongside the large-scale public meetings and demonstrations they showed themselves adept at organising, they also built on the 'spontaneous' organisation of the kitchen and close committees. Regular public meetings were held in halls and theatres around the city to discuss and co-ordinate general activity. The timing of the meetings was significant, weekdays at 3 p.m., a time when it would have been impossible for workers of either sex to attend, but which was eminently suitable for housewives who could still get home in time to make dinner. Apparently mundane matters such as this were important in developing new political techniques and in extending political involvement. What was learnt in the rent strike could be applied elsewhere.

The declaration of war divided the women's suffrage campaign much as it divided the labour and socialist movement, and both the WSPU and NUWSS dropped their agitation. The most famous schism was that within the Pankhurst family as Christabel became jingoistic in her war fervour while Sylvia declared herself against the war and, ultimately, for revolutionary socialism.[106] Similar divisions occurred in Glasgow where Helen Crawfurd left the WSPU because of its pro-war stance and became one of the principal leaders of the anti-war movement. This contrasted sharply with the progress of the woman responsible for attracting Crawfurd to the cause, Helen Fraser, the WSPU's Scottish Secretary who became an arch-patriot and propagandist for the contribution women were making to the war effort.[107]

In the spring of 1915 an International Women's Congress was held in the Hague, out of which was born the Women's International League (WIL), the British Section of which was organised by those who had left the NUWSS and other suffragist women.[108] A Glasgow branch was formed in November incorporating a wide spectrum of political opinion: President of the Branch was Mrs Crosthwaite, a Liberal and non-militant suffragist, while the Secre-

[105] The role played by the GWHA was 'critical and . . . decisive.' S. Damer, 'State, Class and Housing: Glasgow 1885–1919', in J. Melling (ed.), *Housing, Social Policy and the State* (London, 1980), p. 104.

[106] S. Pankhurst, *The Suffragette Movement* (London, 1977), p. 593.

[107] Crawfurd , 'autobiography', p 86; Fraser undertook a speaking tour to the USA in support of American intervention and published a book, *Women and War Work* (New York, 1918).

[108] Pankhurst, *Suffragette Movement*, p. 593; S. Rowbotham, *The Friends of Alice Wheeldon* (London, 1986), pp. 34, 117.

tary was Helen Crawfurd, militant and socialist.[109] The aims of the WIL were opposition to the war and to conscription and to this end the Glasgow members organised conferences, demonstrations and public meetings with national figures like Ethel Snowden as speakers.

However, within the branch there existed, alongside Helen Crawfurd, a small group of socialist and more militantly pacifist women who went on to found a Women's Peace Crusade (WPC) which operated parallel to the WIL.[110] Launched at a conference in Glasgow in June 1916, the WPC called for an immediate negotiated peace and began a summer campaign of street meetings in working class communities.[111] The following summer there was a second, national launch of the WPC with Glasgow, once again, chosen as the centre to start the campaign. From this point activity was sustained until the end of the war and other towns followed Glasgow's example, particularly in the North of England, with perhaps as many as one hundred branches being established.[112]

It was its method of propaganda more than its programme that made the WPC distinctive. While the WIL held regular monthly meetings and dealt with issues other than the war, the WPC concentrated solely on the war, organising street meetings and marches with occasional stunts such as when Helen Crawfurd and Agnes Dollan broke into the City Chambers and showered leaflets on to the heads of the assembled councillors. Highly emotive and religious imagery was utilised with children on demonstrations holding placards such as 'I Want My Daddy', badges depicting the 'Angel of Peace' protecting children, and singing hymns.[113]

Parallels and continuities with the rent strike are very apparent. As with the rent strike there was a great emphasis on the family; on demonstrations women, children and men marched in separate contingents, and contributions came from women who had lost husbands or sons in the war. Like the GWHA, the WPC was an autonomous women's body and its methods of organisation were geared to reaching and involving working class housewives. Although it became large enough to hold its own large-scale public meetings with speakers such as Sylvia Pankhurst and Charlotte Despard, most activity was at street level directed at women in or as near the home as

[109] Crawfurd, 'autobiography', p. 150.

[110] For more detail see J. Smyth, 'Rents, Peace, Votes: Working Class Women and Political Activity in the First World War', in Breitenbach & Gordon, *Out of Bounds*, pp. 174–96.

[111] The very first meetings of the WPC were in Maryhill and Springburn. *Forward*, 5 Aug. 1916.

[112] J. Liddington, 'The Women's Peace Crusade: The History of a Forgotten Campaign', in D. Thompson, (ed.), *Over Our Dead Bodies: Women Against the Bomb* (London, 1983), pp. 180–98; see also D. Mitchell, *Women on the Warpath; the Story of the Women of the First World War* (London, 1966).

[113] This did not save them from attacks in the press or even physical assaults at their meetings – sometimes led by enraged clergymen. Mitchell, *Women on the Warpath*, pp. 310–11.

possible. Echoing the GWHA, regular organisational meetings were held in local halls on weekday afternoons and were closed to men.[114]

The two groups also shared the same cadre of local leaders who were to go on to play prominent roles in other campaigns and in the wider labour and socialist movement. For example at the May Day demonstration on Glasgow Green in 1917, among the platform speakers were Mrs Barbour, Mrs Dollan, Mrs Ferguson and Mrs Laird, all activists in the rent strike and peace movement.[115]

Labour and Women: Wartime and After

With the passing of the Representation of the People Act of 1918 the political parties, regardless of their previous position on women's suffrage, had to make efforts to address the new female electorate. In spite of the restrictions on the women's franchise – deliberately introduced so as to avoid a majority female electorate – the change was, nonetheless, spectacular.[116] From a position of having no votes there were suddenly 194,332 women on the parliamentary register in Glasgow, 37% of the total electorate. At the municipal level women now had more or less parity with men; in 1918 there were 219,743 women local electors, 49% of the total and in almost one third of the wards in the city women comprised a majority.[117]

Those wards with female majorities were overwhelmingly middle class and solidly pro-Moderate, an indication of the class bias in the 1918 franchise as regards women.[118] Nonetheless, this still left a huge new body of working class women voters to whom Labour was now well equipped to appeal.[119] Most obviously Labour was the undisputed champion of the tenant in a situation where housing was a critical issue in both national and local politics. The ILP had made a direct connection between women, housing and voting Labour at the start of the war but after the mobilisation of women in the rent strike and the creation of a mass female electorate that argument had significantly greater resonance. Furthermore, the methods of agitation and propaganda utilised to such effect in the rent strike and also the peace campaign were quickly adopted to electioneering once the war was over. This was vividly illustrated in the municipal election of 1919 in the Woodside

---

[114] For instance see a WPC advert in *Forward,* 16 Feb. 1918.

[115] *Forward,* 5, 12 May 1917.

[116] See M. Pugh, *Electoral Reform in War and Peace 1906–1918* (London, 1978), p. 151 on parliament avoiding a majority of women electors. For the impact of the 1918 reform see M. Dyer, *Capable Citizens and Improvident Democrats: The Scottish Electoral System 1884–1929* (Aberdeen, 1996), pp. 113–7.

[117] *Glasgow Herald,* 1 Nov. 1918.

[118] See Introduction, p. 31, and Chapter Three, pp. 121–2.

[119] See Dyer, *Capable Citizens,* p. 115. The bias towards the Unionists was strongest in suburban and rural seats and weaker in industrial constituencies.

ward where the sitting Labour Councillor, George Smith, was regarded as highly vulnerable due to his being gaoled as a conscientious objector during the war. In the event Smith won by a comfortable margin of over 600 votes, a victory attributed in part to his 'practice for months past of regularly holding meetings during the afternoons in the back courts, whence he addresses the housewives at their kitchen windows.'[120]

Women's experiences of the war were not, however, restricted solely to rents and housing. The most popular image of women in the war is of those working in munitions yet little has been written about women workers in war time Clydeside. Partly this is due to the drama of the rent strike which directs attention to the housewife, and partly it is due to the nature of the shop stewards' movement which was overwhelmingly male. As an organisation of skilled workers the CWC did not include the unskilled or semi-skilled of either sex. However, if there were no women shop stewards there could still be acts of solidarity across the shopfloor, for instance when the CWC threatened a national strike in support of an unofficial stoppage by women at Beardmore's munitions factory.[121]

Munitions was essentially a new industry in Scotland which, apart from Beardmore's, had to be built up from scratch. Moreover, the metal industries on Clydeside were overwhelmingly male; before the war over 185,000 men were employed in the metal trades compared to fewer than 4,000 women and, of these, more than half were employed at the Singer sewing machine works in Clydebank. By the middle of 1916 over 18,000 women were employed in munitions in Glasgow and the West of Scotland and by the end of the war this figure had reached over 28,000. While women were recruited to this work from as far afield as the Outer Hebrides it would appear that most were local. Women transferred from existing jobs such as textiles and domestic service and others took up employment having been non-employed previously, including a significant number of wives and other relations of servicemen.[122]

Amongst these new recruits younger girls would seem to have been more pro-war or at least more easily mobilised into displays of patriotic fervour; for instance when Lloyd George was given the freedom of the City in June 1917 it was young women munitions workers who provided him with a guard of honour.[123] Moreover, among older women, especially the wives of soldiers, there was the perception that trade unions were responsible for the restriction of output. Yet, this did not necessarily lead to hostility to trade unionism since organisation could be seen as a means of defending the

---

[120] *Forward*, 15 Nov. 1919.

[121] J. Hinton, *The First Shop Stewards' Movement* (London, 1973), p. 251; see also J. Foster, 'Strike Action and Working Class Politics on Clydeside 1914–1919', *International Review of Social History*, xxv (1990), p. 51.

[122] The information in this paragraph comes from W.R. Scott & J. Cunnison, *The Industries of the Clyde Valley During the War* (Oxford, 1924), pp. 94–8.

[123] *Glasgow Herald*, 30 Jun. 1917. See Chapter Two p. 90.

conditions of the men until their return.[124] There is evidence that women workers in munitions and elsewhere were prepared to take strike action during the war over wages and conditions and it has been argued that this tends to further negate the view of war-time unrest as existing within separate and opposed spheres of community on the one hand and industry on the other. The view that lessons learned by women at the workplace could then be applied in the community can, however, be reversed: since the mass influx of women into war work did not occur until after January 1916, i.e. after the rent strike, it is just as likely that married women were taking the solidarity of the community into the workplace.[125]

The return to peace-time conditions at the end of the hostilities was made easier by women's own view of their war-time employment as temporary and willingness to be displaced by the returning soldiers. This does not imply that the women were docile but indicates a rational strategy from within a family and community based perspective. Furthermore, it does seem as though the women employed in munitions did have their expectations raised by the experience of better wages and conditions in employment.[126] Although the CWC did not include women within its ranks it did recognise women as workers having a right to employment the same as men.[127] This attitude was continued into the immediate post-war period and the 40 Hours Strike of January 1919. In the pages of *The Strike Bulletin* women were appealed to on the same terms as men; the threat of unemployment also hung over them and their direct involvement as strikers and pickets was made clear.[128] However, this positive militancy could not be sustained once the immediate post-war boom had ended and it ebbed away as unemployment grew. The active inclusion of women in the 40 Hours' Strike contrasts sharply with their position in the General Strike of 1926 where the STUC did not regard women as fellow workers, but gave only a cursory nod to their role as supporters operating from within the home.[129] The limited opportunities available to women workers can be seen in the continuing significance of domestic service after the War. In 1931 'domestic servants

[124] A.W. Kirkaldy, (ed.), *Labour, Finance and the War* (London, 1916), 'Report on the Employment of Women in the Engineering and Shipbuilding Trades' by J.E. & H.E.R. Highton, p. 133.
[125] Foster, 'Strike Action', pp. 40–41. See discussion on this matter in Chapter Two, pp. 81–7.
[126] Kirkaldy, *Labour and War*, p. 136.
[127] This can be seen in the pages of *The Worker*, the CWC journal.
[128] See *The Strike Bulletin* (Organ of the 40 Hours Movement) Jan.-Feb. 1919. Foster, 'Strike Action', p. 55, refers to the 'carnival aspect' of the 40 hours strike and the involvement of 'women and young people'.
[129] *The Scottish Worker* (Official Organ of the STUC) made only one reference to women in an article 'Our Women' published in issue No. 4 Thursday May 13. Compare to *The Strike Bulletin* 12 Feb. 1919, 'Whether as pickets, strikers or counsellors, the women have given sterling service . . .' which is only one of numerous pieces about women's involvement.

(indoor)' was the largest single occupational category for women at 22,739. Although the area and population of the City was much larger in 1931, the proportion of women employed as domestic servants remained the same as 1911 at just under 14%. Some evidence of the shift back to domestic service after the war may be revealed in that the 1931 figure was 7,555 or 50% higher than in 1921.[130]

This industrial retreat in the 1920s mirrored a political retreat, at least from the high point of hopes and aspirations towards the end of the war and the immediate post-war period; as the Glasgow ILP's membership began to decline from around 1920 it was among women and young industrial workers that the fall was most precipitate.[131] At the same time the lofty expectations so many women had shared before the war about the impact women would have on political life once they had the vote appeared to be refuted by the return of the Coalition Government and the new-found strength of the Conservatives and Unionists, obviously due, in part, to female support. The vast potential of women's abilities glimpsed at in the upheavals of war-time emergency was smothered by the post-war anti-feminist reaction and re-assertion of women's primary domestic role.[132]

This retreat was also due to divisions amongst feminists. Once the vote was secured the movement was free to divide into its various political and class elements. Indeed, the war itself had brought sharp and bitter feuds between ex-comrades. Helen Crawfurd found herself no longer defending Mrs Pankhurst from physical assault but angrily denouncing her war-mongering: 'does Mrs Pankhurst speak for us? Has her voice ever been raised since this war started on behalf of the workers of this country against the profiteers and exploiters who have taken advantage of the great crisis to rob and plunder the people.'[133] At the end of the war Mrs Pankhurst's Germano-phobia had become imbued with anti-Bolshevism and just days before the armistice she spoke in Glasgow under the auspices of the Women's Party calling for Lloyd George to stay in power, the Labour Party to be purged of its Bolshevism, pro-Germanism and pacifism and the abolition of 'the tyranny of the shop-steward and the committee.'[134]

Mrs Pankhurst was not an isolated figure but was quite representative of

[130] *Census of Scotland*, City of Glasgow 1911, 1931.
[131] A. McKinlay, ' "Doubtful wisdom and uncertain promise": strategy, ideology and organisation, 1918–1922', in A. McKinlay & R.J. Morris (eds.), *The ILP on Clydeside, 1893–1932: from foundation to disintegration*, (Manchester, 1991), pp. 138–9. From a high point in 1920 when 1,342,000 women nationally were in trade unions there were only 835,000 by 1925, and that figure would not rise above a million again until 1939. N.C. Soldon, *Women in British Trade Unions 1874–1976* (Dublin, 1978), p. 104.
[132] B. Caine, *English Feminism 1780–1980* (Oxford, 1997), p. 181.
[133] This was written in the *Labour Leader*, quoted in Mitchell, *Women on the Warpath*, pp 310–1; see also *Forward* 16 Jun. 1917.
[134] At the same time she claimed she wanted to do away with class distinctions. *Glasgow Herald*, 1 Nov. 1918.

much middle class feminist opinion. Helen Fraser spent some time at the end of the war touting herself as a right-wing candidate. She stood, unsuccessfully, as a National Liberal in Govan in 1922 and had even approached the Unionists in the hopes of being selected by them.[135] In 1917 a National Council of Women's Citizens' Associations was formed with the intention of promoting more women into local government and Local Associations were established throughout the country with many members of suffrage societies shifting their allegiance to these new bodies.[136] In Glasgow the Women's Citizens' Association, maintaining the pre-war opposition of the GWSSWS towards Labour, joined the anti-socialist forces behind the Moderates in the immediate post-war period.[137] Given such developments the formation of a common women's front encompassing middle and working class women was highly unlikely.

In spite of the post-war retreat women were more evident in the Labour Party than ever before and were welcome for the valuable contributions they made. They were not quite so welcome, however, when they tried to promote a distinctly female agenda, for instance over birth control, equal pay and family allowances, against the will of the male majority; 'when they collided the male vision generally won.'[138] Yet, there was not a clear and consistent division between men and women. There could be male support for the women's position on various matters, including birth control, but it was the machinery of the Party, particularly the bloc vote of the big unions, that ensured ultimate defeat.[139] Birth control was certainly the most contentious issue between the sexes in the Labour Party but the general relationship was more complex than men simply ignoring women's demands.

Unlike the National Labour Party the ILP was keen on the idea of family allowances; indeed this demand was an integral part of its underconsumptionist thesis and associated strategy of promoting economic and industrial growth through increasing working class purchasing power.[140] This per-

---

[135] J. Alberti, *Beyond Suffrage: Feminists in War and Peace 1914–28* (London, 1989) p. 159 identifies Fraser standing as a Liberal in 1922, 23 and 24 before resigning from the Party in 1925. However, see SCUA, Glasgow Unionist Association, *minutes,* 30 May 1921, where Fraser is referred to as 'available as a Parliamentary candidate for a Glasgow seat.' In a straight fight against Neil Maclean for Labour Fraser got 38 per cent of the vote in the Govan contest in 1922, F.W.S. Craig, *British Parliamentary Election Results 1918–1949* (Chichester 1983), p. 590.

[136] Alberti, *Beyond Suffrage,* p. 91; Caine , *English Feminism,* p. 201; Leneman, *A Guid Cause,* p. 216.

[137] See Chapter Three, p. 102. In addition 'various women Societies' joined the Good Government League. SCUA, Glasgow Unionist Association, minutes, 30 August 1920.

[138] Thane, 'Women of the Labour Party', p. 140.

[139] Thane, Women of the Labour Party', pp. 137, 141.

[140] W.W. Knox, ' "Ours is not an ordinary parliamentary movement": 1922–1926', in McKinlay & Morris, *ILP on Clydeside,* pp. 170–1; I.S. Wood, *John Wheatley* (Manchester, 1990), pp. 160–1.

spective, strongly supported by Wheatley and Maxton, was close to the views both of socialist women within Labour and middle class feminists outside the Party. Jean Mann, in paying tribute to the pioneering work of Eleanor Rathbone, pointed out while the TUC opposed family allowances, 'From the start she had the support of the ILP, particularly the Clydesiders.'[141] Although there was a common belief in the top echelons of both parties that a female candidate 'cost' 10% of the poll, this does not seem to have bothered the Clydesiders who saw positive benefits in having women as speakers and candidates.[142]

With Jean Mann the ILP were promoting a housewife more than they were promoting a woman. In her memoirs Mann identified a common thread between Hardie's concern for mothers and the Clydesiders' insistence that if Parliament was to be genuinely representative then it would have to contain housewives. Her own, reluctant, promotion into public life by the ILP was based on this premise, 'We must have housewives'.[143] At one level this was a welcome recognition of a neglected constituency, though one which the Glasgow ILP had shown itself increasingly adept at appealing to, especially through the housing issue. At another level it implicitly identified women as wives and mothers only and was not so aware of them as workers or how to appeal to them as such. ILP men like Patrick Dollan could castigate the trade unions for having failed to represent women in the workplace, and call for the industrial organisation of women, even demand equal pay for equal work. At heart, however, there remained the assumption that this was a problem which socialism would solve ultimately by making it unnecessary for women to work.[144]

It was as wives and mothers that the birth control issue directly affected women; there were few voices raised publicly in defence of the single woman's right to contraception. The heart-wrenching collection of letters by Co-operative Guild Women in England published in 1915 revealed the damage done to women by, and the depth of their fears and anxieties of, multiple pregnancies. In her introduction to the collection Margaret Llewelyn Davies pointed out that family limitation was an established fact and was being practised among the working class.[145] The War was in itself something of a catalyst in bringing matters of sex into the open and

---

[141] Mann, *Woman in Parliament*, p. 19.
[142] Mann, *Woman in Parliament*, pp. 117–9.
[143] Mann, *Woman in Parliament*, pp. 170, 232.
[144] *Forward*, 16 May 1914. Given the employment situation in the 1920s the demand for equal pay for equal work actually affected very few women workers and women within the Labour Party had re-focused their demand to a general increase in women's pay to levels commensurate with men's. Essentially equal pay for equal work protected male rates and the notion of the family wage. See P. Graves, *Labour Women: Women in British Working Class Politics 1918–1939* (Cambridge, 1994), pp. 132–5; Thane, 'Women of the Labour Party', pp. 133–4.
[145] 'There is a kind of strike against large families, and it is not, among the workers, a selfish strike.' *Maternity: Letters from Working Women* (London, 1915), p. 14.

encouraging a new outlook on contraception.[146] Although there was no Scottish equivalent to the English Guild's collection there is no reason to believe that the attitudes of women in Scotland were any different. In July 1920 the American birth control pioneer, Margaret Sanger, spoke on the subject in Glasgow as part of the ILP's Sunday lectures series, and later recalled the startled reaction of one male socialist to the number of women who turned up: 'Look . . . the women have crowded the men out of this hall. I never saw so many wives of comrades before.'[147]

The Women's Guild and the Labour Women's Conference declared themselves in favour of maternity and health clinics providing information on contraception to married women who requested it, and this became the basis of the 'birth control resolution' that was to be hotly debated within the Party during the 1920s.[148] Nevertheless, this was an issue that the Labour Party found particularly difficult to give official endorsement to and basically responded by avoiding any discussion at Conference, pleading that the matter was one of individual conscience and to force it would split the Party. The ILP endorsed the birth control resolution at its 1926 Annual Conference but John Wheatley, as Minister of Health in the first Labour Government, had refused to lift the ban on health authorities giving advice on contraception. Wheatley's position was quite clear, as a devout Catholic he supported the Church's opposition to contraception, and wider Catholic hostility is often portrayed as the major reason for the Labour Party's desire to avoid the issue.

As we have already seen, a major controversy erupted in Glasgow local politics in 1927 over birth control. Labour's response to Catholic intervention at the municipal election was to re-assert its view that the matter was one of personal conscience, that it was most certainly not a class issue. *Forward* was almost in despair that birth control should have been permitted to obscure the real issue which, in its opinion, was the employment of direct labour by the Corporation.[149] It is apparent that the possible loss of Catholic votes weighed heavily in Labour's calculation and it was prepared to ignore women's desires rather than risk its electoral position. However, there is more to this than just another illustration of how women's issues were neglected by Labour.

The controversy began early in the year in the unlikely setting of the Corporation Sub-Committee which dealt with literature accessions to the

---

[146] Graves, *Labour Women*, pp. 83–4.
[147] M. Sanger, *An Autobiography* (New York, 1971), p. 274. The chair at Sanger's meeting was taken by the Anarchist Guy Aldred who, along with his partner Rose Witcop, was prosecuted in 1923 for publishing a pamphlet on birth control. Wood, *Wheatley*, pp. 145–6.
[148] Graves, *Labour Women*, pp. 81–98.
[149] 'That Birth Control should receive much greater consideration in our Municipal battles than Direct Labour is a terrible reflection on Glasgow Labour politics.' *Forward*, 5 Nov. 1927.

City's libraries. An offer was made to provide, free, a complete set of *Birth Control News*, published by Marie Stopes' Constructive Birth Control Society. Two Labour Councillors, John S. Clarke and Kate Beaton, moved that the offer be accepted, but this was opposed by the Moderate Chairman, Izett and a Labour member John McBain. By six votes to five the offer was accepted.[150] Izett then raised the matter at the Library Committee of which he was Convenor. Seconded by a female Moderate, Mary Snodgrass, he moved that the minute be disapproved and thus the offer rejected. Clarke and Beaton again moved that the journal be accepted and this time won by a larger margin of seven votes to four.[151] The issue may have been resolved at this point but in March it was raised again, this time at a meeting of the full Corporation.

At this point it became a political issue with a clear division emerging between Labour and the Moderates; Izett, seconded by another Moderate Councillor, Thomson, moved rejection while two Labour members, Charles MacPherson and McBain, in direct contrast to his position in February, moved acceptance. This time the proposal was rejected overwhelmingly, by sixty-two votes to twenty-three. While it has been stated elsewhere that twenty-eight Labour members voted against, the Corporation minutes only indicate that eight did so and this includes the two Catholic members who stood as 'Independent Socialists', while four of the five Councillors who 'declined to vote' were Labour.[152] It is the case, however, that the twenty-three Councillors voting in favour were all Labour members. Not a single Moderate voted for the Libraries being allowed to accept *Birth Control News*.[153] The other dozen or so Labour members most likely tried to avoid publicly committing themselves either way. This certainly seems to have been the strategy adopted by Patrick Dollan who was at the meeting in March and, indeed, spoke on the items immediately before and after the Birth Control debate but whose name is somehow missing from the voting roll. The issue was apparently a complex one.

For a start it is not clear that all Labour women were supporters of birth control; one woman delegate from Glasgow had spoken strongly against the birth control resolution at the ILP conference the previous year.[154] While

[150] *Printed Minutes of the Corporation of Glasgow*, Sub-Committee of the Libraries' Committee on Literature, 17 January 1927.

[151] *Printed Minutes of the Corporation of Glasgow*, Meeting of the Committee on Libraries, 7 February 1927.

[152] *Printed Minutes of the Corporation of Glasgow*, Meeting of the Corporation of the City and Royal Burgh, 3 March 1927. McLean, *Legend*, p. 224 who appears to rely on the *Glasgow Observer* for information on this matter.

[153] Moderate candidates made a virtue of their complete opposition and claimed responsibility for defeating the proposal. See Glasgow University Library, Broady Collection, Election leaflet by Baillie Peter Burt and William G. Niven, joint candidates for North Kelvin, November 1927.

[154] This was Jean Roberts who later became a Labour Lord Provost. T. Gallagher, *Glasgow The Uneasy Peace* (Manchester, 1987, p. 192. As such this may well reflect

both Kate Beaton and Mary Barbour voted in favour of *Birth Control News*, there is no indication as to the position taken by Labour's third woman councillor, Laura McLean. Given Catholic hostility was already very well known a surprising number of Labour councillors in Glasgow were prepared to vote in favour of *Birth Control News* and in doing so were prepared to risk Catholic antagonism or did not regard that threat as significant. Given the complete opposition of the Moderates (presumably not influenced by concern over the Catholic vote) this still left Labour as the most likely political vehicle for women to utilise in support of the cause.[155] Although it has been stated elsewhere that *Forward* refused to run adverts from birth control advocates, this is not the case; certainly prior to the 1927 election it carried advertisements for birth control literature and devices.[156] In 1930 the Second Labour Government quietly allowed health clinics to provide information on contraception on health grounds but, as these could be interpreted quite widely, this was close to the demand for free advice for married women.[157]

It has been argued that male hostility to the issue of birth control in the Party reflected the threat it posed to the authority of working class men within their own families.[158] Yet, alongside sexual power struggles there is also the matter of sheer ignorance to consider, which so many testimonies of working class people at this time attest to.[159] Jennie Lee, the young tyro from Fife who won a parliamentary seat in Lanarkshire at the age of twenty-three, recalled the complete lack of any sex education at all, even her mother never spoke about it. Yet, when she went to Edinburgh University her father, visiting her lodgings, surreptitiously placed a book by Marie Stopes on her bookshelves.[160] What such an incident seems to reveal is both the embarrassment which women and men felt about sex yet, at the same time, a quiet

the situation nationally where women among the Labour leadership went against the wishes of the great majority of the female rank and file, see Graves, *Labour Women*, pp. 86–7.

[155] The Church of Scotland avoided giving any statement on birth control until 1960 when it declared the matter to be one of freedom of conscience, 'which its members had long believed its position to represent.' G.I.T. Machin, *Churches and Social Issues in Twentieth Century Britain* (Oxford, 1988), p. 87. However, the position taken by the Moderates in Glasgow indicates public disapproval among middle class, Presbyterian opinion in the inter-war period at least.

[156] Knox, *Labour Leaders*, p. 33. However, for instances of such advertisements, including literature by Marie Stopes, see *Forward*, 5 Dec. 1925 and 16 Jan. 1926.

[157] Thane, 'Women of the Labour Party', p. 137. By 1930 general opinion had shifted considerably but this resolution can be seen as evidence of covert support for birth control in the Labour Party.

[158] Graves, *Labour Women*, p. 94.

[159] For instance see J. McCrindle & S. Rowbotham (eds.), *Dutiful Daughters: Women talk about their lives*, (London, 1979).

[160] She found the book, as her father intended, 'but it was all a bit remote and unattractive'. And she remained a virgin at 26. J. Lee, *My Life With Nye* (London, 1980), p. 49.

determination by many to consciously limit the size of their families. Even if women at the national level were thwarted by the leadership of the Labour Party there was still a great deal they could do locally. For instance Mary Barbour, who went from leading the rent strike to becoming a councillor, was instrumental in establishing what was basically the first family planning centre in the City, the Women's Welfare and Advisory Clinic, in 1925.[161]

Conclusion

For working class women like Mary Barbour sex and class were inextricably bound together. To repeat the point made by Jean Mann at the beginning of this chapter, '. . . the vital needs of men and women were akin'. Partly there was a continuation of the pre-war situation where prominent female personalities attracted a lot of attention. Within the Scottish ILP Helen Crawfurd was second only to James Maxton in terms of popularity, and when she transferred her allegiance to the Communist Party she became one of its major assets.[162]

Crawfurd was but one of a group of local women activists and, in a sense, the least representative, to emerge out of the war-time struggles. The leadership group identified in the rent strike and peace crusade sustained their activity into the post-war situation: Agnes Dollan was the first woman to stand as a Labour municipal candidate in Glasgow at a by-election in January 1919; in April she, Mrs Laird and Mrs Allan were returned for Labour in the School Board elections; and in the November polls in 1920 the first successful women Town Council candidates were returned for Labour, Eleanor Stewart for Maryhill and, perhaps inevitably, Mary Barbour for her home ward of Fairfield.[163] Although Stewart lost seat the following year Mary Barbour held hers continuously until her retirement from the Council, and from this point there was always a female presence on the Labour benches.

This presence, however, was not a large one, reflecting the minority role still taken by women within the organisations of the labour movement. By the mid 1920s there were some 78, 470 women in trade unions in Scotland who accounted for just under 15% of union membership, although in the Glasgow area 15,487 women represented less than 12% of the total.[164] In the later years of the war and the immediate post-war period there was a

---

[161] I owe this information to Audrey Canning whose her biography of Mary Barbour will appear in the forthcoming *New Dictionary of National Biography* (Oxford, forthcoming).

[162] In the elections to the Scottish Executive she polled more than anyone else apart from Maxton, *Forward*, 11 Jan. 1919; J. Lee, *Life With Nye*, p. 47.

[163] *Forward*, 11 Jan. 1919; *Glasgow Herald*, 7 Apr. 1919, 3 Nov. 1920. Mrs Allan was a sitting member of the School Board.

[164] Scottish Trade Union Congress, *Twenty-Eighth Annual Report* (Glasgow, 1925), 'Extent and Structure of Trade Union Movement in Scotland' p. 34.

significant influx of women into the ILP; in Partick there were over 100 women in the branch. Even so women accounted for around 20% of party membership and only around 10% of delegates to the Glasgow Federation, the central policy-making body.[165] Given that this was the pool from which local candidates were likely to be selected, the odds were still stacked against women. Nonetheless, compared with the situation before 1914, this did represent an advance as women were more numerous and more active than they had been before.[166]

During the 1920s, out of a total membership of 111 representatives, there were between five and seven women on Glasgow Corporation. Alongside the two Labour women elected in 1920 were three women standing as Moderates, and in the early part of the decade there was always a small preponderance of female councillors on the Moderate side. Given that the Moderates held a substantial number of uncontested seats it was, to an extent, easier for them to return a female candidate. By the later 1920s Labour enjoyed a slight lead with a more substantial gap appearing in 1931 when its six women councillors clearly outnumbered the Moderates' two.[167] This was hardly a huge number but still represented a major advance on the pre-war years when there were no women on the Corporation.[168] Counting heads in this way can only be taken so far, however, since on this basis it is the Scottish Protestant League (SPL) – hardly a bastion of feminism – which actually scores best: in 1932 four of its eleven candidates were women and the following year two were elected.[169]

While women did not achieve, or even approach, equality of representation within the Labour Party, nonetheless there were positive developments. Alongside of the prominent women leaders and representatives, such as Mary Barbour and Jean Mann, there was the conscious effort by the STUC to encourage women into the unions. This may have been motivated more by alarm at falling membership rolls in the 1920s than a deliberate pro-feminism, but the Organisation of Women Committee was established in 1926 and became a permanent fixture of the trade union movement; ten years later it would report to Congress that there were thirty-six unions affiliated to the Committee and these had 44,571 female members.[170] This

---

[165] McKinlay , 'Doubtful Wisdom', p. 138.
[166] For instance there are not even estimates of women's trade union membership before the War.
[167] *Glasgow Herald*, 4 Nov. 1931. This gap remained for the rest of the 1930s as the sitting Labour women councillors tended to hold their seats.
[168] The first, unsuccessful, efforts by women to gain election was in 1911. *Glasgow Herald*, 8 Nov. 1911.
[169] As the SPL only had seven councillors this was a relatively high proportion. *Glasgow Herald*, 2 Nov. 1932, 8 Nov. 1933.
[170] S. Lewenhack, *Women and Trade Unions: An Outline History of Women in the British Trade Union Movement* (London, 1977), pp. 193–5; Lewenhack, 'Women in the Leadership', p. 14.; Scottish Trade Union Congress, *Thirty-Ninth Annual Report* (Glasgow, 1936), p. 82.

was not simply the result of an expanding female workforce. While the Censuses of 1921 and 1931 do not, unfortunately, have the same age and sex-specific data as those before WW1, it does not appear that there was a great deal of change in women's experience of employment. The largest single employment category for women remained that of indoor domestic servant; in 1931 there were 22,739 women so categorised which, at just under 14% of the female workforce, was the same proportion as 1911.[171]

In spite of the post-war retreats and the failure of progress to match earlier expectations, women were now part of and active in the movement in a way they had not been prior to 1914. Labour had begun to reassess the potential role of women before the War but it was the rent strike which proved to be the catalyst. Thereafter, and with the reality of a mass female electorate, there were no more complaints about 'old women'. Certainly, Labour was most comfortable with the notion of women as housewives. Nonetheless, the women in the movement were – in no small part – also responsible for shaping the identity of Glasgow Labour.

[171] Indeed there seems to have been a shift back to domestic service in the 1920s given that the 1921 Census reported just over ten per cent of the occupied female workforce as indoor domestic servants. *Census of Scotland* 1911, 1921, 1931.

CHAPTER SIX

Splits and Sectarianism: Labour Takes Control of George Square

At the start of the 1930s Labour remained in the anomalous position of enjoying a majority of Glasgow's parliamentary representation yet operating as the permanent opposition on the City Council. Any view which suggests that Labour was destined to control local government sooner or later, ignores its becalmed position for a decade or more.[1] The irony is that Labour became the majority party in Glasgow at a time when a number of factors appeared to militate against it making any further progress. Firstly there was the ignominious end of the second Labour Government and Ramsay MacDonald's betrayal. In the subsequent general election of October 1931, in which Labour found itself opposing a 'National Government' led by the very leader who had been lionised by the Party for so long, Labour was decimated. Given the extent of the rout nationally (Labour was reduced to fifty-six seats), Glasgow's performance in losing only half its representation (down to five from ten seats) appears almost laudable. In the following year, however, the ILP took the decision to leave the Labour Party and although the majority opinion within Scotland and Glasgow was opposed to disaffiliation and remained with Labour, this was still the most serious split ever to have confronted Labour. The fateful Bradford Conference took place in July 1932 and four months later at the municipal polls Labour and the ILP were confronting each other in most of the municipal wards in Glasgow. The consequences of this civil war ought to have been disastrous, yet within a year there was a Labour administration installed in George Square.

Exit the ILP

The tensions between the ILP and Labour had already spilled over into direct antagonism the previous November. In the general election Labour and ILP candidates were given free runs except in Shettleston where Labour chose to stand against John McGovern. In a four-cornered contest

---

[1] J. Melling, 'Clydeside rent struggles and the making of labour politics in Scotland, 1900–1939', in R. Rodger (ed.), *Scottish Housing in the Twentieth Century*, (Leicester, 1989), p. 74 sees a basic continuity from Labour's parliamentary breakthrough in 1922 and the formation of a Labour Council in the early 1930s.

McGovern increased his majority while the Labour candidate lost his deposit.[2] In the same month Labour and the ILP clashed again in Shettleston, this time at the municipal election. The result here was a victory for the Moderate by an overall though very narrow majority of thirteen votes over the combined Labour and ILP vote. Again, however, the ILP strongly outpolled Labour, by a factor of over four to one.[3] These results, along with the comfortable victories for Maxton and Buchanan in the general election, suggested that a disaffiliated ILP had reasonable hopes of success, in Glasgow at any rate.

In spite of Dollan's claims that the Scottish ILP was more or less unanimous in choosing to retain the link with the Labour Party, it is clear that there was considerable rank and file support for disaffiliation. The Scottish Divisional conference voted solidly against disaffiliation in 1931 by 112 to thirty-five votes, while the following year the same resolution lost by the still substantial but narrower vote of eighty-eight to forty-nine.[4] At least eleven Glasgow branches supported disaffiliation. Nonetheless a clear majority were opposed and shortly after the Bradford Conference they established the Scottish Socialist Party (SSP) which claimed to have the support of 107 branches and half the ILP membership in Scotland.[5] This was essentially a continuation of the ILP under another name and showed the consistency of Dollan and his supporters who were not prepared simply to subsume their separate identity within the Labour Party; the SSP would continue to seek nominations as and support Labour candidates. Dollan castigated the supporters of disaffiliation as young and inexperienced and the split does appear to have had its generational aspect. The vast majority of the ILP's local elected representatives, whom one would expect to be older, refused to follow the Party's decision.[6] At the time of the split there were forty-four Labour councillors in Glasgow, of whom forty were members of the ILP but, of these, only eight remained with the ILP.[7]

In the November polls Labour and the ILP both stood in twenty-five wards and faced each other in direct contests in twenty-one of those. Moreover,

---

[2] F.W.S. Craig, *British Election Results 1918–1949* (Chichester, 1983), p. 597.

[3] *Glasgow Herald*, 4 Nov. 1931. The ILP got over 4,000 votes while Labour managed less than one thousand.

[4] R.E. Dowse, *Left in the Centre: the Independent Labour Party 1893–1940* (London, 1966), pp. 171, 178.

[5] A. McKinlay & J. Smyth, 'The end of the 'agitator workman': 1926–1932', in A. McKinlay & R.J. Morris (eds.), *The ILP on Clydeside 1893–1932*, (Manchester, 1991), p. 198.

[6] Paton saw this as the inevitable consequence of the insistence upon a 'clean break', and claimed that in six months the ILP in Lancashire had only three elected representatives where previously it had 'hundreds'. J. Paton, *Left Turn: The Autobiography of John Paton* (London, 1936), p. 398.

[7] J. McNair, *James Maxton: The Beloved Rebel* (London, 1955), p.231, gives seven as the figure but at the November election the ILP were identified as having eight sitting councillors. *Glasgow Herald*, 4 Nov. 1932.

the Communist Party (CP) took a more active role in the elections than ever before, standing candidates in fourteen wards, all of which were being contested by the ILP and thirteen of which were contested by Labour. Additional complexity was provided by the intervention of the Scottish Protestant League in eleven wards, having already won a seat from Labour the previous year, and four Scottish Nationalist candidates. Somewhat surprisingly there was no drop in the overall Labour and left representation and almost no change in the complexion of the Council. A new seat had been created – Yoker & Knightswood – where Labour took the first two places and the Moderates the third seat. The Protestant League took one seat from the Moderates, giving it a total of three, and the ILP took two seats from Labour, increasing its representation to ten. Even had all the opposition parties combined the Moderate majority on the Council would 'still be at the effective margin of eighteen.'[8]

Given that the potential for disaster had been enormous, Labour had every reason to feel relieved at the outcome in 1932, yet the result could still have been better. The Moderates polled 30% of the total vote, while Labour had polled 31%, the ILP 20% and the Communist Party a further 4.5%. These bald figures, however, do exaggerate the strength of the 'left' vote since they do not include the eight wards in which Moderates were returned unopposed, and the 12% gained by the Protestant League further muddies the waters. Although no seats were lost on split votes, a number of seats may have been gained or regained had there been a single left candidate. For instance in Govan, the sitting Moderate (a surprise victor in 1929) managed to hold on to his seat with a poll of 3,266 votes, while the ILP came second with 2,763, Labour polled 2,528 and a 'Soviet' candidate managed 1,378 votes.[9] In Govanhill, where the ILP again slightly outpolled Labour, the combined vote would have been just above that of the sitting Moderate. In Kinning Park where the SPL came a clear first, a combined Labour-ILP vote would have beaten the Moderate for the second seat. And in the new ward of Yoker & Knightswood the ILP's intervention seems to have done enough to deprive Labour of a clean sweep of all three seats.

Yoker & Knightswood was created out of the existing Whiteinch ward and was an area of good quality council housing in the far west of the city. As a new ward all three seats had to be filled and while Labour and the Moderates stood a full complement of candidates, the ILP presented only two. The result was that Labour took the first two places with the Moderates coming third and, although the ILP candidates polled around 2,000 votes each they came bottom of the poll. This result indicates the difficulty the ILP would have in attempting to build support in new areas. It tried once more

[8] *Glasgow Herald*, 2 Nov. 1932.
[9] *Glasgow Herald*, 2 Nov. 1932. Govan had been and would remain solidly Labour at every election from 1919. The Moderate had only won in 1929 due to the intervention of a 'Republican' candidate taking sufficient votes away from Labour. *Glasgow Herald*, 6 Nov. 1929.

in the following year and again came last; thereafter the ILP never contested Yoker & Knightswood again.

In contrast to this failure, the ILP had managed to take two seats from Labour in 1932, Calton and Shettleston. These were east end wards located in the ILP-held parliamentary constituencies of Bridgeton and Shettleston respectively. The ILP had already defeated Labour in Shettleston in 1931 and in both wards Labour came in a very poor last.[10] Both wards were famous in Labour and ILP history: Calton was John Ferguson's old ward and was where a 'Labour' political presence in Glasgow began in the 1890s; while Shettleston was the seat first held by John Wheatley before the First World War. By winning these wards the ILP was therefore entrenching its position within its traditional strongholds.

In 1933 (as we shall see below) the Labour-ILP clash was overshadowed by the dramatic impact of the SPL and was when Labour at last won control of the Town Council. Labour contested twenty-six wards whereas the ILP only stood in thirteen, and nine of these involved the two parties opposing each other. Again, the fall-out from this discord was minimal; in these contested wards no seats were lost and Labour made three gains from the Moderates. The ILP held the one seat it was defending and managed to make two gains. Again, however, both of these were in the East End – Shettleston and Parkhead – and in neither did Labour field a candidate even though one had been a Labour seat. A pattern was established very quickly which more or less held for the rest of the 1930s; where the ILP contested between eight and eleven wards Labour stood in twenty-nine or thirty, and the number of wards where the two fought each other was either six or seven. There was little turnaround in seats between the parties though, significantly, the ILP found it impossible to take any more seats off Labour.

The ILP's high point, in terms of representation, came in 1935/6 when it had thirteen councillors. This number was reached thanks to gains made at the expense of the Moderates and the SPL in 1934 and 1935. Thereafter the ILP made no further gains at the November polls and lost one seat to the Moderates in 1936 and two seats to Labour in 1937. In 1938, the last election before the outbreak of war, the ILP managed to retain its full complement of ten seats. It successfully defended four seats, Calton, Parkhead, Shettleston and Govanhill, all but the last being East End wards. It would appear that Labour was willing to leave the ILP alone in its den; Labour contested only one of the ILP's four seats, Calton. Govanhill, which had been a surprise ILP victory in 1935, was uncontested by Labour, not because it was a stronghold of the ILP but because the ILP's majority was so narrow.[11] This reflected a realistic assessment by Labour of its own position in the Town

[10] *Glasgow Herald,* 2 Nov. 1932. In Calton the Labour candidate secured only 270 votes compared to the ILP's 3,494.
[11] John S. Clarke won Govanhill for the ILP in 1935 with a majority of only sixty-five over the Moderate. In a straight fight in 1938 he held the seat by eighty-six votes.

Council; although it was by now the largest single party it had only six seats more than the Progressives. In the circumstances it was more sensible to keep a small ILP presence on the Council than risk returning control to the Progressives.

Enter the Protestants

If Labour did not have its troubles to seek in the early 1930s, neither had the Moderates. Firmly embedded in office since 1920 the Moderates had been powerless to halt the decline of the 'Second City'. The almost permanent depression facing the heavy industries, with its attendant unemployment, saw the Town Council caught in a position where social expenditure rose dramatically while the local tax base needed to support this expenditure shrunk. Although the Moderate alliance had been successful in 'saving Glasgow from socialism', by the late 1920s even its 'natural' supporters were growing more critical. Business opinion was hostile to the perceived 'extravagance' of Glasgow's spending on areas like housing and education.[12] The surge in Unionist representation promoted by the formation of the National Government in 1931 did not transfer over to the local arena; the Moderates simply held their own in 1931 and 1932. There had already been some indications that the Moderate alliance was fraying at the edges with 'independent moderate' candidates standing against official Moderates, i.e. those endorsed by the Good Government League,[13] though it was an outside catalyst which ultimately forced a realignment in municipal politics.

The instrument of this change was the Scottish Protestant League (SPL). Led by the flamboyant Alexander Ratcliffe, the SPL was a precocious, albeit temporary, political phenomenon which attracted a significant support by its militant Protestantism and rabid anti-Catholicism directed at the Irish-Catholic population of Scotland.[14] Ratcliffe had been brought up in Leith and imbibed the substance and style of the peripatetic No-Popery, street-corner preachers common to the port. He founded his League in 1920, and

---

[12] By early 1928 the Glasgow Chamber of Commerce was demanding 'retrenchment in civic expenditure' and even the appointment of an outside 'expert' to oversee the financial administration of the City Council. The Council's response of simply allowing the Chamber of Commerce's resolutions to 'lie on the table' caused something of a crisis in relations between the two bodies. *Glasgow Herald*, 28 Feb., 27 Mar. 1928.

[13] In the municipal polls of 1929 and 1930 there were instances of inter-Moderate rivalries. *Glasgow Herald*, 6 Nov. 1929, 5 Nov.1930; Glasgow Unionist Association, *minutes*, 28 October 1929, 27 October 1930.

[14] The story of the SPL is detailed by T. Gallagher in, *Glasgow: the Uneasy Peace* (Manchester, 1987), and 'Protestant Extremism in Urban Scotland 1930–1939: Its Growth and Contraction', *The Scottish Historical Review*, lxiv (1985), pp. 143–167. See also S. Bruce, *No Pope of Rome! Militant Protestantism in Modern Scotland* (Edinburgh, 1984).

in 1925 was elected to the Edinburgh Education Authority. Having stood in Falkirk and Stirling at the general election of 1929, he moved to Glasgow the following year where he established his own Church.[15] In 1931 the SPL contested the municipal elections and won two seats: Dennistoun, where Ratcliffe was returned, and Dalmarnock where Charles Forrester, an ex-communist was successful. Dramatic as these victories were, at this stage it would have been difficult to envisage what sort of longer term impact the SPL might have. The *Glasgow Herald* simply commented that the League's 'participation in the fray introduced the hot spirit of faction.'[16]

If anything, Ratcliffe could most likely have been likened to Scott Gibson in the first decade of the century, a rogue element who could successfully play to the gallery. The SPL secured only 5% of the poll, double what the Communist Party achieved but nothing to trouble Labour's 43% or the Moderates' 47%. However, the League only stood three candidates (the CP had put forward fifteen) and its poll in these three seats was 12,579, or 44%. The third seat contested by the SPL was Partick East and, although the Moderate held it with a clear majority, the Protestant candidate pushed Labour into third place. These three wards all had the highest turnouts of the election, indicating that the SPL could successfully mobilise a latent support. Furthermore, Dennistoun was a safe Moderate ward where Labour had never been successful, and Dalmarnock was equally secure territory for Labour. Both major parties, therefore, seemed to have as much, or as little, to worry about.

The SPL programme was a very simple one – antagonism to all things Catholic. When upbraided by an ILP councillor in 1934 that his party had no policy beyond that of 'Kick the Pope', Ratcliffe replied enthusiastically that was exactly their policy.[17] The main plank of the SPL programme was the call for the repeal of the 1918 Education (Scotland) Act, specifically Section 18 whereby provision was made for the separate Catholic schools to become part of the state system and be financed through the general Education Rates.[18] It was this which produced the rallying cry of 'No Rome on the Rates!' At the same time SPL propaganda exploited the, by now, common fear of hordes of Irish immigrants threatening the limited and increasingly precarious 'Scottish' jobs. As we have already seen the fact that there was no substance to these claims did not prevent them from gaining a wide currency and, in the worst years of the great depression, they seemed to offer an easy explanation and solution to the problem of unemployment.[19] The SPL advanced a combination of legislation to prevent Irish migration to Britain, repatriation of existing Irish and deportation of Irish nationals

[15] Gallagher, *Uneasy Peace*, pp. 150–1.
[16] *Glasgow Herald*, 4 Nov. 1931.
[17] Gallagher, *Uneasy Peace*, p. 155.
[18] See J.H. Treble, 'The working of the 1918 Education Act in Glasgow archdiocese', *Innes Review* xxxi (1980), pp. 27–44.
[19] See Chapter Four, pp. 152–4.

claiming public assistance.[20] In addition the SPL presented itself as a champion of the working man: opposed to the cuts in teachers' salaries imposed by the Moderate council; in favour of cutting the salaries of top council officials but maintaining the wages of most council workers; in favour of building council houses, and reducing rents and rates.[21]

In 1932 the SPL contested eleven wards and gained one more seat and 12% of the total poll. In three contests the SPL came last, yet even in these instances its candidates polled respectably, in every instance securing over 1,000 votes. Somewhat surprisingly, there was no contest in Dennistoun, and the SLP was unable to repeat its success in Dalmarnock, though it was handicapped by the emergence of a rival Protestant candidate. The SPL's success came in Kinning Park where two seats were being contested; the SPL put forward a single candidate but he came top of the poll by over 2,000 votes. Significantly, Kinning Park had been a secure Moderate ward and was one of the seats which the ILP had identified in the early 1920s as critical for Labour to win.[22] Apart from the exceptional year of 1926, Labour had been unable to gain a seat in Kinning Park but, as a result of the SPL intervention, the ward subsequently became solidly Labour. The impact of the SPL in 1932 was, therefore, muted, and largely overshadowed by the internecine strife between Labour and the ILP. The real shocks and the SPL's lasting achievement in Glasgow's political history were to come the following year.

In the local elections in 1933 the SPL stood in twenty-three of Glasgow's wards, winning four seats and securing over 71,000 votes and 23% of the total poll.[23] This was a real show of strength which almost matched the performance of the Moderates who, although contesting twenty-seven wards, only secured 3875 votes and 1.25% more than the SPL.[24] For the Moderates the results were little short of a disaster: going into the election they were on the defensive, as twenty-four of the thirty-four contested wards were held by Moderates but, even so, they could hardly have expected to lose quite so heavily. Apart from the four wards where their candidates were returned unopposed, the Moderates held onto seven seats and in one of these, Kelvinside, the contest was between rival Moderates. Of the remaining six seats, the SPL challenged in two, Sandyford and Langside, and in the latter the Moderate won by the narrow majority of 248 votes. Elsewhere, the SPL intervention spelt defeat for the Moderates. The four seats won by the

---

[20] For an example see report of programme of Miss Edith Fairbairn, SPL candidate in Govanhill in *Glasgow Herald*, 4 Nov. 1933.

[21] For an example see report of speech by Mrs Susan Cameron, SPL candidate in Partick East, in *Glasgow Herald*, 2 Nov. 1931.

[22] See Chapter Three, p. 105.

[23] *Glasgow Herald*, 8 Nov. 1933. See also Gallagher, *Uneasy Peace*, p. 153, and McKinlay & Smyth, 'Agitator workman', p. 199.

[24] Figures taken from the *Glasgow Herald*. It should be noted that the SPL total includes two independent Protestants while the Moderate total does not include eight independent Moderates. If these latter candidates are included the Moderate total share of the vote becomes 29.5%.

League were all in safe Moderate wards, Camphill, Cathcart, Dennistoun and Govanhill. In none of these had Labour ever won a seat and in the first three neither it nor the ILP bothered to stand in 1933.[25] In addition, the Moderates lost twelve seats – eleven to Labour and one to the ILP – where the SPL stood candidates. Only in Provan did Labour secure a direct gain from the Moderates without Protestant help.

The Moderates, therefore, lost seventeen seats in total, but it is the twelve lost due to SPL intervention that are the most interesting. A number of these were in wards where Labour was usually the dominant party: Cowlairs, Kingston, Shettleston & Tollcross, and Woodside. Others were in wards where representation tended to be divided though with a bias towards the Moderates: Ruchil, Townhead, and Whitevale. The remainder were in what were essentially safe Moderate seats: Kinning Park, Maryhill, Partick West, Pollokshaws, and Whiteinch. Labour's debt to the SPL can be gauged from the fact that in all twelve seats with one exception the combined Moderate and Protestant vote was greater than the winning Labour or ILP vote. And in the one case, Maryhill, where Labour had an overall majority, it was by six votes.

In contrast to their impact on the Moderates, the SPL failed to take any seats from Labour. The SPL contested four wards where Labour held the seat, Cowcaddens, Dalmarnock, Fairfield and Govan, and one (Parkhead) where the ILP were the incumbents.[26] In none of these seats were there official Moderate candidates though independent Moderates eventually took the field in all except Dalmarnock where an Independent Protestant stood against the SPL. If this was a ploy by the Moderates to encourage SPL victories in wards where the Moderates considered they had no chance, it did not work: the SPL candidates all polled heavily but Labour and the ILP held their seats quite comfortably. Before the election Labour was aware that the Protestant candidates threatened the Moderate vote more, 'because of the rivalry for the Orange vote.'[27] *Forward* commented that only the 'criminal confusion' created by the ILP and the CP in running their own candidates could prevent Labour gaining an effective majority on the Council, so long as it could win ten seats from the Moderates and hold all of its own.[28] In spite of this, and the fact that the Moderates were very demoralised, it is unlikely that Labour really envisaged such a result; similar optimistic predictions were usually made immediately before the November polls. The difference in 1933 was, quite simply, the SPL. After the election Ratcliffe boasted, 'if the Socialists have a majority in Glasgow Town Council,

[25] Labour may have planned to give the SPL a clear run against the Moderates but these were seats Labour contested either occasionally or very rarely.

[26] There were two seats contested in Parkhead, both of which the ILP held on to. Labour did not stand in Parkhead but the single SPL candidate came third in front of two independent Moderates and two Communists.

[27] *Forward*, 4 Nov. 1933.

[28] *Forward*, 4 Nov. 1933.

they have the Scottish Protestant League to thank for it.'[29] This was no vain
braggadocio but a plain statement of fact.

The scale of the SPL vote in a variety of wards shows that it was capable of
attracting a wide range of support throughout the City; again, the contests
which had the highest turnouts were almost invariably those involving the
SPL. Although Labour had reaped the advantage of the SPL's intervention it
could not afford to be too sanguine about the threat to its own working class
support. After all, Labour had lost Dalmarnock, a ward solidly Labour since
1920, to the League in 1931. And even in 1933 in Shettleston & Tollcross,
while the ILP regained the seat from the Moderates, the combined Moderate, SPL and independent Protestant vote was over 2,000 greater than the
ILP's. Nevertheless, six of the seven SPL victories were in what had been up
to then secure Moderate seats. Apart from Dalmarnock, the SPL councillors
stood for Dennistoun (two), Camphill, Cathcart, Kinning Park and Govanhill. Gallagher identifies these as 'lower middle class districts' and there can
be little doubt that it was from among Moderate voters that the SPL gained
most of its votes.[30] Moderate support cannot, however, simply be identified
as lower middle class. Moderate success since 1920 had been built upon a
degree of working class support with a bed-rock in the middle class suburbs.
While Govanhill and Kinning Park were a mix of lower middle class and
working class, wards such as Cathcart and Camphill were much more solidly
middle class. SPL victories in these latter two and strong showings in
Langside and Pollokshaws show that the genteel suburbs were not immune
to the appeal of rabid sectarianism.

Labour Consolidates its Position, 1933–36

The fissiparous nature of local politics at this time makes it difficult to
identify electoral trends with any certainty; as well as the SPL and the
independent Protestants it had spawned, there were also independent
Moderates, Communist Party, and Scottish Nationalist candidates standing
in the early 1930s. Morever, the varying number of actual contests makes it
difficult to establish reliable comparisons from year to year. From 1932 to
1933 the combined 'left' vote fell from 50% to 43% of the total poll, while
the Moderate share of the vote, including both official and independent
Moderates, remained static at 29.5%.[31] This suggests that the SPL's dramatic
surge from 12% of the poll in 1932 to 23% in 1933 occurred, at least partly,
at the expense of the Left. However, as we saw above, it was the Moderates
who suffered as a consequence of the rise of the SPL.

[29] *The Vanguard*, 15 Nov. 1933, quoted in NLS Acc, 10424/9, SCUA archive.
[30] Gallagher, *Uneasy Peace*, p. 153.
[31] All figures taken from the *Glasgow Herald*. In 1932 Labour accounted for 30% and
the ILP 20%, while in 1933 Labour accounted for 31.5% while the ILP share fell
to 11.3%. In the latter year, however, the ILP contested thirteen wards compared
to twenty-five in 1932.

Because nearly all uncontested seats (which could be as high as a third of the total) were held by the Moderates, overall voting figures tend to diminish their actual strength. A more accurate comparison of what was happening to Moderate support at this time can be gauged from comparing the 1933 election, when there were only four uncontested wards, with 1930, when there were three seats uncontested. In 1930 the Moderates' share of the vote was 58%, which means that its share of the vote in 1933 represented a fall of some 28 percentage points. In contrast the left vote did not exhibit such a wide divergence. In 1930 Labour and all other left-wing candidates (including the CP) secured 42% of the vote, while in 1933 Labour, ILP and Communists together accounted for 46%. The important point from all of this is that at a time of unprecedented uncertainty and confusion, the combined left vote, i.e. Labour and ILP together, proved itself more loyal and cohesive than its opponents. That is why Labour was able to take control of the Council in 1933. However, even when the SPL vote fell, which it did even faster than it had risen, these votes did not simply shift back to the Moderates. Rather, sufficient numbers appear to have transferred over to Labour which registered a significant rise in its share of the vote in the following years.

Almost as soon as it established itself as a power broker in Glasgow politics, the SPL began to self-destruct. The only discipline on its elected councillors was that they vote together on religious (i.e. Catholic) issues. Otherwise, the majority (including Ratcliffe) normally voted with Labour in the council, while two usually supported the Moderates. The main problem, however, was the domineering personality of Ratcliffe and his determination to retain absolute control of the movement. This quickly led to major disagreements with his erstwhile colleagues, and four of the SPL councillors left and presented themselves as independent Protestants.[32] In 1934 the SPL managed to stand only seven candidates and, although they all polled respectably, none were returned. Most damagingly of all, Ratcliffe lost his own seat in Dennistoun, even though he was given a clear run by the official Moderates. In spite of Ratcliffe's claims of being a reformer he came to an arrangement with the Moderates prior to the November poll whereby the two groups would not stand against each other. With the SPL disintegrating beneath his feet Ratcliffe was in no position to sustain the League's upward trajectory, while the Moderates were still in shock after their defeat the previous year and saw such an arrangement as necessary to turn Labour out of office. As the Glasgow Unionists saw it, such a pact meant 'avoiding a split of the Protestant vote in all the thirty-eight Wards.'[33]

This alliance meant that the 1934 election was the most tightly contested ever, with only two councillors (both Moderates) being returned unopposed. The result was another disaster for the Moderates with Labour

---

[32] Gallagher, *Uneasy Peace*, pp. 153–4, 156.
[33] GUA, Local Elections Sub-committee, minutes 22 Oct. 1934.

further entrenching its hold on power. Labour made five gains overall, one from the ILP but, much more significantly, it took four seats from the Moderates. In addition the ILP took one seat from the Protestants and one from the Moderates. For the Moderates salt was rubbed in the wound when an ex-Councillor and Kirk elder, standing as an Independent Moderate and with Catholic support, defeated Ratcliffe by 341 votes.[34] Overall the SPL share of the vote slumped to 7.3% while the Moderate share increased to 39%.[35] However, if we follow the Unionist lead and regard these two together as the 'Protestant' vote, we can see that it fell from 52.5% in 1933 to 46.4%. In contrast, the Labour and ILP combined vote rose from 42.8% to 51%. With this election the SPL more or less disappeared as a political force. Its remaining councillors and those who chose to sit as independent Protestants were defeated in subsequent elections and Ratcliffe failed in his attempt to return to the Council in 1937 when he was defeated in Camphill.[36]

The storm centre of militant Protestantism in Scotland now shifted to Edinburgh where a new grouping, Protestant Action, made a significant electoral impact just as the SPL was falling apart in Glasgow. John Cormack, the founder and leader of Protestant Action was first elected to Edinburgh Town Council for North Leith in 1934.[37] Cormack was as authoritarian as Ratcliffe, which meant that the two regarded each other as rivals rather than potential allies, but was a more successful politician. Although Ratcliffe had closer links to fascist movements, both in Britain and Germany, Cormack's movement had more obvious fascist overtones. He formed a paramilitary wing, dubbed Kormack's Kaledonian Klan (KKK), an obvious reference to the racism of Southern USA. Cormack was even more violently anti-Catholic than Ratcliffe and advocated that Catholics be stripped of the power to vote and be deported. Attacks on Catholic Chapels and on priests became commonplace with the worst incidents occurring in the Summer of 1935 when Cormack and his supporters mobilised thousands of Protestants to attack the Catholic congregation attending the Eucharist Congress held in Morningside, a respectable middle class area of the city.[38]

The douce citizens of Edinburgh were not overly upset by such disorder and intimidation of its Catholic minority. Protestant Action secured almost one quarter of the vote at the local election in 1935 and in the following year

---

[34] Gallagher, *Uneasy Peace*, pp. 156–7. This result was helped by Labour and the ILP deciding not to stand.

[35] Figures taken from the *Glasgow Herald*. The Moderate vote includes four independent Moderate candidates while the SPL vote includes four independent Protestants.

[36] Camphill had been won by the SPL in 1933 and although Ratcliffe polled over 2,500 votes he still lost by over 1500. *Glasgow Herald* 3 Nov. 1937.

[37] *Glasgow Herald*, 7 Nov. 1934. Two other Protestant Action candidates stood but were unsuccessful.

[38] Gallagher, *Uneasy Peace*, pp. 157–66. See also the same author's *Edinburgh Divided* (Edinburgh, 1987).

gained over 30% of the poll and drove Labour into third place on the Council: 'between the two world wars, no other party on the margins of British politics ever did remotely as well in local politics as Protestant Action.'[39] However, like Ratcliffe, Cormack over stretched himself. He insisted on total control of his movement, suffering defections as a result, and in 1937 he made the mistake of standing for two wards and was defeated in both. Unlike Ratcliffe though, Cormack got back on to the Council and represented South Leith from 1938 till his retirement in 1962.

In both Glasgow and Edinburgh militant Protestantism made a dramatic impact upon the political scene in the 1930s.[40] Both drew inspiration from elements deep within Presbyterian Scotland's past, most notably a strident anti-Catholicism, and gave these more modern, fascist overtones. Certainly, the Catholic-Irish provided a suitable scapegoat during a period of unprecedented economic insecurity. They were a numerous and, many feared, a growing minority. Both their religion and national identity marked them out as different and as potentially, if not actually, subversive and disloyal to a Protestant Kingdom. Age-old antipathies were given a new twist by mass unemployment and the apparently simple solution of providing jobs for native Scots by taking them away from Irish Catholics. Without the depression it is impossible to understand this phenomenon.

To a certain extent Ratcliffe and Cormack cancelled each other out. Their rivalry meant that no joint movement would be created; Protestant Action stood candidates in Glasgow in 1935 and Ratcliffe returned the compliment by campaigning against Cormack in Edinburgh in 1937.[41] While Cormack became a permanent feature of Edinburgh local politics, militant Protestantism quickly burned itself out in Glasgow; by 1937 'Protestant' candidates accounted for just over 1% of the vote and in 1938 there were no candidates so designated. However, the rapid melting away of the SPL did not benefit the Moderates. Their attempt to unify the 'Protestant' vote in 1934 had failed and it would appear that the SPL's intervention acted as a conduit for a significant number of electors to transfer their allegiance over to Labour. This becomes more apparent when we examine the changing political complexion of particular wards.

As we saw above, Labour's victory in 1933 owed everything to the direct intervention of the SPL. Some of the gains made were in wards where Labour or the ILP would have normally expected to win, such as Cowlairs and Shettleston, which had only been lost in 1930 and 1931 because of the

---

[39] Gallagher, *Uneasy Peace*, p. 165.

[40] In Liverpool there had been a Protestant Party on the City council since 1903. Though strong enough with three councillors to force some concessions from the majority Conservatives in the 1930s it did not create the same violent excitement as the SPL or Protestant Action. P.J. Waller, *Democracy and Sectarianism: a political and social history of Liverpool 1868–1939* (Liverpool, 1981) pp. 203–5, 339–40.

[41] *Glasgow Herald*, 6 Nov. 1935. Gallagher, *Uneasy Peace*, p. 166.

split on the left. Others were quite remarkable; Pollokshaws and Whiteinch had never returned a Labour candidate before and, with the absence of the SPL, never would again. These wards, along with the middle class areas of Camphill, Cathcart and Dennistoun which had been taken by the SPL, quickly returned to the Moderate fold. In Partick West and Whitevale, both wards where Labour had enjoyed only limited success beforehand, representation was subsequently shared with the Moderates. Of more significance are the larger group of wards which turned Labour in 1933 (thanks to the SPL) and stayed Labour thereafter: Kingston, Kinning Park, Maryhill, Ruchill, Townhead and Woodside. Of particular interest are Kinning Park and Maryhill. Prior to 1933 Kinning Park had only once returned a Labour councillor, when it was one of the temporary gains made after the General Strike. Labour took Maryhill but had only won the ward twice before, in 1929 and in 1920, when it took the last of the three seats. Maryhill was also reputed to have a large Orange vote which explained Labour's relative lack of success in what was a predominantly working class area. That Labour comfortably held Maryhill for the rest of the 1930s suggests that sufficient numbers of Protestant voters either switched to Labour or no longer viewed the return of Moderate candidates as an overwhelming priority.

In their post-mortem on the results in 1933 the Glasgow Unionists concentrated on the impact of the SPL; '. . . the large Socialist gains were not due to their own strength, but to the split in the Anti-Socialist vote through the intervention of the Scottish Protestant League.'[42] However, they were also aware of other contributory causes which led Moderate supporters either to abstain or to switch to the SPL as a protest. These included the failure of the Moderate administration in George Square to enact the full economies they had promised, combined with a significant increase in the rates. In addition a number of other factors operating against the Moderates but in Labour's favour were briefly touched upon. Thus, the large numbers of Council employees were seen as turning to Labour to restore their cuts in wages, Council tenants campaigning for reductions in rents looked to Labour and, lastly, 'the large army of people receiving doles' also saw Labour as the agency which would provide more generous scales of relief.[43] With Labour's continued success in 1934, after accommodation had been reached between the Moderates and the SPL, these more structural explanations were given increased weight.

Five 'main causes of defeat' were identified immediately after the 1934 election. These were: 1) 'the consolidated Roman Catholic vote'; 2) 'the vast army of Corporation employees (over 38,000)'; 3) 'the new housing areas, where in the subsidised houses we find nothing short of hot-beds of Socialism'; 4) 'the question of Public Assistance where the increased dole

[42] NLS, Acc, 10424/9 (xii), 'Report on Glasgow Municipal Elections 1933'.
[43] NLS, Acc, 10424/9 (xii) 'Report on . . . 1933'.

of the Socialists undoubtedly told in very many wards'; 5) 'the influence of Co-operative Societies'.[44] In listing these causes the Glasgow Unionist Association did not, however, develop any ideas about what to do about them. Sir Charles Cleland may have bemoaned the fact that Catholics accounted for 25% of the vote in Glasgow, the same proportion as in Belfast, but, apart from regarding it as 'a very serious problem' which was only likely to get worse given the propensity for Catholics to have large families, he had nothing else to say. Evidently, the Unionists regarded the Catholic vote as a lost cause. The increasing alignment of Co-operators with Labour via the rise in societies affiliated to the Co-operative Party had been causing the Unionists concern for some time. Aware that many Unionists were also Co-operators, the GUA urged that they organise themselves within their Societies to try and combat this growing politicisation.[45] However, there is no evidence that any such action was actively promoted or undertaken.

Conclusion: Towards a Permanent Majority

As regards the other three 'causes', the Unionists had literally nothing to offer. Continuing high levels of unemployment in Glasgow throughout the 1930s would mean the 'dole' remained a live political issue; in December 1938 there still remained almost 83,000 unemployed in the City.[46] The emphasis on Council employees and Council housing echo more contemporary Tory concerns with identifying 'natural' Labour voters, but in the context of Glasgow in the 1930s these were regarded as more or less permanent features of the social and political landscape. Regarding them simply as repositories of Labour supporters ignored the fact that both 'armies' had grown unchecked under a Moderate administration. Just as Labour had become the most active promoter of municipally owned and controlled public services before 1914, did not mean that 'municipal socialism' in Glasgow had been a Labour creation. Similarly, Labour was more vocal in its support of direct labour schemes and building Council houses than any other party, but the 39,000 Council workers and 32,000 Council houses which existed in 1933, had not been built by a Labour administration.[47] The only recommendations put forward by the Unionists

---

[44] NLS, Acc, 10424/74, Glasgow Unionist Association [GUA], minutes, General committee 26 Nov. 1934; also 10424/9 (xii), Ts., n.d. c. 1937.

[45] NLS, Acc, 10424/74, GUA, General committee minutes 7 Jan. 1935, 30 March 1936, 27 April 1936.

[46] J. Cunnison & J.B.S. Gilfillan, *Third Statistical Account of Scotland: Glasgow* (Glasgow, 1958), p. 923.

[47] These were the figures given by the GUA, see NLS, Acc, 10424/9 (xii), 'Report on . . . 1933'. The total number of houses, temporary and permanent, built by the Corporation by the end of 1933 was 33,111. Cunnison & Gilfillan, *Glasgow*, p. 877.

were essentially negative, such as Cleland's suggestion that all municipal employees should be denied the local franchise.[48]

Although it was clear that local politics in Glasgow were primarily a struggle between Labour and Unionist, the strategy of the latter remained that of presenting themselves under the Moderate label. This had become more difficult in 1933 when the Good Government League was wound up because of lack of funds.[49] However, the Unionist response was not to take over the running of candidates themselves, rather they became even more convinced that another such umbrella organisation was necessary to marshal the anti-Socialist forces. A Municipal Society was quickly formed, although it was soon to exhibit the weaknesses of the Good Government League, namely that it had no full-time organisation and only came sporadically to life in the weeks prior to the November polls. The Municipal Society was in turn replaced by a new body, the Glasgow Progressive Party, with its own office and full time staff and, in the 1936 local elections the old Moderate forces now stood and campaigned under the banner of Progressives.[50]

The contests in 1936 were critical since all the gains which Labour made in 1933 had to be defended; this meant that it was the Progressives who were now on the offensive. The result was that the Progressives made seven net gains; while losing one seat to Labour they took four seats from the SPL, three from Labour and one from the ILP.[51] Progressive representation was immediately strengthened by the complete demise of the 'Protestant' element on the Council, but while these gains in predominantly middle class wards were largely expected, it was the contests in the twelve seats which Labour had won in 1933 due to SPL intervention which were critical. In these seats the results were mixed. Labour's loss of Pollokshaws and Whiteinch was certainly no surprise, as was defeat in Partick West and Whitevale, though the latter only occurred on a split Labour-ILP vote. The only major upset was the ILP's surrender of Shettleston & Tollcross. However, as the remaining six wards were all held by Labour, the Progressives still remained some eighteen seats behind the combined forces of Labour and the ILP.

While the Progressives stopped the rot in 1936 and managed to cap Labour's majority, they were unable sufficiently to turn the tide back in their favour. The Glasgow Unionists were divided in their opinion on these results. The Chairman of the Association declared they were 'highly satisfactory', while Cleland regarded them as a 'disappointment'.[52] He was particularly upset that the Progressives had not put up candidates in five seats, the first time that Labour had enjoyed a majority of uncontested

[48] NLS, Acc, 10424/74, GUA, General Committee, minutes, 26 Feb. 1934.
[49] NLS, Acc, 10424/74, GUA, General Committee, minutes, 9 Jan. 1933, 27 March 1933.
[50] NLS, Acc, 10424/9 (xii) Sir Lewis Shedden's file . . . TS, n.d. c. 1937. GUA, General Committee, minutes, 24 Feb. 1936.
[51] *Glasgow Herald*, 4 Nov. 1936.
[52] NLS, Acc, 10424/74, GUA, General Committee, minutes 9 Nov. 1936.

wards. The election in 1937 again saw Labour on the defensive with twenty-three Labour and ILP councillors having to retire, but the Progressives made only a single gain and Labour's majority remained secure with more or less no change in 1938.

The Progressives had managed to make good much of the damage inflicted upon them by the SPL, but they were unable to put all of the pieces back together again. The old Moderate majority had relied upon a total dominance of the middle class wards and an ability to secure a significant representation in a number of working class wards. Although Progressive candidates would, on occasion, win wards such as Shettleston these victories became relatively rare. Of much more significance is the fact that previously secure wards like Maryhill and Kinning Park had been transformed into safe Labour seats. It would appear that the bond which had held the Moderate alliance together had been a common Protestant identity which was implicitly anti-Catholic and anti-Socialist. Ironically, this had been shattered not by a resurgent socialism but by an explicit expression of anti-Catholicism in the form of Alexander Ratcliffe and the Scottish Protestant League. Sectarianism did not die out in Glasgow with the demise of the SPL, but it did not re-emerge as a political force of any significance. And the long term beneficiary of this was not the Glasgow Progressive Party but the Labour Party.

Once in office Labour found it had not inherited the independent municipality of late Victorian and Edwardian Britain; authority and control had increasingly drifted towards London and the Palace of Westminster. The depressed state of the local economy limited the Corporation's ability to act independently as did the necessity for state subsidies for working class housing: the self-contained simplicity of £8 Cottages for Glasgow Citizens belonged to another age. Nonetheless Labour did have some scope for autonomous action and it was able to cancel Moderate plans to cut the wages and conditions of council employees, and attempt to regalvanise the house building programme. In this it was aided by falling interest rates after 1932, and the incoming administration was able to renew a loan under much better terms, and so take some pressure off the rates.[53]

Like the Conservatives nationally, the Moderates in Glasgow in the 1930s were in favour of building slum clearance houses only, and not ordinary subsidy houses.[54] Labour's desire to construct both categories was hamstrung by the National Government's reduction of subsidies in 1933 and their eventual abolition in 1935 other than for slum clearance.[55] The 17,166

[53] *Forward*, 18 Nov. 1933.

[54] Glasgow University Library, Broady Collection, for examples of election leaflets of Moderate candidates in Partick East and Govan in 1933.

[55] Increased subsidies introduced in the 1938 Housing Act were too late to make any impact before the onset of World War Two. J. Butt, Working Class Housing in Glasgow, 1900–1939', in I. MacDougall (ed.), *Essays in Scottish Labour History* (Edinburgh, 1978), pp. 164–5.

houses built between 1934–39, i.e. under a Labour administration, represented just over one third of all council houses built between the wars.[56] Proportionately, then, Labour was not building significantly more houses than its Moderate predecessor though it may be that it would have performed better had it been operating under a more benign central government. One policy Labour could follow was the utilisation of direct labour not just in maintaining houses but in actually building them. This had been a constant demand by Labour, rejected by the Moderates, and from 1936 there was a big expansion of the Corporation's Direct Labour Department, in personnel and the number of houses constructed by it.[57] Labour could make no claim to solving the housing problem but it could demonstrate that it was making an honest effort under the circumstances.

Labour's long march was over. At last it had become the dominant force in Glasgow's municipal affairs. What Labour has done with that power and authority since is the subject of another study – the purpose of this book has been to chart and explain Labour's progress up to the point its majority was secured. As we have shown the journey was an uneven one. Early successes in the 1890s were followed by abject failures in the 1900s. Even the improvement in Labour's position by 1914 must be recognised for what it was – a noticeable presence but a permanent minority. It was only with the Great War that Labour could seriously contemplate taking the leading role in the political life of the City.

After the war there was a greatly expanded electorate but this expansion occurred under very particular circumstances; the radicalising impact of the war, the emergence of class politics, the strengthening of Labour and the collapse of the Liberals. If further suffrage reform had been inevitable it had little to do with Labour but after 1918 Labour was given the opportunity to build support among the whole of the working class – skilled men, poorer workers, women – which it had not shown itself capable of before 1914.

In 1922 Labour secured its parliamentary majority in Glasgow and, despite having lost it temporarily in 1931, became the municipal government in 1933. Compared to some towns and cities this appears quite tardy; Falkirk returned a Labour administration as early as 1920 and Sheffield, in some ways a comparable city, went solidly Labour in the 1920s. Yet, a wider comparison reveals the strength of Labour in Glasgow. None of the other three big Scottish cities went Labour in the 1930s.[58] During the 1920s no English city, other than Sheffield could be regarded as Labour dominated.[59]

---

[56] Information extracted from Cunnison & Gilfillan, *Glasgow*, p. 877.

[57] Corporation of Glasgow, *Review of Operations 1919–1947* (Glasgow, 1948), p. 20–25; J. Mckee, 'Glasgow Working Class Housing Between the Wars 1919–1939' (unpublished M.Litt. thesis, Strathclyde University, 1977), p. 61.

[58] W. Miller, 'Politics in the Scottish City 1832–1982' in G. Gordon (ed.), *Perspectives of the Scottish City* (Aberdeen, 1985), pp. 196–7.

[59] C. Cook, *The Age of Alignment : Electoral Politics in Britain 1922–1929* (London, 1975), pp. 69–70.

In parliamentary elections, by 1935, counting the ILP MPs as still 'Labour', then Glasgow was the most pro-Labour of all the UK's large cities – the location of most of the Party's national support.[60] By the mid-1930s Labour had secured its place as the majority party on Glasgow City Council: a position which continues to this day.[61]

[60] While Labour held four of Sheffield's seven seats, in Glasgow it held nine out of fifteen. The only exception would be the Potteries where all four constituencies were Labour. M. Savage & A. Miles, *The Remaking of the British Working Class 1840–1940* (London, 1994), p. 86.

[61] Contemporary Glasgow is often referred to as the 'One party State', and it is easy to see why. At the combined Assembly and Council elections of May 1999 Labour won all nine of the city's directly elected seats for the Assembly and won 74 of the 79 seats on the City of Glasgow Council. The Scottish National Party is the largest opposition group with two seats. Both the Liberal-Democrats and Conservatives have one seat while, in a faint echo of the separate ILP group of the 1930s, the Scottish Socialist Party also has one seat. *Scotsman,* 8 May 1999.

The Glasgow Electorate in 1911

In direct contrast to those authors who see no class bias operating within the pre-1918 franchise system, the argument here is that the extent of en-franchisement was directly linked to class and status. In the introductory chapter the extent of the variation of adult male enfranchisement within different parts of Glasgow was established for the year 1911. Significant as the differences were between the parliamentary divisions, they were over-shadowed by the massive divergence between municipal wards. The de-scriptive categorisation of wards, partly following the categories used by the City's Medical Officer of Health (MOH), showed clear differences in proportions of adult male electors according to whether a ward was a commercial or business area, middle class residential, 'artisan' or 'poorer working class'.

Establishing a clearer link to the social structure of municipal wards is more difficult since the published Census provides little useful data at such a level and, indeed, nothing at all on occupations and occupational status other than for the City as a whole. However, the Corporation of Glasgow through the offices of the MOH does provide much more detailed informa-tion on the City's wards extracted in part from the Census schedules. Thus in the Annual Reports of the MOH and in the volume *Census 1911* published by the Corporation we are provided with a much more exact age and gender profile of ward populations which, when combined with the numbers of electors given in the annual *Post Office Directory*, allows us to make a fairly precise estimate of the male electorate as a proportion of the adult male population for each ward. Furthermore, the Corporation sources contain a raft of revealing statistics on the housing and health of the wards which, in the absence of any information on occupations, can be utilised as indicators of social structure. It is then possible to correlate the proportionate adult male electorate with these social statistics. We can do this for the twenty-six wards of Glasgow in 1911 but, unfortunately, not for the new wards that were incorporated into the City the following year.

Housing and health are, of course, closely related and Glasgow in our period managed to provide some of the worst statistics for both in the whole of Europe.[1] A pivotal figure in establishing the relationship was James Burn

---

[1] 'Glasgow . . . with some 700,000 people in 1914 living in its three central square miles, the heaviest concentration of people in Europe'. S. & O. Checkland, *Industry and Ethos: Scotland 1832–1914* (London, 1984) p. 185.

Russell, Glasgow's famous MOH in the late nineteenth century, who became convinced that mortality and susceptibility to disease were related to the 'physical differences' between areas, 'especially as to air-space'. Such were the contrasts that he produced in the mid-1880s a four-fold division of Glasgow:

> We can classify the inhabitants of one city so as to produce four cities . . . to amply illustrate the law that the comparative healthiness of sections of the population, whether they be traditionally separated and known by name as distinct communities, or are merely artificial divisions of the same community, is determined by the air-space within and without their dwellings.[2]

Although opposed to socialism, Russell's work would provide material for a generation of socialist propagandists. Death was built into the class structure.[3] The table below provides the levels of adult male enfranchisement for each ward alongside of the proportion of the population living in houses of one or two rooms, the number of persons per room, the death rate, and infant mortality rate.

A cursory glance indicates the closeness of the relationship. Thus the middle class residential wards of Kelvinside, Pollokshields, Langside, Park, Dennistoun, all had high levels of male enfranchisement and enjoyed good housing and health. At the other extreme are the 'poorer working class' areas such as Mile End with desperately poor housing conditions and health problems, and a very low enfranchisement rate. The 'fit' between enfranchisement and housing and health is not perfect and the order in which the wards appear under each category do vary but the statistical correlation between enfranchisement and our chosen social indicators can be established. These are:

- Proportional male electorate with population living in 1 and 2 roomed houses = −.80
- Proportional male electorate with number of people per room = −.82
- Proportional male electorate with death rate = −.91
- Proportional male electorate with infant mortality rate = −.85

In making these calculations the three wards Exchange, Blythswood and Broomielaw have been left out since their exceptionally high levels of plural voters means that their electorate bears very little relationship to the actual population. However, even though the number of cases is quite small, only twenty-three in total, the high values of the correlations establish the closeness of the relationship (a figure of -1 denotes a perfect functional relationship). Thus, an increasing level of enfranchisement is associated

[2] J.B. Russell, *Vital Statistics of the City of Glasgow* (Glasgow, 1885/6) part 2, pp 73–4.
[3] For instance see the pre-war pamphlets by John Wheatley, *Eight Pound Cottages for Glasgow Citizens*, and *A Reply to the Critics of the £8 Cottages* (both Glasgow, n.d.)

with a lower number of people living in one and two roomed houses; with fewer people living per room; with a lower death rate; and a lower infant mortality rate. In short, the wealthier an area the more likely it was to have a higher level of enfranchisement and, conversely, the poorer an area the fewer men were likely to appear on the electoral register.

Glasgow male electorate, housing and health, 1911

Ward Name	Electorate as % of adult males	% of population living in 1 & 2 roomed houses	No. of persons per windowed room	death rates	infant mortality rates
Dalmarnock	46.94	88.89	2.73	18.59	152
Calton	38.88	69.67	2.20	19.35	155
Mile-End	46.67	88.25	2.68	19.04	159
Whitevale	50.94	70.75	2.31	17.38	151
Dennistoun	67.45	47.25	1.63	11.27	99
Springburn	48.05	82.84	2.46	15.82	117
Cowlairs	57.54	76.04	2.35	14.94	130
Townhead	54.18	68.53	2.16	16.51	161
Blackfriars	51.61	63.37	2.18	18.39	180
Exchange	282.90	30.02	1.20	16.75	200
Blythswood	272.01	10.52	0.92	12.88	160
Broomielaw	67.27	52.87	1.99	22.66	234
Anderston	53.43	66.47	2.12	17.78	126
Sandyford	57.31	48.36	1.63	15.43	145
Park	64.96	12.40	0.99	11.39	85
Cowcaddens	36.83	66.50	2.13	19.59	163
Woodside	58.56	66.47	1.92	14.49	144
Hutchesontown	47.13	88.82	2.63	18.06	140
Gorbals	46.55	47.89	1.93	15.64	145
Kingston	55.28	52.30	1.99	18.33	145
Govanhill	66.38	66.53	2.02	13.34	76
Langside	86.68	19.53	1.13	9.31	59
Pollokshields	85.16	7.27	0.78	10.45	86
Kelvinside	83.88	4.09	0.75	8.89	29
Maryhill	56.59	67.00	1.81	12.75	106
Kinning Park	53.97	82.13	2.57	16.82	145

Bibliography

Manuscript Sources

Broady Collection, Glasgow University Library.

Crawfurd, H., 'unpublished autobiography', n.d., Marx Memorial Library, London (copy in Gallagher Memorial Library, Glasgow Caledonian University Library)

Glasgow ILP Federation Collection, Mitchell Library Glasgow.

Joseph Duncan, Letters 1905–08, National Library of Scotland, Acc 5490.

Scottish Conservative and Unionist Association, Records, National Library of Scotland, Acc 10424.

Archives of the Independent Labour Party, including the Francis Johnston Correspondence, London School of Economics, published in microform edition by Harvester Press.

Scottish Workers Representation Committee (SWRC), minutes and letters 1900–1909, National Library of Scotland, microfilm mss 141 (held in Scottish Trades Union Congress collection).

Printed Primary Sources

A. REPORTS &c.

Burgh of Glasgow, *Electoral Registers*.

Burgh of Glasgow, *Valuation Rolls*.

Corporation of Glasgow, *Census 1911: Report on Glasgow and its Municipal Wards* (Glasgow, 1912).

Corporation of Glasgow, *Review of Operations 1919–1947* (Glasgow, 1948).

Glasgow Corporation, *Report of the Medical Officer of Health* (Glasgow, various).

Glasgow Post Office Directory.

Glasgow Trades Council, *Annual Reports* (Glasgow, various).

Presbytery of Glasgow, *Report of Commission on the Housing of the Poor in Relation to Their Social Condition* (Glasgow 1891).

Glasgow Municipal Commission on the Housing of the Poor, *Minutes of Evidence* (Glasgow 1903).

Glasgow Municipal Commission on the Housing of the Poor, *Report* (Glasgow, 1904).

Labour Party 13th. Annual Conference, Glasgow 1914, *Souvenir*, (Published by the Glasgow Labour Party).

Printed Minutes of the Corporation of Glasgow.

Russell, J.B., T*he Vital Statistics of the City of Glasgow 1881–1885* (published in 3 parts, Glasgow 1885/6).
Scottish Advisory Council of the Labour Party, *Annual Reports 1915–1921.*
Scottish Trade Union Congress, *Annual Reports.*
Scottish Workers' Representation Committee, *Annual Reports 1901–1909.*
Rules of the Blackfriars and Hutchesontown Labour Representation Committee (n.d.).

B. PARLIAMENTARY PAPERS AND OFFICIAL PUBLICATIONS

Board of Trade, *An Industrial Survey of the South-West of Scotland* (London, 1932).
Ministry of Labour, *Local Unemployment Index.*
Census of Scotland, *Report* 1911, 1921, 1931.
PP 1908, CVII *Cost of Living of the Working Classes (1908)* .
PP 1913, LXVI, *Cost of Living of the Working Classes (1912).*
PP 1901, XXVII, PP1907, XXXVII *Annual Reports of the Local Government Board for Scotland.*
PP 1917, XIV, *Report of the Royal Commission on the Housing of the Industrial Population of Scotland Rural and Urban.*

C. NEWSPAPERS

Forward
Glasgow Commonweal
Glasgow Herald
Glasgow Observer
Labour Leader
Scottish Co-operator
Scottish Leader
The Scottish Worker
The Socialist Review
Star
The Strike Bulletin (Organ of the 40 Hours Movement)
Vanguard
The Worker

D. MEMOIRS, CONTEMPORARY ACCOUNTS &c

ALDRED, G., *John MacLean: Martyr of the Class Struggle* (Glasgow, 1932).
BELL, T., *John MacLean: a Fighter for Freedom* (Glasgow, 1944).
BELL, T., *Pioneering Days* (London, 1941).
BUCHAN, A., *History of the Scottish Co-operative Women's Guild* (Glasgow, 1913).
CONNELL, J., *Glasgow Municipal Enterprise* (Glasgow & London, 1899).
DOLLAN, P.J., *History of the Kinning Park Co-operative Society Ltd.* (Glasgow, 1923).

FLANAGAN, J.A., *Wholesale Co-operation in Scotland: the Fruits of Fifty Years Efforts* (Glasgow, 1920).

FRASER, H., *Women and War Work* (New York, 1918).

GALLACHER, W., *Revolt on the Clyde* (London, 1936).

GALLACHER, W., *Last Memoirs* (London, 1966).

GEORGE, H., *Progress and Poverty: an Inquiry into the Cause of Industrial Depressions, and Increase of Want with Increase of Wealth* (first published 1879, London, 1906 edition).

HARDIE, J. KEIR, 'The Independent Labour Party', in A. Reid (ed.), *The New Party* (London, 1895).

HARDIE, J. KEIR, *From Serfdom to Socialism* (London, 1907).

History of the Ministry of Munitions (London, 1920).

JOHNSTON, T., *The Case for Women's Suffrage and Objections Answered* (Glasgow, 1907).

JOHNSTON, T., *Memories* (London, 1952).

KESSACK, J. O'CONNOR, *Is Drink the Cause of Poverty? A Reply to the Temperance Party* (Glasgow, 1907).

KIRKALDY, A.W., (ed.), *Labour, Finance and the War* (London, 1916).

KIRKWOOD, D., *My Life of Revolt* (London,1935).

LEE, J., *My Life With Nye* (London, 1980).

LOWE, D., *Souvenirs of Scottish Labour* (Glasgow, 1919).

McGOVERN, J., *Neither Fear Nor Favour* (London, 1960).

McSHANE, H., & SMITH, J., *No Mean Fighter* (London, 1978).

MANN, J., *Woman in Parliament* (London, 1962).

MUIR, J.H., *Glasgow in 1901* (Glasgow & Edinburgh, 1901).

PATON, J., *Left Turn: The Autobiography of John Paton* (London, 1936).

PANKHURST, S., *The Suffragette Movement* (London, 1977).

SANGER, M., *An Autobiography* (New York, 1971).

SCOTT, W.R., & CUNNISON, J., *The Industries of the Clyde Valley During the War* (Oxford, 1924).

WHEATLEY, J., *The Single Tax v. Social Democracy: Which will most benefit the people?* (London, 1889).

(——) J., *Eight Pound Cottages for Glasgow Citizens* (Glasgow, 1913).

(——) *A Reply to the Critics of the £8 Cottages* (Glasgow, 1913).

(——) *Municipal Glasgow: Its Evolution and Enterprises* (Glasgow, 1914).

(——) *Maternity: Letters from Working Women* (London, 1915).

SECONDARY SOURCES

ADAMS, T., 'The Formation of the Co-operative Party Re-considered', *International Review of Social History*, xxxii (1987).

ABRAMS, M., & ROSE, R., *Must Labour Lose?* (London, 1960).

ALBERTI, J., *Beyond Suffrage: Feminists in War and Peace 1914–28* (London, 1989).

ANDERSON, P., *Arguments within English Marxism* (London, 1980).

ASPINWALL, B., 'The Catholic Irish and Wealth in Glasgow', in Devine, *Irish Immigrants and Scottish Society.*

BENN, C., *Keir Hardie* (London, 1992).

BENNETT, G., '*A most extraordinary and mysterious business': the Zinoviev Letter of 1924* (Foreign and Commonwealth Office, History Notes No. 14, London, 1999)

BHAUMICK, S., 'Glasgow', in M. Morris (ed.), *The General Strike* (London, 1980).

BLEWETT, N., 'The Franchise in the United Kingdom 1885–1918', *Past and Present*, xxxii (1965).

BREITENBACH, E. & GORDON, E. (eds.), *Out of Bounds: Women in Scottish Society 1800–1945* (Edinburgh, 1992).

BROTHERSTONE, T., 'The Suppression of Forward', *The Journal of the Scottish Labour History Society*, i (1969).

BROWN, A., McCRONE, D., PATERSON, L., *Politics and Society in Scotland* (Basingstoke 1996).

BROWN, G., The Labour Party and Political Change in Scotland: the Politics of Five Elections (unpublished Ph.D. thesis, University of Edinburgh, 1982).

BROWN, S.J., ' "Outside the Covenant": The Scottish Presbyterian Churches and Irish Immigration, 1922–1938', *Innes Review*, xcii (1991).

BROWN, S.J., 'The Social Vision of Scottish Presbyterianism and the Union of 1929', *Records of the Scottish Church History Society*, xxiv (1992).

BRUCE, S., *No Pope of Rome: Anti-Catholicism in Modern Scotland* (Edinburgh 1985).

BUDGE, I. & URWIN, D.W., *Scottish Political Behaviour* (London, 1966).

BURNESS, C., 'The Long Slow March: Scottish Women MPs, 1918–45', in Breitenbach & Gordon, *Out of Bounds.*

BUTLER, D., & BUTLER, G., *British Political Facts 1900–1985* (London, 1986).

BUTT, J., 'Working Class Housing in Glasgow 1900–1939', in MacDougall, *Scottish Labour History.*

CAINE, B., *English Feminism 1780–1980* (Oxford, 1997).

CAMPBELL, A. B., *The Lanarkshire Miners: A Social history of their Trade Unions 1775–1874* (Edinburgh, 1979).

CAMPBELL, R. H., *Scotland since 1707* (Edinburgh, 1985).

CARTER, P., 'The West of Scotland', in J. Skelley (ed.), *1926: The General Strike* (London, 1976).

CHALLINOR, R., *The Origins of British Bolshevism* (London, 1977).

CLARKE, M.G. & DRUCKER, H. M., *Our Changing Scotland: A Yearbook of Scottish Government 1976–77* (Edinburgh, 1976).

CLARKE, P.F., 'The electoral position of the Liberal and Labour Parties, 1910–1914', *English Historical Review*, xc (1975).

CLOSE, D. H., 'The realignment of the British electorate in 1931', *History*, lxvii (1982).

COLE, G.D.H., *A History of the Labour Party From 1914* (London, 1948).

COLLINS, B., 'The Origins of Irish Immigration to Scotland in Nineteenth and Twentieth Centuries', in Devine, *Irish Immigrants and Scottish Society.*

COOK, C., *The Age of Alignment: Electoral Politics in Britain 1922–29* (London, 1975).

COOPER, S., John Wheatley: A Study in Labour History (Unpublished Ph.D. thesis, University of Glasgow, 1973).

CORR, H., 'An Exploration into Scottish Education', in Fraser and Morris, *People & Society.*

CRAIG, F.W.S., *British Parliamentary Election Results 1885–1918* (London, 1974).

CRAIG, F.W.S., *British Electoral Facts, 1885–1975* (London, 1976).

CRAIG, F.W.S., *British Parliamentary Election Results 1918–1949* (Chichester 1983).

CRAIG, F.W.S., *British Electoral Facts 1832–1987* (Aldershot, 1989).

CRONIN, J.E., *Labour and Society in Britain 1918–1979* (London, 1984).

CRONIN, J.E., *The Politics of State Expansion* (London, 1991).

CUNNISON, J., & GILFILLAN, J.B.S. (eds.), *Glasgow: The Third Statistical Account of Scotland* (Glasgow, 1958).

DAMER, S., 'State, Class and Housing: Glasgow 1885–1919', in Melling, J. (ed.), *Housing, Social Policy and the State* (London, 1980).

DANGERFIELD, G., *The Strange Death of Liberal England* (London, 1966, first published 1935).

DARRAGH, J., 'The Catholic Population of Scotland, 1878–1977', in McRoberts, *Modern Scottish Catholicism.*

DAVIDSON, R., 'War-Time Labour Policy 1914–16: a Re-appraisal', *Scottish Labour History Society Journal*, viii (1974).

DEVINE, T. M. (ed.) *Irish Immigrants and Scottish Society in the Nineteenth and Twentieth Centuries* (Edinburgh, 1991).

DONNACHIE, I., 'Scottish Labour in the Depression', in Donnachie, Harvie & Wood, *Forward!*

DONNACHIE, I, HARVIE C. & WOOD I. S. (eds.), *Forward! Labour Politics in Scotland, 1888–1988* (Edinburgh, 1989).

DOWSE, R. E., *Left in the Centre: the Independent Labour Party 1893–1940* (London, 1966).

DUNBABIN, J.P.D., 'British Elections in the nineteenth and twentieth centuries, a regional approach', *English Historical Review*, xcv (1980).

DYER, M., *Capable Citizens and Improvident Democrats: The Scottish Electoral System 1884–1929* (Aberdeen, 1996).

EDWARDS, O. D., 'The Catholic Press in Scotland since the Restoration of the Hierarchy', in MacRoberts, *Modern Scottish Catholicism.*

ENGLANDER, D., *Landlord and Tenant in Urban Britain 1838–1918* (Oxford, 1983).

ENGLANDER, D., *Poverty and Poor Law Reform in 19th. Century Britain, 1834–1914* (London, 1998).

FIELDING, S., *Class and Ethnicity: Irish Catholics in England, 1880–1939* (Birmingham, 1993).

FINLAY, R., *Independent and Free: Scottish Politics and the Origins of the Scottish National Party 1918–1945* (Edinburgh, 1994).

FOSTER, J., 'Strike Action and Working Class Politics on Clydeside 1914–1919', *International Review of Social History*, xxxv (1990).

FRASER, W.H., Trades Councils in England and Scotland 1858–1897 (unpublished Ph.D. thesis, University of Sussex, 1967).

FRASER, W.H., 'Trades Councils in the Labour Movement in Nineteenth Century Scotland', in MacDougall, *Scottish Labour History*.

FRASER, W.H., 'The Labour Party in Scotland', in K.D. Brown (ed.), *The First Labour Party 1906–1914* (London, 1985).

FRASER, W.H., 'Labour and the Changing City', in G. Gordon (ed.), *Perspectives of the Scottish City* (Aberdeen, 1985).

FRASER, W.H., 'Municipal Socialism and Social Policy', in R.J. Morris & R. Rodger (eds.), *The Victorian City: A Reader in Urban History, 1920 – 1914* (London, 1993).

FRASER, W.H., & MAVOR, I. (eds.), *Glasgow, Volume Two: 1830–1912* (Manchester, 1996).

FRASER, W. H. and MORRIS R. J., (eds.) *People and Society in Scotland, Volume II, 1830–1914* (Edinburgh, 1990).

FRASER, W.H., 'The Working Class', in Fraser & Mavor, *Glasgow, 1830–1912*.

FRY, M., *Patronage and Principle: A Political history of Modern Scotland* (Aberdeen, 1987).

GALLAGHER, T., 'Protestant Extremism in Urban Scotland 1930–1939: Its Growth and Contraction', *Scottish Historical Review*, lxiv (1985).

GALLAGHER, T., *Glasgow: The Uneasy Peace* (Manchester, 1987).

GLASGOW LABOUR HISTORY WORKSHOP, 'The labour unrest in West Scotland, 1910–14', in Kenefick & McIvor, *Roots of Red Clydeside*.

GORDON, E., Women's Employment in Scotland (unpublished paper, Glasgow University, 1979).

GORDON, E., 'Women's Spheres', in Fraser & Morris, *People and Society in Scotland*.

GORDON, E., *Women and the Labour Movement in Scotland 1850–1914* (Oxford, 1991).

GRAVES, P., *Labour Women: Women in British Working Class Politics 1918–1939* (Cambridge, 1994).

HANDLEY, J.E., *The Irish in Modern Scotland* (Cork, 1948).

HARRISON, R., *Before the Socialists: Studies in Labour and Politics 1861–1881* (London, 1965).

HART, T., 'Urban Growth and Municipal Government: Glasgow in a Comparative Context, 1846–1914', in A. Slaven & D. H. Aldcroft (eds.), *Business, Banking and Urban History* (Edinburgh, 1982).

HARRIS, J., *William Beveridge: A Biography* (Oxford, 1997).

HARVIE, C., *No Gods and Precious Few Heroes* (London, 1981, 2nd. edition Edinburgh 1992).

HARVIE, C., 'Before the Breakthrough, 1886–1922', in Donnachie, Harvie & Wood, *Forward!*

HINTON, J., 'The Clyde Workers Committee and the Dilution Struggle', in A. Briggs & J. Saville (eds.), *Essays in Labour History 1886–1923* (London, 1971).

HINTON, J., *The First Shop Stewards' Movement* (London, 1973).

HINTON, J., 'The Suppression of the *Forward* – a note', *The Journal of the Scottish Labour History Society,* vii (1974).

HINTON, J., *Labour and Socialism: A History of the British Labour Movement 1867– 1974* (Sussex, 1983).

HOBSBAWM, E.J., *The Forward March of Labour Halted?* (London, 1981).

HOLLIS, P., *Ladies Elect: Women in English Local Government 1865–1914* (Oxford, 1987).

HOLTON, R., *British Syndicalism 1910–1914: Myths and Realities* (London, 1976).

HOLTON, S., *Feminism and Democracy: Women's Suffrage and Reform Politics in Britain 1900–1918* (Cambridge, 1986).

HOWELL, D., *British Workers and the Independent Labour Party 1888–1906* (Manchester, 1984).

HOWELL, D., *A Lost Left: Three Studies in Socialism and Nationalism* (Manchester, 1986).

HUNT, E.H., *Regional Wage Variations in Britain 1850–1914* (Oxford, 1973).

HUNT, E.H., *British Labour History 1815–1914* (London, 1985).

HUNT, K., *Equivocal Feminists: The Social Democratic Federation and the Woman Question 1884–1911* (Cambridge, 1996).

HUTCHISON, I.G.C., *A Political History of Scotland 1832–1924: Parties, Elections and Issues* (Edinburgh, 1986).

HUTCHISON, I.G.C., 'Glasgow Working Class Politics', in R. A. Cage (ed.), *The Working Class in Glasgow 1750–1914* (London, 1987).

KEATING, M., *The City That Refused To Die* (Aberdeen, 1988).

KELLAS, J.G., 'The Mid Lanark By-Election (1888) and the Scottish Labour Party (1888–1894)', *Parliamentary Affairs,* xviii (1965).

KELLAS, J.G., *Modern Scotland: The Nation Since 1870* (2nd. Edition, London, 1980).

KENEFICK, W & McIVOR A. (eds.), *Roots of Red Clydeside, 1910–1914: Labour Unrest and Industrial Relations in West Scotland* (Edinburgh, 1996).

KENDALL, W., *The Revolutionary Movement in Britain 1900–21: The Origins of British Communism* (London, 1969).

KIBBLEWHITE, E., The Impact of Unemployment on the Development of Trade Unions in Scotland, 1918–1939: some aspects (unpublished Ph.D. thesis, University of Aberdeen, 1979).

KINLOCH, J.A., The Scottish Co-operative Wholesale Society 1868–1918 (unpublished Ph.D. thesis, University of Strathclyde, 1976).

KINLOCH, J.A., & BUTT, J., *History of the Scottish Co-operative Wholesale Society Limited* (Manchester, 1981).

KING, E., 'The Scottish Women's Suffrage Movement', in Breitenbach & Gordon, *Out of Bounds.*

KNOX, W.W., (ed.) *Scottish Labour Leaders 1918–1939: A Biographical Dictionary* (Edinburgh, 1984).

KNOX, W.W., *James Maxton* (Manchester, 1987).

KNOX, W.W., 'The Political and Workplace culture of the Scottish Working Class, 1832–1914', in Fraser & Morris, *People and Society .*

KNOX, W.W., '"Ours is not an ordinary Parliamentary movement": 1922–26', in McKinlay & Morris, *ILP on Clydeside.*

KNOX, W., McKINLAY, A., & SMYTH, J.J., 'Industrialisation, Work and Labour Politics: Clydeside, c. 1850–1990', in R. Schulze (ed.), *Industrial Regions in Transformation* (Essen, 1993).

LANCASTER, B., *Radicalism, Co-operation and Socialism: Leicester Working Class Politics 1860–1906* (Leicester, 1987).

LAYBOURN, K. & REYNOLDS, J., *Liberalism and the Rise of Labour 1890–1918* (London, 1984).

LENEMAN, L., *A Guid Cause: The Women's Suffrage Movement in Scotland* (Aberdeen, 1991).

LEVITT, I., *Poverty and Welfare in Scotland 1890–1948* (Edinburgh, 1988).

LEWENHACK, S., 'Women in the Leadership of the STUC 1897–1970', *Scottish Labour History Journal,* vii (1973).

LEWENHACK, S., *Women and Trade Unions: An Outline History of Women in the British Trade Union Movement* (London, 1977).

LIDDELL, P.H., The Role of the Trades Council in the Political and Industrial Life of Glasgow 1858–1976 (unpublished M.Sc. thesis, University of Strathclyde, 1977).

LIDDINGTON, J., & NORRIS, J., *One Hand Tied Behind Us: The Rise of the Women's Suffrage Movement* (London, 1978).

LIDDINGTON, J., 'The Women's Peace Crusade: The History of a Forgotten Campaign', in D. Thompson (ed.), *Over Our Dead Bodies: Women Against the Bomb* (London, 1983).

LUCAS, B.K., *The English Local Government Franchise: A Short History* (London, 1952).

McCAFFREY, J.F., 'The Irish Vote in Glasgow in the Later Nineteenth Century', *Innes Review,* xxi (1970).

McCAFFREY, J.F., 'Politics and the Irish community Since 1878', in MacRoberts, *Modern Scottish Catholicism.*

McCAFFREY, J.F., 'Irish Issues in the Nineteenth and Twentieth Century: Radicalism in a Scottish context?', in Devine, *Irish Immigrants and Scottish Society.*

McCAFFREY, J.F., 'Political Issues and Developments', in Fraser & Maver, *Glasgow, 1830–1912.*

McCRINDLE, J. & ROWBOTHAM, S. (eds.), *Dutiful Daughters: Women talk about their lives,* (London, 1979).

McDermid, J., 'Catholic working class girls' education in Lowland Scotland, 1872–1900', *Innes Review,* xlviii (1996).

MacDougall, I. (ed.), *Essays in Scottish Labour History: A Tribute to W. H. Marwick* (Edinburgh, 1978).

McFarland, E., *Protestants First: Orangeism in 19th Century Scotland* (Edinburgh, 1990).

MacIntyre, S., *Little Moscows* (London, 1980).

McKee, J., 'Glasgow Working Class Housing Between the Wars 1919–1939 (unpublished M.Litt. thesis, Strathclyde University, 1977).

McKibbin, R., *The Evolution of the Labour Party 1910–1924* (London, 1974).

McKinlay, A., Employers and Skilled Workers in the Inter-War Depression: engineering and shipbuilding on Clydeside 1919–1939 (unpublished D. Phil. thesis, Oxford 1986).

McKinlay, A., & Morris, R.J. (eds.), *The ILP on Clydeside 1893–1932: from foundation to disintegration* (Manchester, 1991).

McKinlay, A., ' "Doubtful wisdom and uncertain promise": strategy, ideology and organisation, 1918–1922', in McKinlay & Morris, *ILP on Clydeside.*

McKinlay, A. & Smyth, J.J., 'The end of "the agitator workman": 1926–32', in McKinlay & Morris, *ILP on Clydeside.*

McLean, I.S., *The Legend of Red Clydeside* (Edinburgh, 1983).

McNair, J., *James Maxton: The Beloved Rebel* (London, 1955).

McRoberts, D. S. (ed.), *Modern Scottish Catholicism, 1878–1978* (Glasgow, 1979).

Machin, G.I.T., *Churches and Social Issues in Twentieth Century Britain* (Oxford, 1988).

Marquand, D., *Ramsay MacDonald* (London, 1977).

Marshall, T.H., *Sociology at the Crossroads and other Essays* (London, 1963).

Matthew, H.C.G., McKibbin, R., & Kay, J.A., 'The Franchise Factor in the Rise of the Labour Party', *English Historical Review,* xci (1976).

Matthew, H.C.G., 'The Liberal Age', in K.O. Morgan (ed.), *The Oxford Illustrated History of Britain* (Oxford, 1986).

Mavor (Sweeney), I., 'Local Party Politics and the Temperance Crusade: Glasgow 1890–1902', *Scottish Labour History Society Journal,* xxvii (1992).

Mavor, I., 'Glasgow's Civic Government', in Fraser & Mavor, *Glasgow, 1830–1912.*

Mavor, I., ' Glasgow's municipal workers and industrial strife', in Kenefick & McIvor, *Roots of Red Clydeside.*

Melling, J., *Rent Strikes: People's Struggle for Housing in West Scotland 1890–1916* (Edinburgh, 1983).

Melling, J., 'Clydeside rent struggles and the making of labour politics in Scotland, 1900–1939', in Rodger, *Scottish Housing.*

Melling, J., 'Whatever happened to Red Clydeside? Industrial Conflict and the Politics of Skill in the First World War', in *International Review of Social History,* xxxv (1990).

MELLING, J., 'Work, culture and politics on 'Red Clydeside': the ILP during the First World War', in McKinlay & Morris, *The ILP on Clydeside.*

MILLER, W., 'Politics in the Scottish City 1832–1982', in G. Gordon (ed.), *Perspectives of the Scottish City* (Aberdeen, 1985).

MILTON, N. (ed.), *John MacLean: In the Rapids of Revolution* (London, 1978).

MITCHELL, D., *Women on the Warpath; the Story of the Women of the First World War* (London, 1966).

MOORHOUSE, H.F., 'The Marxist Theory of the Labour Aristocracy', *Social History*, iii (1978).

MORGAN, K.O, *Keir Hardie: Radical and Socialist* (London, 1975).

MORGAN, N.J., ' "£8 cottages for Glasgow citizens": Innovations in municipal house-building in Glasgow in the inter-war years', in Rodger, *Scottish Housing.*

PACKER, I., 'The Land Issue and the Future of Scottish Liberalism in 1914', *Scottish Historical Review*, lxxv (1996).

PELLING, H.M., *Social Geography of British Elections, 1885–1910* (London, 1967).

PELLING, H.M., *A History of British Trade Unionism* (Middlesex, 1976).

PHILLIPPS, G.A., *The General Strike: The Politics of Industrial Conflict* (London, 1976).

PUGH, M., *Electoral Reform in War and Peace 1908–1918* (London, 1978).

PUGH, M., *Women and the Women's Movement in Britain 1914–1959* (London, 1992).

PURDIE, B., Outside the Chapel Door: the Glasgow Catholic Socialist Society 1906–22' (Unpublished thesis, Ruskin College, 1976).

Radical Scotland, xxii (August/September 1986).

RAMELSON, M., *The Petticoat Rebellion: A Century of Struggle for Women's Rights* (London, 1972).

REID, A., 'The Division of Labour and Politics in Britain, 1880–1920' in W.J. Mommsen & H. Husung (eds.), *The Development of Trade Unionism in Great Britain and Germany, 1880–1914* (London, 1985).

REID, A., 'Glasgow Socialism', *Social History*, xi (1986).

REID, F., *Keir Hardie: the Making of a Socialist* (London, 1978).

RIPLEY, B.J., & McHUGH, J., *John MacLean* (Manchester, 1989).

ROBERTS, E., *A Woman's Place: An Oral History of Working Class Women 1890–1914* (London, 1984).

RODGER, R. (ed.), *Scottish Housing in the Twentieth Century* (Leicester, 1989).

RODGER, R., 'Crisis and confrontation in Scottish housing 1880–1914', in Rodger, *Scottish Housing.*

RODGER, R., 'The Labour Force', in Fraser & Mavor, *Glasgow, 1830–1912.*

ROWBOTHAM, S., *The Friends of Alice Wheeldon* (London, 1986).

RUBIN, G., *War, Law and Labour: The Munitions Acts, State Regulation and the Unions, 1915–1921* (Oxford, 1987).

SASSOON, D., *One Hundred Years of Socialism: The West European Left in the Twentieth Century* (London, 1997).

SAVAGE, M., *The Dynamics of Working Class Politics: The Labour Movement in Preston 1880–1914* (Cambridge, 1987).

SAVAGE, M., 'Whatever happened to Red Clydeside?', in J. Anderson & A. Cochrane (eds.), *A State of Crisis* (London, 1989).

SAVAGE, M., & MILES, A., *The Remaking of the British Working Class 1840–1940* (London, 1994).

'SECTARIANISM IN SCOTLAND', a film by George Rosie, part of the Secret Scotland series broadcast by Scottish Television (1997).

SHEPPARD, M.G. & HALSTEAD, J.L., 'Labour's Municipal Election Performance in Provincial England and Wales 1901–13', *Bulletin of the Society for the Study of Labour History*, xxxix (1979).

SLAVEN, A., *The Development of the West of Scotland: 1750–1960* (London, 1975).

SMITH, F.B., *The Making of the Second Reform Bill* (Melbourne, 1966).

SMITH, J., 'Labour Tradition in Glasgow and Liverpool', *History Workshop*, xviii (1984).

SMITH, J., 'Taking the leadership of the labour movement: the ILP in Glasgow, 1906–1914', in McKinlay & Morris, *ILP on Clydeside*.

SMOUT, T.C., *A Century of the Scottish People 1830–1950* (London, 1986).

SMYTH, J.J. & RODGERS, M., 'Peter Petroff and the Socialist Movement in Britain, 1907–18', *Immigrants and Minorities*, ii (1983).

SMYTH, J.J., Labour and Socialism in Glasgow 1880–1914: the electoral challenge prior to democracy' (unpublished Ph.D. thesis, University of Edinburgh, 1987).

SMYTH, J.J., 'The ILP in Glasgow 1888–1906: the struggle for identity', in McKinlay & Morris, *ILP on Clydeside*.

SMYTH, J.J., 'Rents, Peace, Votes: Working Class Women and Political Activity in the First World War', in Breitenbach & Gordon, *Out of Bounds*.

SMYTH, J.J., ' "From Industrial Unrest to Industrial Debacle?": the labour left and industrial militancy 1910–14', in Kenefick & McIvor, *Roots of Red Clydeside*.

SOLDON, N.C., *Women in British Trade Unions 1874–1976* (Dublin, 1978)

Spare Rib, xxxii (1975).

SWENARTON, M., *Homes Fit For Heroes: The Politics and Architecture in Early State Housing in Britain* (London, 1981),

TANNER, D., 'The Parliamentary Electoral System, the 'Fourth' Reform Act and the Rise of Labour in England and Wales', *Bulletin of the Institute of Historical Research*, lvi (1983).

TANNER, D., *Political Change and the Labour Party 1900–1918* (Cambridge, 1990).

THANE, P., 'The Women of the British Labour Party and Feminism, 1906–1945', in H.L. Smith (ed.), *British Feminism in the Twentieth Century* (London, 1990).

THERBORN, G., 'The Rule of Capital and the Rise of Democracy', *New Left Review*, ciii (1977).

THOMPSON, P., *Socialists, Liberals and Labour: The Struggle for London 1885–1914* (London, 1967).

THORPE, A., *A History of the British Labour Party* (London, 1997).

TICHELAR, M., 'Socialists, Labour and the Land: the Response of the Labour Party to the Land Campaign of Lloyd George before the First World War', *Twentieth Century British History*, viii (1997).

TREBLE, J.H., 'The Market for Unskilled Male Labour in Glasgow 1891–1914', in Macdougall, *Scottish Labour History*.

TREBLE, J.H., 'The working of the 1918 Education Act in Glasgow archdiocese', *Innes Review* xxxi (1980).

TREBLE, J.H., 'The Seasonal Demand for Adult Labour in Glasgow, 1890–1914', *Social History*, iii (1978).

TREBLE, J.H., 'Unemployment in Glasgow, 1903–1910: Anatomy of a crisis', *Scottish Labour History Society Journal*, xxv (1990).

TROTSKY, L., *My Life* (London, 1979).

TUCKETT, A. *The Scottish Trades Union Congress: The First 80 Years, 1897–1977* (Edinburgh, 1986).

TURNER, J., *British Politics and the Great War: Coalition and Conflict 1915–1918* (London, 1992).

URWIN, D., 'The Development of the Conservative Party Organisation in Scotland until 1912', *Scottish Historical Review*, xliv (1965).

WALKER, G., 'The Protestant Irish in Scotland', in Devine, *Irish Immigrants and Scottish Society*.

WALKER, G., 'The Orange Order in Scotland Between the Wars', *International Review of Social History*, xxxvii (1992).

WALKER, W.M., 'Irish Immigrants in Scotland: Their Priests, Politics and Parochial Life', *Historical Journal*, xv (1972).

WALLER, P.J. *Democracy and Sectarianism: A Political and Social History of Liverpool, 1868–1939* (Liverpool, 1981).

WOOD, I.S., 'Irish Immigrants and Scottish Radicalism, in MacDougall, *Scottish Labour History*.

WOOD, I.S., 'John Wheatley, the Irish and the Labour Movement in Scotland', *The Innes Review*, xxxi (1980).

WOOD, I.S., 'Hope Deferred: Labour in Scotland in the 1920s', in Donnachie, Harvie & Wood, *Forward! Labour Politics in Scotland 1888–1988*.

WOOD, I.S., *John Wheatley* (Manchester, 1990).

WRIGLEY, C., *David Lloyd George and the British Labour Movement* (Brighton, 1976).

Index